The KGB, Russian Academic Imperialism, Ukraine, and Western Academia, 1946–2024

The KGB, Russian Academic Imperialism, Ukraine, and Western Academia, 1946–2024

Sergei I. Zhuk

LEXINGTON BOOKS
Lanham • Boulder • New York • London

Published by Lexington Books
An imprint of The Rowman & Littlefield Publishing Group, Inc.
4501 Forbes Boulevard, Suite 200, Lanham, Maryland 20706
www.rowman.com

86-90 Paul Street, London EC2A 4NE

Copyright © 2024 by The Rowman & Littlefield Publishing Group, Inc.

All rights reserved. No part of this book may be reproduced in any form or by any electronic or mechanical means, including information storage and retrieval systems, without written permission from the publisher, except by a reviewer who may quote passages in a review.

British Library Cataloguing in Publication Information Available

Library of Congress Cataloging-in-Publication Data

Names: Zhuk, Sergei I., 1958– author.
Title: The KGB, Russian academic imperialism, Ukraine, and western academia, 1946–2024 / Sergei I. Zhuk.
Description: Lanham, Maryland : Lexington Books, [2024] | Includes bibliographical references and index. | Summary: "This book is a study of Soviet and Russian intelligence operations against the centers for Soviet studies in North American academia. Special attention is paid to the historical roots of contemporary Russian intelligence operations targeting American-Russian academics and promoting Russian state interests in the ongoing war against Ukraine"— Provided by publisher.
Identifiers: LCCN 2024020043 (print) | LCCN 2024020044 (ebook) | ISBN 9781666943672 (cloth) | ISBN 9781666943689 (epub)
Subjects: LCSH: Education, Higher—Political aspects—United States. | Education, Higher—Political aspects—Russia (Federation) | Intelligence service—Soviet Union—History. | Intelligence service—Russia (Federation)—History. | Soviet Union. Komitet gosudarstvennoĭ bezopasnosti. | Soviet Union—Foreign relations—United States. | United States—Foreign relations—Soviet Union. | Russian Invasion of Ukraine, 2022.
Classification: LCC LC89 .Z48 2024 (print) | LCC LC89 (ebook) | DDC 378.73—dc23/eng/20240521
LC record available at https://lccn.loc.gov/2024020043
LC ebook record available at https://lccn.loc.gov/2024020044

Contents

Introduction: Russian Academic Imperialism in the West and
Soviet/Russian Intelligence ... vii

Chapter 1: The KGB and Founding of the Soviet Studies Centers in
Capitalist America, 1946–1960 ... 1

Chapter 2: The KGB and International Academic Connections in
the USSR Academy of Sciences ... 17

Chapter 3: The "KGB People" and Soviet Americanists in
International Academic Exchanges ... 49

Chapter 4: The KGB Spies, Infiltration into American Society, and
KGB "Sleeper Cells/Illegals" ... 71

Chapter 5: The KGB, Ukrainian Diaspora in America, and
Academic Exchanges ... 91

Chapter 6: "Academic Imperialism": Writing Soviet and
Post-Soviet History Without Ukraine and the Role of the
Russian Post-Soviet Immigration to the West ... 125

Chapter 7: "The Agents of Influence": Post-Soviet Oligarchs,
Russian Intelligence Service, and Slavic Studies Centers in the
West ... 155

Epilogue: KGB Legacy and Failed "Westernization" of Russia ... 187

Appendix: List of Interviews ... 201

Selected Bibliography ... 203

Index ... 209

About the Author ... 217

Introduction
Russian Academic Imperialism in the West and Soviet/Russian Intelligence

When, on February 24, 2022, the Russian Federation started the full-scaled military invasion of Ukraine, openly blaming the West and especially the US for using Ukraine against Russia, it was a shock for many political observers and scholars in the West, who used to emphasize the Westernization and Americanization of post-Soviet Russia and its integration into the Western political system. Now the same observers suddenly noted how Putin's "Americanized" Russia openly became the enemy of the West, some Western observers even discovered how the Russians interfered in Western politics and cultural and educational systems. Surprisingly, some former Western Sovietologists even began criticizing "Russian academic imperialism" after February of 2022.[1] To some extent, the events of the Russian war against Ukraine played "the eyes-opening factor" for many Western specialists, who suddenly discovered that the Russians interfered not only in the Western politics, promoting the interests of Putin's regime, but also in the Western academia, promoting pro-Russian cultural and educational concepts.[2] Unfortunately, those Western observers forgot that the Russians, especially their intelligence service organizations, never stopped their interference in the Western, especially American, politics and academia, especially in various centers of Slavic/Russian/Soviet studies in the United States. These practices of interference were just a continuation of the old strategies of Soviet intelligence from the times of the Cold War.

"BUTINA-FEDYASHIN-CARMEL" CONNECTIONS

The most scandalous case of Russian intelligence's interference in the functioning of American centers for Russian studies was the story of the Carmel Institute of Russian Culture at American University in Washington, D.C.[3]

In July of 2018, in one of the apartments in northwest Washington, D.C., FBI agents arrested Maria Butina, "an attractive redheaded Russian student in her twenties," who "just finished a master's at American University." She was indicted as a spy, or as the FBI "alleged as a 'covert Russian agent,'" directed by Russian intelligence "as part of an 'influence operation.'"[4] The US Department of Justice charged Butina, who acted "as an agent of Russia inside the United States by developing relationships with U.S. persons and infiltrating organizations having influence in American politics, for the purpose of advancing the interests of the Russian Federation."[5]

This arrest was the result of a special FBI investigation, which revealed the most scandalous case of Russian intelligence's interference not only in the American politics, but also in the American academia.[6] It turned out that Butina's academic adviser at American University was Associate Professor Anton Fedyashin, who had direct personal (family) connections to the Soviet and Russian intelligence. His father, Andrey Fedyashin, was a staff reporter at the Soviet news agency TASS first in the UK and then in the US during the mid-1980s, when all Soviet journalists, working in the West, had "the professional KGB connections." His grandfather, Georgy Fedyashin, was a general at the First Chief Directorate of the KGB.[7]

According to some commentators, Anton Fedyashin's publications and media interviews gave an impression he was "a professional Kremlin propagandist, who is well trained in turning the logic on its head and proving to his audience that black is in reality white, and vice versa." During 2015–2017, he was a visiting professor at the prestigious elitist Moscow Institute of International Relations.[8] And, of course, Anton Fedyashin became linked to the alleged Russian spy Maria Butina, who studied at American University, took all of Fedyashin's classes and seminars, and "could work with Fedyashin (and the Rossotrudnichestvo office in Washington, D.C.) on selecting potential Russian intelligence recruits from the university's student body."[9] Moreover, those Butina-Fedyashin's connections demonstrated another source of Russian influences in American University and other academic centers in Washington, D.C. Anton Fedyashin was also an executive director of the Carmel Institute of Russian Culture and History at American University. This institute was created in 2011 by a "DC socialite and millionaire," Susan Carmel Lehrman, who "donated $2 million to American University to launch the Initiative for Russian Culture." In 2015, Lehrman changed the name into the Carmel

Institute of Russian Culture and History.[10] It turned out that the entire idea of this organization came from another "KGB man" in Washington, D.C., Russian Ambassador Sergey Kislyak, who "inspired" Lerman to do this. Susan Carmel Lehrman became very active in "enhancing greater relations between Russians and Americans, particularly among younger generations" expressing her "personal desire to continue to assist in creating stronger cultural bonds and greater understandings between people of different cultures [of Russia and America]."[11] Eventually, she involved in her activities not only the Library of Congress, but also the Kennan Institute of the Wilson Center and the John F. Kennedy Center for the Performing Arts, inviting the Russian artists and musicians, who openly supported Putin's war against Ukraine. In 2017, Susan Carmel sponsored the American-Russian Cultural Cooperation Foundation, collaborating with pro-Putin Russian oligarchs, such as Victor Vekselberg, Petr Aven, Mikhail Fridman, Len Blavatnik, and Vagit Alekperov. As a result of her activities, despite her open "anti-Ukrainian and anti-Cold War pro-Russian sympathies," in November 2015, the Kennan Institute awarded Susan Carmel with "the Woodrow Wilson Award for Public Service in recognition of her philanthropy benefiting Russian Studies." As the official institute's site explained, "In addition to her generous support of U.S.-Russian cultural engagement in general, Ms. Lehrman recently endowed the Carmel Institute of Russian Culture and History within the College of Arts and Sciences at American University. The Carmel Institute, and the Initiative for Russian Culture which preceded it, has attracted over 15,000 students to events on Russian culture, including film screenings, lectures, and musical performances."[12] A year later, in 2016, Lehrman was awarded with the Russian Order of Friendship, which was personally handed to her by Putin at the Kremlin.[13]

Since 2011, Susan Carmel and Anton Fedyashin, as a director of the Carmel Institute of Russian Culture and History, had participated in and organized various conferences on Russian culture and history, using sponsorship of Russian funding agencies such as Rossotrudnichestvo and the Gorchakov Fund, which many scholars connected to the Russian intelligence.[14] Both of them were actively involved in "Russia Forum New York," which was sponsored by the Gorchakov Fund and organized by the Russian Center NY at the Princeton Club in New York City on April 21, 2016. One of the major ideas of this meeting was to justify post-Soviet Russian diplomacy, including its anti-Ukrainian position.[15] This meeting in 2016 revealed another personal connection of Susan Carmel to the major organizer of this forum, Elena Branson, who on March 8, 2022, was charged by US Department of Justice as "acting illegally as a Russian agent in the United States." According to the FBI investigation, Elena Branson, "a dual Russian and U.S. citizen," "beginning in at least 2011, . . . worked on behalf of the Russian government and

Russian officials to advance Russian interests in the United States, including by coordinating meetings for Russian officials to lobby U.S. political officials and businesspersons, and by operating organizations in the United States for the purpose of publicly promoting Russian government policies." As the FBI officers explained, "At the direction of the Russian government, she led a years-long campaign to identify the next generation of American leaders, cultivate information channels, and shape US policy in favor of Russian objectives."[16]

All those "Butina-Fedyashin-Carmel" connections, according to the FBI investigation, demonstrated the serious involvement of the Russian government, especially the Russian intelligence, and the Russian oligarchs, in the American (and in general, Western) educational institutions and think tanks. As a former KGB officer commented about this case, "the very fact that the Western, especially, American, academia is a target of Putin's intelligence now, reminds us of the revival of the old KGB strategy for its operations in the West. What we need to do is to trace down the origins and developments of such a strategy, to understand what to expect in the future."[17]

THE OLD KGB STRATEGY, RUSSIAN INTERFERENCE, AND WESTERN ACADEMIA

In March of 2019, in Kyiv, Ukraine, one of the retired KGB officers, who after the Chernobyl catastrophe of 1986 took a patriotic pro-Ukrainian and anti-Kremlin position, made an important observation in his conversation with me. According to him,

> Under a new Soviet leadership of Nikita Khrushchev after 1953, the KGB still targeted as their main adversaries the mostly English-speaking countries, especially the USA, Canada, and the United Kingdom. At the same time, the USSR became "more open" to a dialogue with these countries of the capitalist West under the new conditions of the Khrushchev's Thaw and new policy of "peaceful co-existence," with the massive engagement of Soviet diplomats in various diplomatic institutions, the beginning of the academic and cultural exchanges and numerous tourist visits. Now the KGB leadership had to include in their operations the new targets, which presented not only various international venues, such as the United Nations Organization (UNO), but also various centers of Soviet Studies (Sovietology), which appeared in the capitalist West during the Cold War. It became especially obvious during the period of Brezhnev's détente of the 1970s, when Soviet leaders tried to promote the positive, pro-Soviet images and perceptions among the Western audiences. Various centers of Slavic Studies, especially in the USA, Canada, and the UK, attracted a KGB attention as the important venues of promoting pro-Soviet ideas and practices in studying

Russian/Soviet culture and history. For the KGB, it was especially important not only to cultivate the useful assets/agents of influence among the Western Slavists, who supported and promoted the positive perceptions of the Russian/Soviet past, but also to reject any negative anti-Soviet notions, such as the Ukrainian resistance to Russian occupation, or the rumors about the artificial famine, created by Stalin in 1932 in Ukraine. This trend of KGB operations in the West [to target the centers of Slavic Studies] survived the collapse of the USSR and still exists in the international activities of the post-Soviet Russian successor of the KGB—FSB. It became obvious, especially after so-called "colored revolutions," which challenged a domination of the Russian Federation in a former Soviet geopolitical space. Now, using its intelligence service, Russia is fighting for its control of not only a space, but also a knowledge production about this space. We need now more specialized research of this KGB/FSB trend, for our better understanding of Russian relations with the Western centers of Slavic Studies today.[18]

So, this book is an attempt to address this officer's concerns and to follow his suggestions to explore how Soviet/Russian intelligence with their spies and other "agents of influence" not only promoted Russian academic imperialism in the West, but became influential in the development of various centers for Soviet/Russian/Ukrainian studies in the West since the early days of the Cold War in the 1940s to the Russian war against Ukraine in 2022.

The best study of the intellectual history of the Soviet studies centers in the United States during the Cold War, written by David C. Engerman, was entitled *Know Your Enemy*. To some extent my book is a response to his fascinating project, but from a different perspective, which was completely ignored by Engerman. This perspective is about an involvement of the Soviet and Russian intelligence in a history of those centers. In his book of 2009, Engerman confessed that he had certain limitations with primary sources. He admitted that he lacked the documents from the Soviet side about the exchange program between the Soviets and the West. At the same time, he noted that "looming questions about the involvement of Soviet and American security services in exchanges cannot be answered with documentary evidence, at least not yet." As he explained, "While I heard many participants describe their encounters or near-encounters with CIA and/or KGB officers, I could not adequately reflect these in the text without more documentation."[19]

Ten years later, in 2019, in his conversation with me, a retired Ukrainian KGB officer, who worked undercover in the West during the 1970s, confirmed the fact of the KGB controlling the international academic exchanges and attempting to influence Western centers of Slavic studies,

People now forgot that Soviet intelligence's major goal working in the West, especially in America, was not just spying and stealing new technologies there, but influencing the public opinion, using media, politicians, and various universities' educational centers (including Slavic studies programs) in pro-Soviet, pro-Russian direction, promoting the main Soviet geopolitical interests. Academic exchanges with capitalist America were used especially for establishing Soviet/Russian influences in the existing centers for Slavic Studies in the West.[20]

Using the recently opened KGB documents at SBU Archive in Kyiv, Ukraine, archival collection of such US funding agencies as the American Council of Learned Societies (ACLS) and the International Research and Exchange Board (IREX), memoirs, and the personal interviews with the former (retired) KGB officers in post-Soviet Ukraine, this book is an attempt to add a KGB story to a history of various centers for Soviet studies in major English-speaking (mainly in Northern America) countries. Soviet and later Russian intelligence always tried to use those centers for their own operations or active measures, starting with the beginning of the exchange program between the USSR and the US in 1958. This strategy of "using their enemies" for their own Soviet or Russian interests became especially obvious in KGB/Russian intelligence attitudes to the problems of Ukrainian nationalism and Ukrainian independence. Moreover, a story of this strategy is not just an object of the abstract historiographic interest, but on the background of the Russian war against Ukraine; first at the stage of limited aggression in 2014, and finally at the open massive Russian invasion of Ukraine in 2022, this story is now a part of the military strategy of the Russian Federation in its confrontation with the civilized West.

During the Cold War, the KGB began targeting various Western centers of Slavic studies/Sovietology, especially in the US and Canada, with the aim of influencing and shaping Western experts' views and historical narratives to serve the objectives of Soviet/Russian foreign policies and political interests. Thus, in North America, KGB agents focused on amplifying the split between radical Ukrainian nationalists and a more moderate part of the Ukrainian American diaspora. The KGB was quite successful in their operations against Western centers of Slavic studies and managed to infiltrate their agents into these centers and to use Soviet visiting scholars, especially so-called Americanists (Soviet experts in US/Canada studies), for establishing fruitful working relationships between the KGB and Western Slavists.

This book also analyzes the old KGB Cold War operations and traditions of establishing the foundation for future intelligence work of the KGB and GRU (the so-called "sleeping cells") in educational and research Slavic centers in the US and Canada, and also explores post-Soviet and most recent strategies of the KGB's successor, the Russian FSB, of using Russian emigrants-Slavists, as part of various centers of Russian studies in America and Europe, to promote pro-Kremlin and pro-Putin myths and concepts. Special attention will be paid to the historical roots of contemporary Russian intelligence operations, targeting American-Russian academics, participants of the Valdai Discussion Club and/or the Russkii Mir Foundation, and promoting Russian state interests.

What is unique in this book, which could be a sequel to my recent study of KGB operations in Soviet Ukraine,[21] is a combination of an analysis of Soviet/Russian intelligence operations against Western academia with the intellectual history of the Soviet/Slavic/Russian/Ukrainian studies in the West. Despite the publication of serious general studies of the Cold War and Soviet/Russian intelligence activities in the West by John Lewis Gaddis, John Earl Haynes, Oleg Kalugin, Christopher Andrew, and many others, the recent historiography is still missing an archival-based research work about various forms of the Soviet and Russian interference and influencing the Western academia, especially in various centers for Slavic/Russian/Soviet studies in the West.[22] This book of mine will be the first serious attempt to address this very important chapter in a history of Soviet/Russian intelligence influences in the Western academia. The book will be not only a significant contribution to this history, but also a good and practical reference tool for Western policymakers who witnessed recently the massive Russian meddling in both American and European politics. At the same time, my book will play a very important role in educating the general audience about the Soviet roots of recent Russian meddling in the Western politics and education, especially those Russian state-funded efforts to promote Russian academic imperialism in the West.

HISTORIOGRAPHY OF RUSSIAN INTERFERENCE IN WESTERN ACADEMIA

KGB and Russian intelligence operations against Western academia could be considered as the special "active measures" of Soviet and Russian intelligence services. As early as the beginning of the 1980s, the CIA documents had already addressed some of the KGB "active measures" as "Soviet covert operations."[23] Some observers defined KGB "active measures" as the "actions of political warfare conducted by the Soviet and Russian security services (Cheka, OGPU, NKVD, KGB, FSB) ranging from media manipulation to outright violence."[24] Many scholars had already described various aspects of KGB active measures. As Thomas Rid noted, "Spreading anarchy and chaos and disrupting order have long been a strategy embedded in active measures."[25] In 2017, a group of Ukrainian political scientists and politicians even prepared a special pamphlet about the USSR active measures against the US. Unfortunately, this document quoted only the most famous cases without a referral to the collection of the KGB archive in Kyiv. The major emphasis of this document was on using "the active measures" by Russia against Ukraine after the Maidan Revolution.[26] Another expert in Russian intelligence, Olga Bertelsen, emphasized the important aspects of active measures. According to her,

> They [active measures] had two dimensions, domestic and foreign. Their task was to enforce and reinforce a Soviet version of the story, a discourse, and rhetoric across geographical and political lines. During the Cold War, the stability and omnipresence of the chekist narrative and discourse guaranteed change in public opinion, and this change had to be universal. The prevalence of this discourse ultimately suppressed and marginalized other voices, truths, or discourses (domestically and overseas) that were inadmissible for the Soviet regime.[27]

Overall, active measures were interwoven into the regular KGB operations on retrieving and analyzing the intelligence information, which involved traditional spying activities.[28] Among many definitions of this term, which appeared after 1995, Seth G. Jones, in 2018, offered the most inclusive and shortest description of such KGB activities. According to him,

> During the Cold War, the Soviet Union developed a broad campaign to influence populations across the globe, which was best captured in the phrase ... "active measures." Active measures encompassed a range of activities, which were different from typical espionage and counterespionage activities. Examples included: written and oral disinformation (or *dezinformatsiya*); forgeries and false rumors; "gray" (unattributed) and "black" (falsely attributed) propaganda; manipulation and control of foreign media assets; political action and the use of agents-of-influence operations; clandestine radio stations; use of foreign Communist Parties and international front groups for pursuing Soviet foreign policy objectives; support for international revolutionary and terrorist organizations, including national liberation movements; political blackmail and kidnapping; targeted assassinations, including the killing of defectors.[29]

The scholars of Russian intelligence also present the Russian operations, which target Western academics and use for this Russian intelligence's "front organizations" such as the Russkii Mir (The Russian World) Foundation and *Rossutrudnichestvo*, as Russian "active measures."[30] The story of these Russian organizations and how they target the Western academics, became the research topic for various participants of Western think tanks, such as Chatham House in the UK and the Kennan Institute in the US, the participants, who personally witnessed the Russian interference in their own organizations.[31] One of those scholars, Orysia Lutsevich, concentrated on so-called

Russian "agents of influence" abroad. According to her, "these agents of influence abroad can be separated into three distinct tiers":

1. Major state federal agencies, large state-affiliated grant-making foundations, and private charities linked to Russian oligarchs; 2. Trusted implementing partners and local associates like youth groups, think tanks, associations of compatriots, veterans' groups, and smaller foundations that are funded by the state foundations, presidential grants, or large companies loyal to the Kremlin; and 3. Groups that share the Kremlin's agenda and regional vision but operate outside of official cooperation channels—these groups often promote an 'ultra-radical and neo-imperial vocabulary' and run youth paramilitary camps.[32]

Olga Bertelsen and other scholars emphasized the danger of those Russian organizations as "cover up" or "front organizations" for the Russian intelligence.[33]

At the same time, so-called "Russian academic imperialism" became another subject of the recent research, which demonstrated the direct Russian interference in teaching in the Western system of college education and in the research of various Western think tanks. Many scholars and journalists noted the increase and intensity of Russian interference (including Russian intelligence's interference) in Western politics and academia after 2000, when Vladimir Putin, a former KGB officer, became the President of Russia. Some of those scholars, like Taras Kuzio and Andriy Zayarnyuk, connected Russian academic imperialism to the Russian misinformation campaign, which is sponsored by the Russian state.[34]

After the beginning of the Russian war against Ukraine, more scholars tried to concentrate their research on the connections of Russian academic imperialism with the Russian intelligence operations against Western academia.[35] The recent literature on the Soviet/Russian intelligence and its influence in Western politics and academia is growing.[36] What is missing in this literature is a historical perspective, a historical analysis of the old Soviet KGB operations in Western, especially American, academia, the operations of which used a system of academic exchanges; and tracing the connections between Soviet academic imperialism and Putin's public diplomacy, which is still using the connections between Western academia and Russian think tanks and educational institutions, which are the "front organizations" of Russian intelligence. This book is an attempt to bring such a historical perspective.

SOURCES AND STRUCTURE OF THE BOOK

Concentrating on the period of the Cold War after Stalin, when the academic exchange programs started between the Soviet Union and the West, and combining the counterintelligence documents from fund 1 of the SBU archive (Kyiv, Ukraine) with the official KGB correspondence and reports to the political leadership of Soviet Ukraine from fund 16 of the same archive, my book offers a historical analysis of the Soviet and Russian intelligence interference in Western academia. A variety of these archival KGB documents is the first and major historic source for the book. Additional KGB documents came from the "open internet" sources, such as "The Chekist Monitor," a blog on the operations and personalities of the Soviet and Russian state security and intelligence organizations, a blog, organized and run by Filip Kovacevic.[37] Another group of archival documents covered the foreign travels of Soviet visiting scholars in the United States which are available from the collection of US funding agencies such as the American Council of Learned Societies (ACLS) and the International Research and Exchanges Board (IREX).

The second group of "unexpected" sources for this book consists of my recorded conversations/interviews with the retired KGB officers in the cities of Kyiv and Dnipro during the period from 1991 to 2019. In June of 2012, Leonid Leshchenko (1931–2013), Ukrainian Americanist and my colleague, introduced me in Kyiv to three former KGB officers, who were engaged in various KGB operations, including those that were connected to US President Nixon's visit to Kyiv in 1972 and the opening of US Consulate in Kyiv afterward. Frankly speaking, after those meetings with Leshchenko's friends, I decided to engage those interviews in my research. Therefore, later, in 2019, while doing my research in Kyiv archives, I interviewed Leshchenko's friends and used their notes and observations in my analysis of the real archival documents about the same events they had covered in our conversations. I promised to my interviewees that I would use only their first names in my publication, and that I would not reveal their real officer rank and position during their service in my book. I used those interviews in my first book about KGB operations in America.[38] After publication of that book, I realized that I still have transcripts of the precious material about Russian interference in Ukrainian and Western academia, and how the KGB and Russian intelligence contributed to Russian academic imperialism today. Therefore, I decided to incorporate their interviews in this book as well.

To some extent, the major source basis for this book is also personal interviews and oral histories, which I had begun recording as early as April of 1990, asking Nikolai Bolkhovitinov in Moscow and Arnold Shlepakov in Kyiv the questions about KGB connections among Soviet Russian experts in US-Canadian studies, known as Soviet Americanists.[39] My position of a former graduate student of Nikolai Bolkhovitinov at the Institute of World History (the USSR Academy of Sciences in Moscow) in 1983–1987 allowed me to approach other prominent Soviet Americanists in the USSR/Russian Academy of Sciences and MGU and interview them during the 1990s and the 2000s. As it turned out, the most interesting result of my interviews was an accumulation of various details of personal stories of Soviet Americanists, demonstrating their personal connections to the KGB, GRU, and to Russian intelligence today. I conducted more than one hundred personal interviews with former Soviet Americanists in Russia and Ukraine (and recently in the US and Canada), beginning with my first recorded conversations with my first academic mentor, Professor Viktor Kalashnikov, in Dnipropetrovsk, Ukraine. I checked correctness/plausibility of every critical statement by my interviewees either with documents, or with a testimony of at least two different witnesses. I also interviewed (by phone or email) active representatives of the academic dialogue between American and Soviet scholars, such as Basil Dmytryshyn, John Lewis Gaddis, David Goldfrank, Valery Golovskoy, Allen H. Kassof, Frank Sysyn, Donald J. Raleigh, Yale Richmond, late Richard Stites, Andrei Znamenski, Vladislav Zubok, Valery Tishkov, Ivan Kurilla, and many others about their encounters with the officers of Soviet and Russian intelligence. Some of those former Soviet Americanists (like Leonid Leshchenko and Vladislav Zubok) even admitted in their interviews the attempts of the KGB officials to use them in the system of academic exchanges with the United States.

All Soviet Americanists had various connections to the KGB. With a few exceptions, such as the obvious cases of Grigorii Sevostianov, a former KGB/intelligence officer, who became head of the famous Moscow center of American studies, and his favorite student, Nikolai Sivachev, MGU professor of US history, it is very difficult to trace "the direct KGB connections" in Soviet academia. Nevertheless, the experienced archivists in Moscow and Kyiv defined the "apparent" KGB connections of those Soviet scholars who traveled abroad before 1991, according to four major criteria: (1) their personal files had been removed (from archival collection) in accordance with the official stamp of *Osobyi (Pervyi) otdel*; (2) they had an extensive record of service as supervisors (*Soprovozhdaiushchii*, or *Starshii groupy*) of tourist groups, which traveled abroad, especially to capitalist countries, and/or as Deans of Foreign Students (*prorektor po rabote s inostrantsami*) in their schools; (3) their dossier included an extensive record of service as invited reviewers or members of review panels, which examined the applications of those Soviet officials who intended to travel abroad, especially to capitalist countries; and (4) they had accumulated an unusually frequent (e.g., twice a year) number of trips to capitalist countries, and enjoyed a simplified procedure regarding official approval for such trips. These classifications, devised by the Moscow and Kyiv archivists, helped to identify "the KGB connections" of those former Soviet scholars, who had publicly denied any association with the "directive organs." Post-Soviet archivists in Russia, some American Sovietologists, like late Richard Stites, and former Soviet Ukrainian Americanists, like late Leonid Leshchenko, emphasized the very important so-called "family relations" with KGB and Russian intelligence among many post-Soviet emigrants from the former Soviet geopolitical space, who became integrated in Western academia, like Anton Fedyashin from American University in Washington, D.C.[40] As Leonid Leshchenko noted,

> My American friends from various Canadian and American colleges, accepting as their new colleagues from Russia, the Post-Soviet emigrants, who came from the KGB officers' families, always denied such Russian intelligence influences, comparing those Russians' position to their American colleagues, who came from the CIA officers' families. My American colleagues always tried to dismiss my conversation about the KGB family connections, telling me: you cannot say that the American scholars, who came from the CIA families, are also the CIA agents. But they forgot the basic differences between the Soviet closed totalitarian society, controlled by the KGB, and the American open democratic society, where the CIA is not such a controlling force, as the Soviet KGB. Even many years after the collapse of the USSR, the KGB "family" connections, especially in the Russian Federation, where the President Putin represents the KGB, still exist and influence everything, especially political, business, and academic careers not only in Russia, but also in the West, where many "KGB children" emigrated and found their new jobs there, especially in Canada and the USA.[41]

Other sources for this book are the published memoirs of the contemporaries of the events, covered by the book. Among many books of memoirs, the best sources of the information for my research were memoirs of Soviet Ambassador to the United States Anatoly Dobrynin, and a book, written by a former general of the KGB Oleg Kalugin, a head of the KGB political operations in the United States. Besides memoirs, this book uses various contemporary periodicals, a few personal diaries, and the published collections of the KGB documents, such as "Mitrokhin Archive."

All those materials and archival documents are engaged in the text of this book, which follows the chronological and thematic order. The first chapter tells a story of the first Soviet studies centers in the United States after WWII and the Soviet intelligence's reaction to the beginning of Sovietology in the "capitalist West." The second chapter focuses on the KGB's role in influencing and structuring the research institutions of the USSR Academy of Sciences, as well as monitoring their connections with Western academia. The third chapter is about the activities of the "KGB people," especially Soviet Americanists, in international academic exchanges, during Khrushchev's thaw and Brezhnev's détente. Next, the fourth, chapter deals with the KGB spies, so-called "illegals"/"sleeper cells," who infiltrated American society, including American academia. Chapter 5 is about KGB operations against the Ukrainian American community, concentrating on the role of the Ukrainian studies centers in the US and Canada, and how Soviet/Russian intelligence monitored those centers through the 1970s until now. The sixth chapter concentrates on Russian academic imperialism in history writing and how Russian intelligence uses Russian emigrant-scholars in Western academia. The last, seventh, chapter explores the role of so-called "agents of influence" of Russian intelligence in Western think tanks and various Russian front organizations such as the Valdai discussion club and the Russkii Mir Foundation. Using the Russian intelligence services and finances of the Russian oligarchs, Putin's regime managed to influence not only Western politicians but also Western academics.

NOTES

1. See a publication of Todd Prince about the new academic trend among former Western Slavists and Sovietologists to criticize "Russian academic imperialism": https://www.rferl.org/a/russia-war-ukraine-western-academia/32201630.html.
2. Ibid.
3. This book will use the traditional Russian abbreviation for Soviet/Russian/Ukrainian intelligence agencies. The KGB is a committee of state security of the USSR (*komitet gosudarstvennoi bezopasnosti*), the FSB is a federal service of security of Russia (*federal'naia sluzhba bezopasnosti*), and the GRU is a state military intelligence of the USSR/Russia [Main Intelligence Directorate] (*gosudarstvennoie razvedyvatel'noe upravlenie*). SVR is a Service of Foreign Intelligence of Russia (*sluzhba vneshnei razvedki*). SBU stands for a service of security of Ukraine (*sluzhba bezpeky Ukrainy*).
4. Gordon Corera, *Russians Among Us: Sleeper Cells, Ghost Stories, and the Hunt for Putin's Spies* (New York: William Morrow Paperbacks, 2021), 371. See: "Maria Butina, 29, a Russian citizen residing in Washington D.C., was arrested on July 15, 2018, in Washington, D.C.": https://www.justice.gov/opa/pr/russian-national-charged-conspiracy-act-agent-russian-federation-within-united-states.
5. See https://www.justice.gov/opa/pr/russian-national-charged-conspiracy-act-agent-russian-federation-within-united-states.
6. See https://www.hstoday.us/subject-matter-areas/intelligence/in-the-wake-of-a-foreign-agent-fallout-and-lessons-from-the-case-of-maria-butina.
7. *The Soviet Invasion of Czechoslovakia in 1968: The Russian Perspective* (The Harvard Cold War Studies Book Series), edited by Jozef Pazderka (Lanham,

MD, and Boulder, CO: Rowman and Littlefield's Lexington Books, 2019), 134, 142, 280. See also https://english.gordonua.com/news/exclusiveenglish/my-name-is-fedyashin-anton-fedyashin-who-is-anton-fedyashin-and-what-was-he-teaching-maria-butina-investigation-by-yuri-felshtinsky-342703-342703.html.

8. See https://english.gordonua.com/news/exclusiveenglish/my-name-is-fedyashin-anton-fedyashin-who-is-anton-fedyashin-and-what-was-he-teaching-maria-butina-investigation-by-yuri-felshtinsky-342703-342703.html.

9. Kateryna Smagliy (with Ilya Zaslavskiy), "Hybrid Analytica: Pro-Kremlin Expert Propaganda in Moscow, Europe and the U.S. A Case Study on Think Tanks and Universities," pp. 50–51. See https://www.underminers.info/publications/hybridanalytica and compare with Josh Meyer's publication: https://www.politico.com/story/2018/07/28/mariia-butina-russia-kremlin-suspected-spy-746043.

10. See https://www.american.edu/cas/carmel/faculty.cfm.

11. See https://english.gordonua.com/news/exclusiveenglish/my-name-is-fedyashin-anton-fedyashin-who-is-anton-fedyashin-and-what-was-he-teaching-maria-butina-investigation-by-yuri-felshtinsky-342703-342703.html.

12. See https://www.wilsoncenter.org/article/wilson-center-honors-petr-aven-and-susan-carmel-lehrman.

13. See https://www.4freerussia.org/kislyaks-spider-web-of-networks-of-oligarchs-and-putins-apologists-in-the-u-s.

14. See https://www.american.edu/cas/news/susan-lehrman-chair-in-russian-history-and-culture.cfm.

15. See https://russian-americans.org/russia-forum-new-york-2016.

16. See https://www.justice.gov/usao-sdny/pr/dual-us-russian-national-charged-acting-illegally-russian-agent-united-states.

17. Interview with Leonid K., a retired KGB officer, March 3, 2019, Kyiv, Ukraine.

18. Interview with Ivan Grigorovich K., a retired KGB officer, March 4, 2019, Kyiv, Ukraine.

19. David C. Engerman, *Know Your Enemy: The Rise and Fall of America's Soviet Experts* (New York: Oxford University Press, 2009), 9.

20. Interview with Stepan Ivanovich T., a retired KGB officer, January 30, 2019, Kyiv, Ukraine. This officer became instrumental in opening the KGB archives in Kyiv for the public in 2015, after post-Soviet Russia began its first war against Ukraine.

21. Sergei I. Zhuk, *KGB Operations against the USA and Canada in Soviet Ukraine, 1953–1991* (London and New York: Routledge [Taylor & Francis] Publishing Company, 2022).

22. See John Lewis Gaddis, *The Cold War: A New History* (New York: Penguin Books, 2006); Christopher Andrew and Vasili Mitrokhin, *The Sword and the Shield: The Mitrokhin Archive and the Secret History of the KGB* (New York: Basic Books, 1999). See also John Earl Haynes, Harvey Klehr, and Alexander Vassiliev, *Spies: The Rise and Fall of the KGB in America* (New Haven: Yale University Press, 2009), Oleg D. Kalugin, *Spymaster: My Thirty-Two Years in Intelligence and Espionage Against the West* (New York, NY: Basic Books, 2009).

23. See especially Richard H. Shultz and Roy Godson, *Dezinformatsia: Active Measures in Soviet Strategy* (New York: Pergamon-Brassey's International Defense Publishers, 1984).

24. Vladimir Bukovsky, *Judgment in Moscow: Soviet Crimes and Western Complicity*, translated by Alyona Kojevnikov (Westlake Village, CA: Ninth of November Press, 2019), 629.

25. Thomas Rid, *Active Measures: The Secret History of Disinformation and Political Warfare* (New York: Farrar, Straus and Giroux, 2020), 9, 11.

26. D. Dubov, A. Barovska, T. Isakova, I. Koval, V. Horbulin; General editorship by D. Dubov. *"Active Measures" of USSR against USA: Preface to Hybrid War. Analytical Report* (Kyiv: The National Institute for Strategic Studies, 2017).

27. Olga Bertelsen, "Introduction: A Blind Spot of Active Measures," in *Russian Active Measures: Yesterday, Today and Tomorrow*, edited by Olga Bertelsen (New York: ibidem Press and Columbia University Press, 2021), 15–35, citation is from p. 2. She also described how Soviet traditions still affected post-Soviet Russian intelligence: "First, they cast challenges to their narratives and alternative narratives as actions on the 'extreme end of the Cold War spectrum.' Second, any critique of Russian foreign policy or Russia's encroachments into other states' political and cultural spheres are identified as nationalistic manifestations of ultra-right neo-fascist governments or groups that have an ax to grind with Russia." Op. cit., 18.

28. See more information about the KGB active measures in detail in Edward Mickolus, *The Counterintelligence Chronology: Spying By and Against the United States From the 1700s Through 2014* (Jefferson, NC: McFarland & Company, Inc., 2015); Kevin N. McCauley, *Russian Influence Campaigns Against the West: From the Cold War to Putin* (North Charleston, SC: CreateSpace Independent Publishing Platform, 2016); Jolanta Darczewska, Piotr Żochowski, "ACTIVE MEASURES: Russia's key export," *Point of View*, June 2017, no. 64 (Warsaw: Center for Eastern Studies), pp. 5–71; Richard Stengel, *Information Wars: How We Lost the Global Battle against Disinformation & What We Can Do About It* (New York: Atlantic Monthly Press, 2019).

29. Seth G. Jones, "Going on the Offensive: A U.S. Strategy to Combat Russian Information Warfare," quoted from https://www.csis.org/analysis/going-offensive-us-strategy-combat-russian-information-warfare. See also his book *A Covert Action: Reagan, the CIA, and the Cold War Struggle in Poland* (New York: W.W. Norton, 2018).

30. See Marcel H. Van Herpen, "The Many Faces of the New Information Warfare," *Russian Active Measures: Yesterday, Today and Tomorrow*, edited by Olga Bertelsen (New York: ibidem Press and Columbia University Press, 2021), 37–59, especially p. 50 about "The Russian World" Foundation and *Rossutrudnichestvo*; and Massimiliano Di Pasquale and Luigi Sergio Germani, "Russian Influence on Italian Culture, Academia, and Think Tanks," in *Russian Active Measures*, 263–308, especially pp. 273, 286, 291, 296.

31. I refer to Orysia Lutsevych, "Agents of the Russian World. Proxy Groups in the Contested Neighborhood," Chatham House, April 2016, https://www.chathamhouse.org/publication/agents-russian-world-proxy-groups-contested-neighbourhood, and

Kateryna Smagliy (with Ilya Zaslavskiy), "Hybrid Analytica: Pro-Kremlin Expert Propaganda in Moscow, Europe and the U.S. A Case Study on Think Tanks and Universities," pp. 1-52. See https://www.underminers.info/publications/hybridanalytica.

32. Orysia Lutsevych, "Agents of the Russian World. Proxy Groups in the Contested Neighborhood," Chatham House, April 2016, https://www.chathamhouse.org/publication/agents-russian-world-proxy-groups-contested-neighbourhood. Compare with Carolina Vendil Pallin and Susanne Oxenstierne, "Russian Think Tanks and Soft Power," FOI—Swedish Defense Research Agency, August 2018, https://www.foi.se/rest-api/report/FOI-R--4451--SE.

33. Olga Bertelsen, "Russian Front Organizations and Western Academia," *International Journal of Intelligence and Counterintelligence*, vol. 36, no. 4 (2023), 1184–1209.

34. See especially Taras Kuzio, *Crisis in Russian Studies? Nationalism (Imperialism), Racism and War* (Bristol, England: E-International Relations, 2020), Taras Kuzio, *Russian Nationalism and the Russian-Ukrainian War: Autocracy-Orthodoxy-Nationality* (London and New York: Routledge [Taylor & Francis] Publishing Company, 2022), and Andriy Zyarnyuk, "Historians As Enablers? Historiography, Imperialism, and the Legitimization of Russian Aggression," *East/West: Journal of Ukrainian Studies*, vol. ix, no. 2 (2022): 191–212. Compare with the recent studies about the "memory wars" in Putin's Russia: Jade McGlynn, *Memory Makers: The Politics of the Past in Putin's Russia* (London: Bloomsbury, 2023) and idem, *Russia's War* (New York: Polity, 2023).

35. See publications of Mark Galeotti, especially *Putin's Wars: From Chechnya to Ukraine* (London: Osprey Publishing, 2022), and of Olga Bertelsen, especially "Russian Front Organizations and Western Academia," and *Russian Misinformation and Western Scholarship: Bias and Prejudice in Journalistic, Expert, and Academic Analyses of East European and Eurasian Affairs*, edited by Taras Kuzio (Stuttgart, Germany: ibidem-Verlag / ibidem Press, 2023).

36. Mark Hollingworth, *Agents of Influence: How the KGB Subverted Western Democracies* (London: Oneworld Publications, 2023); *Russian Cultural Diplomacy Under Putin: Rossutrudnichestvo, the "Russkii Mir" Foundation, and the Gorchakov Fund in 2007–2022*, edited by Nadiia Koval and Denys Tereshchenko (Stuttgart: ibidem-Verlag, 2023). Compare with the best analysis of the new geopolitical situation in Jim Sciutto, *The Return of Great Powers: Russia, China, and the Next World War* (New York: Dutton, 2024).

37. See Filip Kovacevic's unique collections of KGB and Russian intelligence materials on the Wilson Center's website: https://www.wilsoncenter.org/person/filip-kovacevic.

38. Sergei I. Zhuk, *KGB Operations against the USA and Canada in Soviet Ukraine, 1953–1991.*

39. Eventually, I used a part of this "oral history" collection of mine for my book about cultural consumption in Soviet Ukraine during the Brezhnev era. See about my methodology of oral history and my list of questions in Sergei I. Zhuk, *Rock and Roll in the Rocket City: The West, Identity, and Ideology in Soviet Dniepropetrovsk, 1960–1985* (Baltimore, MD: Johns Hopkins University Press & Washington,

D.C.: Woodrow Wilson Center Press, 2010), 15–16, 318–320. An overwhelming majority of my interviews (especially those conducted in the 1990s) were transcribed in my numerous notebooks. Many of the recent interviews are still on my voice recorder.

For this particular book, I decided that all interview subjects, related to the Soviet intelligence service, have been anonymized or will be referred to using pseudonyms, to avoid any threat to my interview subjects from the Russian intelligence actions today.

40. I refer to my interview with Richard Stites, Philadelphia, at the 40th National Convention of the American Association for Advanced Slavic Studies, November 21, 2008; and to my interview with Leonid Leshchenko, June 25, 2013, Kyiv, Ukraine.

41. I quote my interview with Leonid Leshchenko, June 25, 2013, Kyiv, Ukraine.

Chapter 1

The KGB and Founding of the Soviet Studies Centers in Capitalist America, 1946–1960

From the early beginning of the Cold War, Soviet intelligence monitored the first centers of Soviet studies in the West, especially in "capitalist America" as the American spy schools, the CIA creation in the "American secret war" against the Soviet Union. Soviet intelligence especially targeted the members of those centers, who were the Russian emigrants and just "the apparent Soviet supporters," such as communists and anti-war activists. According to the former KGB analysts, since 1946, Soviet intelligence organizations "had begun targeting all centers of Slavic/Russian/Soviet Studies, considering them the CIA spy schools for CIA undercover operations against the USSR. From the start, Soviet intelligence agents found their 'agents of influence'— Russian emigrants and various 'Leftists'—inside those American centers and used them all the time."[1]

THE FIRST SOVIETOLOGY CENTERS IN THE "CAPITALIST AMERICA"

For the first time, the KGB administration noticed the beginnings of the special American centers for the studies of the Soviet Union as early as 1945–46. The Soviet spies informed the KGB offices about the connections between the US Army/American intelligence and the special military training centers, such the Naval School of Military Government and Administration (NSMGA) at Columbia University in New York City and the Army Specialized Training Program (ASTP), which was based in the numerous (227) American universities and colleges all over the US. These centers, founded during 1942, eventually became the foundations for a few Russian studies centers and Russian Institutes at Cornell, Columbia, and Harvard Universities.[2]

According to the NKVD/KGB sources, a few instructors of the Russian studies courses from Cornell University, which laid a foundation for a future Russian Institute at Columbia University (known as the W. Averell Harriman Institute for the Advanced Study of the Soviet Union since 1982), were so-called "Soviet sympathizers." One of them, a Russian emigrant named Vladimir Kazakevich, who taught Soviet economics at Cornell University, became the very important KGB source about a creation of the first Soviet studies center in the US. As some KGB veteran officers noted, Kazakevich was the "most precious Soviet source of information" about the American efforts to create the first Soviet studies centers in the 1940s.[3] During WWII, Kazakevich worked for the National Association of Manufacturers, trying to identify pro-Soviet propaganda in America. After coming to Cornell, Kazakevich, in his public lectures, praised Soviet educational and economic achievements and emphasized the Soviet experience to consolidate the country before the war, destroying the so-called "fifth column" of opposition. In 1944–47, many American journalists called him a "communist."[4] Despite the rumors that Kazakevich was "red professor" without any academic credentials, who promoted "the virtues of the Soviet system" among his students at Cornell University, its administration still defended him as their "best choice" for teaching not only Soviet economics, but also other courses at ASTP. According to Kazakevich's students, such as Richard Pipes, his lectures were "pure communist propaganda."[5] Eventually, Vladimir Kazakevich moved to the Soviet Union in 1949, and he offered the precious information to the KGB about the CIA influences during the first attempts to organize the centers of the Soviet studies in the US.[6] Kazakevich's case was one of many stories that allowed the Soviet intelligence to trace the origins of the "anti-Soviet studies" centers as connected to the US intelligence organizations such as the CIA. As early as 1947, Soviet ideologists and the KGB officials called those academic centers, "created to study the USSR and its socialist allies," as "the spy centers" of "imperialist aggressors," who "planned to destroy the socialist countries." This narrative was included in both political practices and propaganda of the Soviet administration.[7]

KGB administration knew also about how American Slavic centers treated suspiciously the emigrants of Slavic origin, and about their suspicions of those Slavic (especially Russian) emigrants having the possible connections to the Soviet "intelligence networks." Therefore, for future intelligence work, the experts from the KGB and GRU planned their operations relying on the American "pro-Soviet" members of those centers, rather than on the former Russian emigrants. Moreover, the KGB was aware that such Slavic studies centers, like one at Harvard University, were using various "enemies of the Soviet state" such as Vlasovites for engaging them (through those Slavic centers) in the spying activities against the Soviet Union. Soviet intelligence planned the special operations against those Vlasovites as early as 1946, using various lists of them from all available sources, including the information from the "left, pro-Communist" faculty members of Harvard University as well.[8]

Another concern of the KGB was a direct connection between the American Slavic centers and the "big capitalist corporations," such as Rockefeller Foundation, which invested money in such a center at Columbia University. KGB experts especially emphasized the "dangerous influences and interactions between" the capitalist corporations and the military organizations of the United States, using the example of NSMGA transformed into Columbia's new School of International Affairs, which became a center of "anti-Soviet activities" immediately after WWII.[9] The KGB officials also knew that a founder of the so-called Russian Institute at Columbia University, Professor Geroid Robinson, was connected directly to "American espionage," working as a chief of the USSR Division at the Office of Strategic Services (OSS), America's wartime intelligence agency (the predecessor of the CIA).[10] When Columbia's Russian Institute tried to approach the Soviet administration in 1946 and asked them about a possibility to send a few prominent Soviet "academics" as "the exchange scholars" to Columbia University, the KGB interpreted this American action as a "political provocation," involving "scholarship in American system of total espionage." As early as 1946, Soviet intelligence analysts informed Soviet leadership about the financial support of all main experts in Sovietology, like Robinson, by capitalist corporations. For them, Robinson and his American colleagues were the CIA agents on the payroll of American corporations.[11]

At the same time, from the beginning, the KGB agents were aware of the role of the "politically left," pro-communist scholars (like Marxist Herbert Marcuse) in the functioning of Soviet studies centers, such as Columbia's Russian Institute, and tried to use them, promoting Soviet political interests in American academia as well.[12,13] KGB administration understood that this institute became "the founder of modern Russian Studies" in the US, involving the Russian emigrants in its programs, and using various Russophiles among scholars of Columbia's various departments.[14] This trend of supporting Russophiles was noted by the KGB analysts, and later on it was used by them against various non-Russian national groups in Columbia and other "Russian Studies" centers in the US and Canada. One of those Russophiles was Ernest Simmons, a former professor of Russian from Cornell University, who moved to Columbia University in 1945 to teach Russian language and literature there. The same year the Rockefeller Foundation gave the American Council of Learned Societies (ACLS) a $50,000 grant for the development of

Slavic studies, "the primary purpose of which was to send Ernest Simmons to the Soviet Union and Eastern Europe"[15] to establish the exchange program between the Soviet bloc and the United States. When, in June of 1947, Simmons began his mission, he immediately attracted the attention of the KGB, which tried to monitor his travels and prevent him from establishing the contacts with the Soviet scholars. As a result of the Soviet resistance to his efforts, Simmons failed to establish any kind of exchange program with the USSR. But, still, the KGB followed his activities and became aware of Simmons's role in the creation of the first American organization of Soviet studies, the Joint Committee on Slavic Studies (founded in 1948), and the *American Slavic and East European Review*, the research journal with a strong focus on Russia and the USSR.[16]

According to the Soviet intelligence, the CIA planned to establish in Washington, D.C., a special Eurasian Research Institute, which used the resources of the Library of Congress, for organizing the "anti-Soviet provocations and spying operations" in Europe. The KGB operatives were aware that the special funds provided by the Rockefeller Foundation and the Ford Foundation for the Eurasian Research Institute led to the creation of some "spy centers" in Europe, such as a similar institute in Munich, Germany, "with overt CIA funding and no academic cover."[17] In 1954, the Ford Foundation quickly outspent Carnegie and Rockefeller Foundations combined in the field of area studies, especially in Slavic studies. Despite the growth of the Russian area specialists in the US during the 1950s, there were still few if any experts on non-Russian nationalities in the USSR, let alone on the peoples of "socialist European countries."[18] Paradoxically for the KGB observers, who criticized those American programs in Slavic studies, as the CIA "research centers," such programs in Columbia University suffered as "pro-Soviet" ones during Senator Joseph McCarthy's investigations. By late 1954, three of Columbia's five core faculty (including Ernest Simmons) faced accusations of disloyalty. This climate of fear led to changes in research priorities in those Slavic research centers, like Columbia: scholars were opting for "safe" topics, "students were opting" to study different regions, or seminar participants were taking extra care "not to appear pro-Soviet."[19]

Another focus of Slavic/Russian studies after WWII was on social sciences rather than on humanities; and Harvard University became the center of this new focus, which would shape the entire development of Slavic/Sovietology centers in the US for the years to come.[20] In 1946, Frederick Osborn, a trustee of the Carnegie Corporation of New York, decided to ask the American social scientists, especially psychologists, to help with understanding and "deciphering" the "unpredictable and unreasonable Soviet behavior." He began looking for a location to fund the research of "Russian behavior." Eventually, by July 1947 Osborn selected Harvard University, which received $75,000 for this kind of research. As the KGB analysts figured out, all those efforts led to the creation of the new Russian Research Center at Harvard, also involving the activities of not only US social scientists from that university, but also the intelligence officers from the CIA and the US Air Force. At the same time various research projects, such as the Soviet Vulnerability Project, led by economic historian W. W. Rostow, combined efforts of the intelligence officers with scholars from Harvard and MIT, including social relations faculty Raymond Bauer, Alex Inkeles, Clyde Kluckhohn, and Barrington Moore Jr., as well as historian Richard Pipes and political scientist Adam Ulan. Such projects combined both analysis and policy recommendations.[21] Their major goal was to develop a plan for "how to destroy the Soviet government's control over its population and territory through a combination of propaganda and diplomacy," supporting the secession of some of the key Soviet republics, especially Ukraine and Armenia, triggering the anti-Soviet and anti-Russian rebellions there.[22]

PROLIFERATION OF AMERICAN RESEARCH PROGRAMS IN SOVIETOLOGY AND DELAYED KGB REACTION

Another project of Harvard scholars targeted displaced persons (DPs), living in Germany, mainly in Bavaria in the American occupation zone.[23] They decided to use those DPs of Soviet origin as a source of their information about Soviet life.[24] Scholars from the University of Michigan tried to do this in 1948–49, and then in 1948 Talcott Parsons and then George Fischer from Harvard tried to interview Soviet refugees, which became the beginning of a large-scale interview project. The activities of Fischer contributed to the functioning of the Institute for the Study of the History and Culture of the USSR in Munich, Germany, funded by the CIA.[25] According to some researchers, this institute started as a special "Russian Library" that served as the "Harvard Project's" legal European office, which by 1954 "employed roughly eighty people." The first president of its Learned Council was Borys Martos. Other prominent members were B. Yakovlev, Ivan Bakalo, Mykhailo Miller, Petro Kurinny, Ivan Mirchuk, and Borys Krupnytsky. The institute had a varied publication program of periodicals, monographs, and conference proceedings in several languages, including the journals *Ukraïns'kyi zbirnyk* (17 issues, 1954–60) and *Ukrainian Review* (9 issues, 1955–60). Among its publications were works by Panas Fedenko, Vsevolod Holubnychy, Hryhory Kostiuk, Nataliia Polonska-Vasylenko, Dmytro Solovei and other Ukrainian scholars. By 1960, it had forty-five full and twenty-nine corresponding members. The institute was dissolved in June 1972.[26] According to contemporaries and scholars, the open confrontation between the emigrants of Russian ethnic origin and the ethnic Ukrainians began in this "Munich Institute," when the CIA representatives in October 1953 tried to involve in its activities the members of the Ukrainian Free Academy of Sciences, which was founded in 1945 in Augsburg, Germany. Both the CIA and the KGB officers who monitored the activities of this institute stressed Russian-Ukrainian conflict even between anti-Soviet emigrants, who were employed by the American supervisors. Eventually, this conflict led to demise of this "academic intelligence" operation.[27]

The KGB administration knew about the CIA plans "behind all Sovietologist centers in the US," especially at Columbia and Harvard. Moreover, the KGB analysts expected to use "pro-left sympathies" of many scholars, who were used by "those centers." As the recent American researchers explained, the US intelligence also knew "about the leftward political leanings of early Sovietologists":

> [While none of their] security questionnaires listed memberships in the Communist Party or other left-wing parties of the 1930s and 1940s, almost half had a connection to one or another group whose history was intertwined with that of the Communists. Two groups in particular attracted the attention of authorities: the American Student Union and the American Veterans Committee. About half of the interviewers who attended American universities belonged to one or the other. The two organizations encapsulate the trajectory of the Communist Party's "Popular Front" policies in the late 1930s and beyond. The student group was born of a joint Socialist-Communist effort in 1935; it split into factions within two years and came under Communist control in 1939.[28]

The KGB administration in Kyiv became informed about a new academic project of "the spy surveying" of the Soviet emigrants by the American research centers of "the Soviet Studies." As former KGB officers recalled, the most alarming fact of that project was how "the American researchers used non-Russian, especially Ukrainian, emigrants (former DPs) for their interviews."[29] The KGB became aware of the special research project by Harvard University to "explore the problems of political allegiance and disaffection among Soviet citizens" and "the extent of home front support in the USSR in a military conflict between the Soviet and American troops in a future war." The KGB agents informed the Soviet leaders that a special group of researchers from Harvard University traveled from the United States to Germany in the fall of 1950 to interview the former Soviet citizens, who were interred in DP German camps. The KGB realized that for more than nine months in 1950 and 1951, the American researchers collected their information through the interviews with DPs in Germany, subsequently providing their material for various US "spying" organizations. But details of this research project became "public" only later via numerous TV shows and publications by the participants of this Harvard project.[30] The failure of the KGB to find the information about this project "in advance," eventually pushed the KGB administration to pay more close attention to the Western centers of Sovietology (especially in the US) at the different colleges and universities during the 1950s and the 1960s.[31]

At the same time, the KGB administration in Kyiv, which was always obsessed with "a threat of Ukrainian nationalism to integrity of Soviet Ukraine," was relieved after reading the major results of the Harvard research project, based on numerous interviews of the former Soviet citizens. As the retired KGB officers noted,

> Overall, the representatives of Soviet intelligence administration were happy that US intelligence and the American experts in Soviet Studies were misled and confused by the results of that project, which obviously ignored the 'nationalist factor' and focused from now on the Russian aspects of Soviet developments. For us, it meant that the CIA and other Western intelligence agencies had less funding for Ukrainian and Jewish nationalist activities inside Ukraine, and that American experts in Soviet Studies became more Russia-oriented and completely ignored the massive Russification of non-Russian Soviet republics.[32]

The KGB officers quoted the published observation by the American researchers that "the basic social and political values of our [Soviet DPs] respondents, their attitudes toward the Soviet regime, and their life experiences and life chances were on the whole strikingly little determined by nationality as compared with their social origins or their class position."[33]

Paradoxically, the similar observation about a Russia-focused analysis of the Soviet geopolitical space was made by many American scholars, who researched the development of Slavic/Soviet studies centers in the United States. One of them, David C. Engerman, wrote,

> While American scholars devoted much of the 1950s to hand-wringing over the need for more work on non-Russian (and especially non-Slavic) peoples in the Soviet Union, the data from the RIP [Harvard Refugee Interview Project] offered evidence that nationality was a minor issue in the USSR. For all of the hand-wringing, the view that nationality was not a key factor in Soviet life held sway for decades.... [T]he Harvard project cast doubt on two American hopes for the dissolution of the USSR—a military coup or the secession of minority nationalities.[34]

Another KGB failure was a delayed reaction to an institutionalization of Slavic/Soviet studies in the US. The KGB agents had already reported about the first attempt in 1948 to create the American Association for the Advancement of Slavic Studies (AAASS). Only after 1964, when AAASS had its first annual convention, the KGB administration realized the direct influence and connection of those Harvard and Columbia professors, whom they studied through their publications in the 1950s, on and with the US intelligence operations against the USSR.[35] As a result, during the first official academic exchanges with the US, Soviet intelligence began targeting those American universities, which were prominent in organizing the first American centers of Sovietology, such as Columbia University, but at the same time ignoring the professional Western organizations of Slavists and Sovietologists, such as AAASS.

SOVIET SPIES INSIDE THE FIRST ACADEMIC EXCHANGE WITH AMERICA

Officially, Soviet-American cultural and academic exchanges started in 1958. After the long and controversial negotiations between the USSR and the US, which began on October 29, 1957, in Washington, D.C., William S. B. Lacy, President Eisenhower's Special Assistant on East-West Exchanges, and Georgiy Z. Zarubin, Soviet Ambassador to the United States, signed a special document, in fact, the first US-USSR exchanges agreement, entitled "Agreement between the United States of America and the Union of Soviet Socialist Republics on Exchanges in the Cultural, Technical and Educational Fields" on January 27, 1958.[36] As Soviet newspaper *Pravda* interpreted this document:

> Two sides agreed that during 1958 they will exchange four delegations of the university professors and college teachers, representing the university education in natural sciences, engineering technologies and humanities, and for learning about the systems of higher education in the Soviet Union and the United States, which will include 5–8 persons for a period of visit of 2–3 weeks. Two sides will provide an exchange of the delegations of university professors and college teachers between Moscow and Columbia Universities, Leningrad, and Harvard Universities. The future exchanges of the university professors and college teachers of other universities of the USSR and the USA will be decided by both sides, if it is necessary. Both sides will provide the student exchange between Moscow and Leningrad Universities, on the one hand, and US universities, on the other, with twenty students on each side during 1958/59 academic year. For 1959/60 academic year such an exchange will be with thirty students on each side. Composition of these student groups will be defined by each side. Each side will provide an exchange of the delegations of educators (8–10 persons) for a thirty-day at the end of 1958.[37]

This exchange started in 1958 with twenty Soviet students. Their travels in America were officially sponsored by the Fulbright Scholarship Program, which originated in 1946. This student exchange was recorded in the official documents for academic year of 1958–59, although most of these students began their studies only in January of 1959; and their visits ranged from four to twelve months. The US sent twenty American scholars to the USSR and the "initial agreement called for increasing to thirty scholars each way in 1959–1960."[38]

From this early beginning of the new Soviet-American relations, the KGB used a variety of the American funded exchanges programs (from ACLS, International Research and Exchange Board [IREX] to Fulbright) as a cover for sending their agents to America. For many young KGB officers, such a trip to the US in a role of "a Soviet student of American studies" became the first foreign assignment, which helped them to join the Soviet intelligence network in America.[39] Traditionally, this first KGB assignment for such "Soviet Americanists" was a simple one:

> Just lay the foundation for future work—the KGB supervisor instructed such agents before their "academic exchange trip" to America. . . . But don't overstep the line. Now that you've been picked to go to America, make it your business to learn more about the country. Buy yourself good maps. Improve your English. Find out about their way of life. Communicate with people and make as many friends as possible.[40]

Such KGB practices affected international academic exchange programs, especially when they involved various Soviet experts in American studies. The presence of the KGB people characterized all Soviet exchanges with America from the early beginning. As one member of the first Soviet group of "student exchange with America"[41] (four of them were "Americanists" sent to Columbia University) recalled, they met in Moscow by early September of 1958 at the headquarters of the Communist Youth League (Komsomol) for special instructions before their travel to the United States:

> Of the eighteen Soviets in our group, half were officers of the KGB or Soviet military intelligence, known as GRU; the other half could be counted on to cooperate with us. Four students were assigned to Columbia University. One was from GRU, two of us were from the KGB, and the fourth was from the Central Committee of the Communist Party. His name was Alexander Yakovlev, and he would go on to forge a close relationship with Mikhail Gorbachev and become one of the architects of perestroika.[42]

As memoirs of the participants in the first academic exchanges demonstrated, it was a normal practice to mix the communist party functionaries with the KGB/intelligence operatives in the groups of Soviet Americanists.

According to the official American documents, the first four Soviet exchange students, sponsored by the US government, arrived in the US during late November of 1958 to study at Columbia University:

> They were "Gennadiy P. Bekhterev—a constitutional lawyer who [is] interested in (the US) local and state governmental administration; Oleg D. Kalugin—a philologist and student of English [especially American] literature who [is] enrolled in the International Division of the School of Journalism; Yuli N. Stozhkov—a student of the Pedagogical Institute interested in American history especially during and after World War II, and Alexander N. Yakovlev—also a student at the Pedagogical Institute, also interested in American history during and after World War II."[43]

Technically speaking, all these participants in the first academic exchange were Soviet students of American studies, described in the official documents as "Soviet Americanists." All of them were communists, cleared by the KGB, and two of them, Bekhterev and Kalugin were KGB officers, and Stozhkov was a GRU (Main Intelligence Directorate) officer. And one of their goals was to establish connections with American scholars who were specializing in Russian and Soviet studies at Columbia University.[44] This became a normal practice for the Soviet academic guests who visited the United States. As Nikolai Bolkhovitinov and Aron Gurevich, Soviet historians, used to joke during the 1990s, "it was a correct proportion for Soviet academic delegation—one among four Soviet participants in the exchange program [during the Brezhnev era] with the capitalist countries was a regular KGB officer, and other three—just the KGB informers." But in 1958–59, at the beginning of this program, as we see, it was a different ratio—three out of four Soviet academic visitors were the intelligence officers.[45]

All those Soviet "Americanists," like KGB officer Kalugin, became the most active participants in the academic exchange program, who were supported by their American college supervisors, many of them being the experts in Slavic/Soviet studies. Because of their communicative talent and intellect, Soviet exchange students like Kalugin attracted the attention of their American colleagues who praised their good linguistic skills and intellectual abilities.[46] Paradoxically, from the early beginning of these exchanges, all official American reports praised those Soviet guest scholars who happened to be either the "undercover" KGB officers, or the KGB "collaborators." In 1959, American officials positively described Kalugin, applauding his fluency in English, contrasting his intellectual abilities with "very bad

English skills" of his "partner" Yakovlev. At some point, a Foreign Student Admissions Officer from Columbia University even noted that Kalugin had "gone so far as to learn to type in English to meet one of the requirements of the program. This is considerable as he had never typed in Russia before."[47]

The first American report of 1959 noted the trend, which, overall, characterized all Soviet visitors (including the obvious KGB agents) to America. These visitors demonstrated "[despite their supposed anti-American feelings] their sincere curiosity about and even fondness [sometimes even an obvious fascination with] of America and Americans":

> They [Bekhterev, Kalugin, Yakovlev, and Stozhkov] are all very interested in America and Americans. They have taken full advantage so far as I can see of numerous opportunities to visit American homes and churches.... They wish to do more and have asked me as a friend to arrange trips to American secondary schools and colleges for the spring.... They are most anxious to see the rest of the United States and have asked me to enquire about a tour.[48]

Paradoxically, during 1959–60, the American supervisors, the experts in Soviet studies, encouraged and supported those Soviet exchange students, like Kalugin, suspecting their KGB connections. Those American "Sovietologists" tried to incorporate the Soviet scholars into the international academic community, starting with "opening a dialogue between the Soviet and American scholars, who participated in the first wave of academic exchanges, and trying to avoid the open ideological confrontation, pursuing a peculiar sort of political correctness in their relations with Soviet academic visitors."[49]

Many years after, the late Professor Richard Stites from Georgetown University, who knew personally those American scholars, the former supervisors of the studies for the first Soviet student visitors in Columbia in 1959–1960, noted that:

> The "left liberal" organizers of the first American centers for Soviet Studies in Columbia and Harvard not only encouraged and maintained the new opportunities for academic exchanges with the Soviet students after Stalin, but also tried not to notice those Soviet students' well-known connections with the KGB. Moreover, this kind of attitude would create a very ambiguous situation in those schools, like Columbia and Harvard, which would be used by the Soviet intelligence for building the important personal connections between the Soviet guests (mostly "KGB people") and American hosts inside American academia, using the structures and influences of the first American centers for Slavic/Soviet Studies.[50]

For many years to come, starting in 1959, this tradition of establishing the personal connections between American and Soviet scholars via the American centers for Slavic/Soviet studies will become the most important result of the academic exchanges, which the Soviet intelligence will be using for its operations inside American academia through the entire history of the Cold War. From the early beginning, the presence of "left-oriented" American scholars and researchers of the Russian ethnic origin in the first American Slavic centers would be used by the KGB operatives for their own special operations and promoting various pro-Soviet notions and practices.

As a retired KGB officer recalled in 2019,

> At the beginning, the KGB administration did not treat the first American organization for Slavic/Soviet studies (AAASS) seriously [after 1948—SZh.] as a just "academic superficial" cover for training the future American spies against the USSR. Instead, the KGB analysts concentrated on planning their operations [and active measures] against the most famous American universities, with their faculty, who specialized in Sovietology, such as Harvard and Columbia Universities. That is why, the first KGB agents [like Kalugin and Bekhterev—SZh.] were sent to those schools during the first wave of the academic exchanges in 1959. Only after 1964, with the first annual public meetings of AAASS, Soviet intelligence began paying more attention to such Slavic Associations in the West, trying to influence them in pro-Soviet direction as well. Moreover, since the end of the 1960s, under Brezhnev and Andropov, Soviet intelligence [both KGB and GRU—SZh.] had begun targeting, especially during the 1970s and 1980s, various Sovietology centers in the America. If before the 1970s, major participants of the Soviet programs of academic exchange with America were predominantly scientists and engineers, connected to the KGB, who were engaged mainly in industrial and technological espionage in the US and stealing various American engineering innovations, during the 1970s, more and more Soviet exchange scholars, who traveled to the US, the UK, and Canada represented humanities and social sciences, especially such fields like American Studies (Amerikanistika). Moreover, various research institutions in the fields of humanities, so-called Institutes of the USSR Academy of Sciences, specializing in a variety of field studies—from African and Slavic studies to American studies—were formed under a direct influence of the KGB to provide a "base" and education for the KGB agents and professional spies, who could be active abroad, especially in Western academia.[51]

As we see, various Soviet academic research institutions became the new KGB "actors" in the academic and cultural Cold War. Those traditions of KGB connections with and KGB supervision of the Soviet academic institutions have survived through the years of transformation of Soviet system of college education and the USSR Academy of Sciences from the years of late Stalinism through Khrushchev's, Brezhnev's, and Gorbachev's rule and still exist in post-Soviet space. The next chapter will explore those connections, concentrating mainly on Soviet academic institutions, related to the field of American studies.

NOTES

1. Interview with Bohdan Josypovych K., a retired KGB/SBU Officer, February 9, 2019, Kyiv, Ukraine.
2. David C. Engerman, *Know Your Enemy*, 17–18; Gary May, *Un-American Activities: The Trials of William Remington* (New York: Oxford University Press, 1994), 71–72.
3. See Soviet intelligence documents tracing Kazakevich as early as 1944 in https://www.wilsoncenter.org/sites/default/files/media/documents/publication/White_Notebook_No.2_Translated1.pdf.
4. See publications in *Time* magazine in 1944: https://content.time.com/time/subscriber/article/0,33009,850859,00.html, and in *The Harvard Crimson* in 1947: https://content.time.com/time/subscriber/article/0,33009,850859,00.html.
5. Interview with Ivan Grigorovich K., a retired KGB officer, March 3, 2019, Kyiv, Ukraine; "Accused Russian Returns to Soviet," *New York Times*, January 18, 1950; Richard Pipes, *Vixi: Memoirs of a Non-Belonger* (New Haven, CT, 2003), 49–50; David C. Engerman, *Know Your Enemy*, 21.
6. Interview with Ivan Grigorovich K.; "Accused Russian Returns to Soviet"; David C. Engerman, *Know Your Enemy*, 355. Eventually, Kazakevich resumed his teaching in Moscow, the USSR. In 1958, Canadian and American scholars met him teaching as a professor of economics at prestigious Institute of the World Economy and International Relations of the Soviet Academy of Sciences (IMEMO) in Moscow. See Harold Gordon Skilling, *Education of a Canadian: My Life as a Scholar and Activist* (Ottawa: Carleton University Press, 2000), 144, 189–190.
7. Among numerous Soviet publications about the "American Soviet studies spy centers," see V. Minaev, "Total'nyi shpionazh v novom izdanii," *Novoe vremia*, September 10, 1947, p. 7.
8. See about Vlasovites, the members of Vlasov Army, the Russian Liberation Army (ROA), which collaborated with Nazi Germany in WWII, in Benjamin Tromly, *Cold War Exiles and the CIA: Plotting to Free Russia* (New York: Oxford University Press, 2019), 103–104. Compare with a description of those KGB operations in Sergei I. Zhuk, *KGB Operations against the USA and Canada in Soviet Ukraine, 1953–1991* (London and New York: Routledge, 2022), 7, 14, 16, 19, 20ff.
9. David C. Engerman, *Know Your Enemy*, 25–26.
10. Ibid. Among many interviews the most important was one with Ivan Grigorovich, retired KGB officer, and especially an interview with Leonid K., a retired KGB officer, March 3, 2019, Kyiv, Ukraine.
11. David C. Engerman, op. cit., 31. Soviet KGB officers discussed the role of such centers in the 1950s as well. See Sergei Zhuk, *KGB Operations*. I quote my interview with Leonid K., a retired KGB officer, March 3, 2019, Kyiv, Ukraine.

12. Personal collection of Leonid K.
13. Interview with Leonid K. Compare with David C. Engerman, op. cit., 33, 35–36.
14. Ibid., 36. Interview with Igor T., a former KGB officer, July 18, 2001, Dnipro, Ukraine.
15. David C. Engerman, op. cit., 36.
16. Ibid., 38. Interviews with Ivan Grigorovich and Stepan Ivanovich K.
17. Ibid., 40; Charles T. O'Connell, *The Munich Institute on the USSR: Origin and Social Composition*, The Carl Beck Papers in Russian and East European Studies, no. 808 (Pittsburgh, PA: University of Pittsburgh Press, 1990). Interview with Stepan Ivanovich K.
18. Ibid., 41.
19. Ibid., 42. Interview with Stepan Ivanovich K.
20. Ibid., 43–45.
21. Ibid., 48–50. Soviet KGB officers called those American scholars "academic spies." See my interview with Leonid K., a retired KGB officer, March 3, 2019, Kyiv, Ukraine.
22. David Engerman, op. cit., 50; and Gregory Mitrovich, *Undermining the Kremlin: America's Strategy to Subvert the Soviet Bloc, 1947–1956* (Ithaca, NY: Cornell University Press, 2000), 117–120.
23. See the Russian study of displaced persons: P. M. Polian, *Zhertvy dvukh diktatur: trud, unizhenie i smert' sovetskikh voennoplennykh i ostarbaiterov na chuzhbine i na rodine* (Moscow: ROSSPEN, 2002).
24. David Engerman, op. cit., 51–52. Compare with the Russian research about this project in E.V. Kodin, *Garvardskii proekt* (Moscow: Rosspen, 2003), chapter 5.
25. Ibid., 52–53. See also Charles T. O'Connell, Op. cit., and Benjamin Tromly, *Cold War Exiles and the CIA*, 1–2, 103, 150–153. Tromly called this institute "a byproduct of the Harvard Project on the Soviet Social System, the sociological study of Soviet refugees." See op. cit., 150.
26. E.V. Kodin, *Miunkhenskii institut po izucheniiu istorii i kul'tury SSSR, 1950–1972 gg.: evropeiskii tsentr sovetologii?* (Smolensk: Izd-vo SmolGU, 2016), 16. See also A. V. Popov, "Miunkhenskii institut po izucheniiu istorii i kul'tury SSSR i vtoraia emigratsiia," *Novyi istoricheskii vestnik*, 10, no.1 (2004): 54–70. See also chapter 1 of my book, Sergei Zhuk, *KGB Operations*, 3–23.
27. See especially Benjamin Tromly, op. cit., 152–153. Interview with former KGB officer Leonid K.
28. David Engerman, op. cit., 57–58.
29. Interview with retired KGB officer Leonid K.; compare with David Engerman, op. cit., 60.
30. Among those numerous publications, the KGB officers especially quoted (in Russian translation) a book by Raymond Augustine, Alex Inkeles, Clyde Kluckhohn, *How the Soviet System Works: Cultural, Psychological and Social Themes* (Cambridge, MA: Harvard University Press, 1956).
31. See about this in my book, Sergei Zhuk, *KGB Operations*, chapters 1, 2, 3.
32. See my interview with Leonid K.

33. Raymond Augustine, Alex Inkeles, and Clyde Kluckhohn, *How the Soviet System Works*, 239, 243.
34. Engerman, op. cit., 67, 68.
35. I refer to Leonid K. Three of the AAASS six founding board members were involved in the Harvard refugee interview project (Joseph Berliner, Merle Fainsod, and Alex Inkeles), and two of them (Joseph Berliner and Alexander Dallin) served as presidents of AAASS. See Engerman, op. cit., 69.
36. See about this and following US-USSR exchanges agreements in the books of those who organized these exchanges from the US side: Robert F. Byrnes, *Soviet-American Academic Exchanges, 1958–1975* (Bloomington, IN: Indiana University Press, 1976), 46–47, 48ff., and Yale Richmond, *U.S.-Soviet Cultural Exchanges, 1958–1986* (Boulder, CO: Westview Press, 1987), 2, 4ff. Compare with the Russian publications, especially A.S. Krymskaia, "K istorii nauchno-obrazovatel'nykh obmenov mezhdu SSSR i SSHA v kontse 1950-kh–1960-e gg.," *Noveishaia istoriia Rossii*, 2011, no. 2, 99–106. See also in Norman E. Saul, "The Program That Shattered the Iron Curtain: The Lacy-Zarubin (Eisenhower-Khrushchev) Agreement of January 1958," *New Perspectives on Russian-American Relations*, edited by William Benton Whisenhunt and Norman E. Saul (London and New York: Routledge, 2015), 229–239.
37. This is a citation from "Soglashenie mezhdu SSSR i SSHA ob obmenakh v oblasti kul'tury, tekhniki i obrazovaniia," Chapter 10 "An Exchange of the University Delegations" published in *Pravda*, 1958, January 29, no. 29, 6. See also Walter L. Hixson, *Parting the Curtain: Propaganda, Culture and the Cold War, 1945–1961* (New York: St. Martin Press, 1998), 151–183.
38. David Engerman, op. cit., 89. In 1956, Americans created a special program for providing grants for American scholars, who traveled abroad, called Inter-University Committee on Travel Grants (IUCTG). Using Soviet-American agreement on cultural exchanges in 1958–1960, IUCTG "sent sixty-eight students to the USSR and hosted a similar number in the United States. To the constant frustration of the Americans involved, the USSR sent laboratory scientists who had little direct bearing on Sovietology as practiced by social scientists and humanists. Another frustration for IUCTG was its effort to decentralize Sovietology, which was at best a partial success in the early years; close to half of the participants came from Columbia and Harvard." Ibid. See also in Yale Richmond, *Cultural Exchange and the Cold War: Raising the Iron Curtain* (University Park, PA: Penn State University Press, 2003), pp. 30–35.
39. See also the good portrayals of Kalugin's and other KGB people participation in the exchange program in Yale Richmond, *Cultural Exchange and the Cold War: Raising the Iron Curtain* (University Park, PA: Penn State University Press, 2003), pp. 32–35 (about Oleg Kalugin), and 36–38 (about Boris Yuzhin).
40. Oleg D. Kalugin, *Spymaster: My Thirty-Two Years in Intelligence and Espionage Against the West* (New York, NY: Basic Books, 2009), 23.
41. Kalugin called this exchange program "made under the auspices of a Fulbright Foundation student exchange." See Oleg D. Kalugin, *Spymaster*, 23.
42. Oleg Kalugin, *Spymaster*, 24. As Kalugin recalled later, because he needed a cover story for his student exchange, he (a senior lieutenant of the KGB with a salary

of 300 rubles) posed "as a graduate of the Philology Department of Leningrad University." And he continued, "This ruse was eventually swallowed by the *New York Times* and others in the United States. I travelled to Leningrad to cook up a past and spent a month at the university, familiarizing myself with the campus and picking a topic for my nonexistent senior thesis. After several weeks, I 'graduated' from Leningrad University and became the proud holder of degree number 981064, dutifully signed by one Professor Alexandrov, member of the USSR Academy of Sciences." Ibid., 23. See also a good biography of Alexander Yakovlev and his first visit to US in: Christopher Shulgan, *The Soviet Ambassador: The Making of the Radical Behind Perestroika* (Toronto: McClelland & Stewart, 2008), 34ff.

43. Library of Congress. Archival Manuscript Collection. International Research and Exchanges Board [hereafter LC. IREX], RC 94, F 23, Letter on January 15, 1959, by Stephen Viederman, Foreign Student Admissions Officer, to Professor Henry L. Roberts, Russian Studies at Columbia University.

44. See Kalugin's memoirs: Oleg Kalugin, *Spymaster*, pp. 21–33, about his KGB operative work in New York City; and pp. 398–399 about "Gennadi Bekhterev, one of [his] KGB colleagues from [his] Columbia University days." See my interview with Yale Richmond via phone, Muncie, Indiana, May 9, 2012. Both Bekhterev and Kalugin were promoted to the rank of the general of KGB by 1990. Compare with Christopher Shulgan, op. cit., 34–35.

45. Conversation with Nikolai N. Bolkhovitinov and Aron Ya. Gurevich during our trip to Madrid, Spain, August 25, 1990, for the 17th Congress of the Historical Sciences. As Kalugin recalled, "The KGB had infiltrated the [Soviet] Foreign Ministry to the same extensive degree that it controlled the Soviet media. Nearly half the Soviet diplomats stationed overseas were officers of the KGB or military intelligence." And he added that since 1965 "of the hundred or so people stationed at the [Soviet] embassy [in Washington], about forty were KGB officers." See Oleg Kalugin, *Spymaster*, pp. 71–72, and 73.

46. Both Yale Richmond and Donald Raleigh acknowledged this fact. See also my interview with Donald J. Raleigh via phone, Muncie, Indiana, May 11, 2012.

47. See in LC. IREX. RC 94, F 23, Letter by Stephen Viederman, January 15, 1959, pp. 1–2.

48. Ibid., p. 3. See also in Oleg Kalugin, *Spymaster*, 27, 29.

49. Interview with Richard Stites, Philadelphia, 2008.

50. Interview with Richard Stites.

51. Interview with a retired KGB officer Leonid K., Kyiv, April 3, 2019.

Chapter 2

The KGB and International Academic Connections in the USSR Academy of Sciences

One of the first institutes of the USSR Academy of Science, which was created under close supervision of the Soviet intelligence in 1947, was the Institute of Slavic Studies and Balkan Studies (*Institut slavianovedeniia* in Russian). The major goal of this venue was not only to study, but to monitor the international connections of the Soviet Union with the newly created Slavic socialist states in Eastern Europe, such as Poland and Yugoslavia. The KGB sent to this institute its representative, Ilia Solomonovich Miller (1918–1978), who became a head of the special group, which later was renamed as a sector of the international connections among the Slavic nations (*sector mezhslavianskikh svaizei*). Miller was a former officer of the SMERSH (*smert' shpionam*—death to the spies) group, which was created by the NKVD, the predecessor of the KGB, for the fight against the German spies and Nazi collaborators during WWII.[1]

Ilia Miller, like Grigorii Sevostianov from the Institute of World History and many other professional KGB officers, not only represented the KGB in the academic institutions in Moscow, but also was responsible for the KGB control of all international connections and links in their institutions. These Moscow KGB curators controlled the provincial national institutions of the USSR Academy of Sciences as well. Miller personally "curated" (controlled) the Institute of History of the Ukrainian Academy of Sciences in Kyiv. Among many of the Ukrainian scholars controlled through those connections there were famous Soviet Ukrainian historians such as Arnold Shlepakov and Stanislav Kulchytsky.[2]

According to contemporaries, the Institute of the World Economy and International Relations of the Soviet Academy of Sciences (IMEMO) in Moscow also became the infamous Soviet "academic center for retirement" of the former KGB and GRU officers, who worked as Soviet spies abroad. Among the pioneers of the Soviet intelligence service was Zalman Litvin (1908–1993), who worked as a Soviet spy for the GRU in China, Japan, and the US until 1946. Upon returning to Moscow, Litvin continued his GRU service, now with the rank of colonel. He also reportedly made several "special" trips to Europe and later taught at the Military and Diplomatic Academy of the General Staff of the Soviet Armed Forces (a higher military school specializing in training military intelligence officers). In the spring of 1953, at the height of an anti-Semitic campaign in the USSR, Litvin was discharged from the Army "as a Jew" and lost his teaching job at the Military and Diplomatic Academy. He would tell his friends years later that in those days he had feared arrest. For three years, he could not find a job, and earned his living by taking on freelance translation assignments. In 1956, during Khrushchev's Thaw, Litvin became a senior scholar at IMEMO, where he worked until his death in 1993. He was remembered by his colleagues as a "brilliant expert in the United States and the Far East." Another Litvin colleague, Vladimir Kazakevich, also worked for Soviet intelligence and lived in the United States, before joining IMEMO faculty.[3]

Another institution supervised by the KGB was the Institute of African Studies (*Institut Afriki*), created in 1959 in the system of the USSR Academy of Sciences, whose first director was Ivan Potekhin (1959–1964). From the early start of existence of this institution, its experts not only provided Soviet leadership and KGB analysts with professional information about African countries, but also participated in the special operations of the KGB and GRU against Western intelligence, including the American CIA, which became an important assignment for many Soviet scholars-Africanists who worked under the new director, Vasily Solodovnikov (1964–1972). This second institute's director, Solodovnikov, was a KGB agent, who worked undercover as a Soviet diplomat in Africa. He brought those KGB connections to the Institute of African Studies, which became the training ground for many professional Soviet intelligence officers, who worked not only in Africa, but also later in America.[4]

During the 1970s, Soviet professional spies, after their retirement, like Iosif R. Grigulevich (Lavretskii), a famous Soviet expert in Latin American studies, continued their careers at various academic institutes in Moscow, advising their academic colleagues and supervising academic exchanges with the capitalist West. After 1979, when Iosif Grigulevich was elected as a new corresponding member of the USSR Academy of Sciences, he became the active leading figure in the KGB and the GRU, controlling and monitoring the foreign connections of the Institute of Ethnography and the Institute of Latin America of the USSR Academy until his death in 1988 in Moscow. Eventually, the Institute of Latin America, which was founded in

1961, became the important center of the Soviet and Russian espionage in Latin American countries, led by such famous scholars-spies like Grigulevich (Lavretskii).[5]

Two other centers (for "American Studies") in the USSR Academy of Science were also created under direct KGB supervision. Chronologically, the first special center for the "studies of American countries" was organized in 1953 by the Soviet government at the Institute of History of the USSR Academy of Sciences. The presidium of the USSR Academy of Sciences prepared a special decree about this, which was published on March 20, 1953, "On the Scientific Activity and Status of Staff at the USSR Academy of Science Institute of History." Following this decree, a new department on the history of American countries was organized at the Institute of History that same year by B. N. Krylov, who was one of the trained specialists in the theory of communist and working-class movements and officially represented the Central Committee of the Communist Party of the Soviet Union (CPSU) at the institute.[6]

GRIGORII SEVOSTIANOV AND THE FIRST SOVIET CENTER OF AMERICAN STUDIES

At the same time, the official KGB "curator" of this center (like Ilia Miller at the Institute of Slavic Studies) represented the interests of the Soviet intelligence. This KGB "curator" was Grigorii Sevostianov, a professional Soviet spy and intelligence/KGB officer, who during WWII conducted Soviet espionage in the Far East. Grigorii Sevostianov was born into a Don Cossack family on the Russian Cossack farmstead of Pleshakovo (the region of Rostov-na-Donu) on March 23 (April 5), 1916. After losing his parents in 1924, Sevostianov stayed with his grandfather and his older sister, living on a small peasant farm in the region of Rostov. After graduation from the high school in a neighboring town, Sevostianov, who had already joined a local Komsomol organization, moved to the city of Novocherkassk, where he entered the local technical college (Polytechnical Institute). In December of 1940, a recent graduate from this college, Sevostianov joined the Red Army. During the Second World War, in July of 1941, Sevostianov's regiment was surrounded by Nazi troops near the city of Minsk in Soviet Byelorussia. By October of 1941, Sevostianov had not only organized the resistance of his own regiment to the Nazi occupants, but also established relations with Soviet intelligence representatives sent by Moscow to Byelorussia. In March of 1942, Sevostianov became head of a special intelligence group "Chekist" (meaning "the officer of the Soviet political police") among local Byelorussian resistance activists and anti-Nazi partisans. Until July of 1944,

Sevostianov served as an NKVD officer (Soviet police operative) among Soviet partisans, demonstrating his organizational skills and unique leadership abilities.[7]

Sevostianov not only played a prominent role in organizing a guerrilla (partisan) movement in Soviet Byelorussia against Nazi occupants, he also became one of the organizers of a new post-war Soviet government in liberated Byelorussia from July of 1944 through September of 1945. Then, for a short period of time, Sevostianov was sent to the Far East where he was in charge of the special Soviet "spy infrastructure," whose goal was to fight against Japanese agents in northern China, liberated by the Soviet Army and Chinese communists. After his "spy career," in 1945, Sevostianov was sent by the KGB to the High Diplomatic School of the USSR Ministry of Foreign Affairs, from which he graduated in 1947. The next year he was admitted to graduate school in the USSR Academy of Sciences' Institute of History. In 1950, using his short "spy experience" in China, Sevostianov defended his freshly written *kandidatskaia* dissertation, entitled as *American Imperialism Is An Accomplice of the Japanese Aggression in China, 1931–33*. In March of the same year, he was recommended by the KGB to be hired by the Institute of History. In 1960 he defended his doctoral dissertation entitled *Imperialist States' Politics in the Far East, July 1937–December of 1941*, and was appointed in September of 1967 as an acting head of the sector of history of the US and Canada at the same Institute. In April of 1969, Sevostianov was officially approved as a chair of this sector. He replaced an older chair, Boris Mikhailov, a former apparatchik from the Central Committee of the CPSU, an expert in the working-class movement.[8]

From the outset, this sector united experts in Latin American and US/Canadian history. Following the division of the Institute of History in 1968 into two separate institutes, World History and USSR History, the center for the "studies of American countries" was eventually compartmentalized as well. All specialists in Latin American history left this center. After this subsequent division in 1968, the center was transformed into a new "sector of history of the USA and Canada" at the new Institute of World History (hereafter IVI) under the leadership of Grigorii Sevostianov. He was finally replaced in 1988 by Nikolai Bolkhovitinov, who was not connected to the KGB.[9] This became standard institutional policy at all centers for American studies in the Soviet Union: all directors of these centers were approved by the KGB or had direct connections to this organization.

GEORGI ARBATOV AND THE SECOND SOVIET CENTER OF THE AMERICAN STUDIES

The second Soviet center of American studies was created in May 1967 as a special Institute of the USA at the USSR Academy of Sciences (it was renamed in 1975 as the Institute of the USA and Canada [hereafter ISKAN]) under the leadership of Georgi Arbatov.[10] Many prominent Soviet experts on the US economy and politics, including Nikolai Inozemtsev, the first Soviet expert on American contemporary economic history, were employed by IMEMO (Moscow's Institute of World Economy and International Relations, the USSR Academy of Sciences)—formerly the center of Soviet economic theory, closed by Stalin in 1949 and re-opened during the Khrushchev thaw.[11] Some Soviet Americanist experts moved from IMEMO to ISKAN. Arbatov, who also had two years' experience of working at IMEMO, began organizing this new institute of American studies in November of 1967. Officially, he was appointed as ISKAN director on December 20, 1967.[12] At first, a presidium of the USSR Academy of Sciences issued an order about an organization of this institute as a part of the Department of Economy of the USSR Academy of Sciences in December of 1967. This decision was officially approved by the Politburo of the CPSU Central Committee in October of 1968, and on November 15, 1968, this institute received its official name of the Institute of the USA and its right to have the special graduate school in American studies.[13] As ISKAN director Georgi Arbatov wrote in his memoirs, a "majority of our specialists [in American studies]" had yet to overcome "pervasive ideology . . . [of] propaganda and fear." Speaking for himself, he recalled that, when named in 1967 the head the Institute of the USA, his

> knowledge was insufficiently deep . . . I had never been to the United States. I had no contacts or acquaintances among Americans . . . [but] harder to acquire than acquaintances . . . was a feeling for the country, a partly rational, partly intuitive sense that we could only acquire through regular professional contact with a wide variety of specialists from the United States and with representatives from government and business.[14]

Eventually, Georgi Arbatov, a director of ISKAN, became the major figure, serving as an important link between Soviet administration and the American officials.

Arbatov was born in the city of Kherson, in Soviet Ukraine, on May 19, 1923, into the family of a prominent Communist functionary and Soviet official. After serving in the Soviet Army from 1941 to 1944 during the Second World War, Arbatov entered Moscow State Institute of International Relations (MGIMO), from which he graduated in 1949. Since 1949, he had worked at the Foreign Literature Publishing House in Moscow, at the various editorial boards of the communist party's periodicals like *Kommunist*, and then at MGIMO. Arbatov was a member of the Central Committee of CPSU, and since 1967 he had been an ISKAN director, serving as an adviser on US affairs to top Soviet policymakers.[15] As an ISKAN director, he made his first trip to the United States in January of 1969, visiting Harvard University, the Massachusetts Institute of Technology, Columbia University, the Rand Corporation, and other places. This trip "opened his mental horizons" and "immediately expanded [his] circle of acquaintances both in the academic world . . . and among politicians." After this trip Arbatov again visited America in April-May 1970, September 1970, May 1971, November 1971, February 1973, and then he accompanied Leonid Brezhnev to the United States for the June 1973 summit talks.[16]

In 1969, after only one year of its actual existence, ISKAN was transferred from the CPSU Central Committee to the USSR Academy of Sciences and became the major Soviet center for North American studies. By 1970, Arbatov had managed to gather about seventy researchers and support staff. According to contemporaries, "Arbatov's staffing problems at the beginning were not made easier by the fact that he himself did not have the influence [in Soviet academia] and reputation of either a distinguished academician or powerful politician." As Arbatov and his colleagues explained, "the Institute was created not only with the task of supplying information on the U.S. to Soviet officials, but, and perhaps more importantly, to build good relations with American scholars and propagandize the Soviet position to them in the most appropriate way."[17]

From the very beginning, the major function of ISKAN was political advising of the Soviet government based on the thorough research of the original sources from the United States and Canada. As Arbatov recalled in his memoirs,

> The people who worked in the [USSR] Defense Ministry and in the military-industrial complex (as well as the majority of Foreign Ministry officials and even academic experts) were intellectually unprepared for a dialogue with the Americans and for serious talks going beyond the bounds of political declarations. At first they could not properly grasp American concepts and terminology concerning strategic and disarmament issues. . . . They were neither prepared for nor capable of seizing the initiative, of making their own well-grounded proposals, let alone of introducing new ideas. . . . But [ISKAN] fund of knowledge made our institute unique and encouraged others to seek its help. Due to the institute's pioneering efforts, a new type of expert was created—the civilian expert on strategic-military, political-strategic, and arms-control issues.[18]

Arbatov also worked out an agreement between the USSR Academy of Sciences and the USSR Foreign Ministry permitting ISKAN researchers and students to be assigned to the Soviet Embassy in Washington or to the Soviet Mission to the United Nations in New York. As Arbatov's colleagues explained,

> The research done at ISKAN initially took the form of short analytical reports drawn from a variety of first-hand sources. The reports were to be free of ideological bias and propaganda elements. Requests for reports came mostly from the Central Committee's International Department, the Foreign Ministry and the KGB. After the Institute's transfer to the Academy of Sciences, reports were also written for that body's Presidium, but these reports were not considered as important as those written for the Central Committee.[19]

By the end of the 1970s, there were six departments at ISKAN for studies of the US: Foreign Policy, Domestic Policy, Economics, Information, Ideology, Military and one department for studies of Canada (added in 1974).[20] Following the recommendations of the Central Committee of CPSU, Arbatov was appointed as a chairman of the Scientific Council on the Economic, Political and Ideological Problems of the United States of America, an organization established in 1973 under the USSR Academy of Sciences to guide and coordinate the research activities of Americanists all over the Soviet Union.[21]

Western experts described the important functions of such centers as ISKAN and IMEMO, calling them Soviet "spy institutes":

> The role of these institutes in foreign policy-making is a subject of contention in the American academic and political community. They are not simply propaganda outlets to the West. They perform an important staff function for the leadership. They contribute to the Central Committee's evaluations of international events and trends. At the same time, they provide an unofficial channel of communication to foreign political and scholarly communities.[22]

Some of the Western guests painted a pretty rosy picture of those institutions. For such American guests, the main Soviet center for American studies and the most important Soviet center for international academic exchange, especially during the détente of the 1970s, was Arbatov's institute in Moscow, ISKAN. According to Strobe Talbott,

> Over the years, the institute performed three important services: it made available to the leadership analysis and advice that were often better than what it received from the Party apparatus and the ministries; it kept open a channel to the West that was especially useful when government-to-government relations

were strained; and it offered sanctuary to a number of intellectuals who had run afoul of the authorities and who were later able, thanks in part to Arbatov's protection, to emerge as constructive figures in the reforms of the eighties.[23]

In Kyiv, the capital of Soviet Ukraine, under the leadership of Ukrainian scholar Arnold Shlepakov, a department of modern and contemporary history at the Institute of History of the Ukrainian Academy of Science was transformed into a new Soviet center of American studies during 1969–1978. In 1978, this center overgrew its small department and became a new institute of the Ukrainian Academy, with an official name of the Institute of Social and Economic Problems of the Foreign Countries.[24] As early as 1973, G. G. Shevel, the Ukrainian Minister of Foreign Affairs, complained to the new Ukrainian communist party leadership about the absence of the special research institutions of international diplomacy in the Ukrainian SSR, and about the lack of the Ukrainian experts in the international relations and diplomacy. Then, referring to the improving relations of the Soviet Union with the United States, Shevel suggested to organize such a research center, with special departments devoted to American studies, in Kyiv. According to the memoirs of Volodymyr Shcherbytskyi's aide, the first secretary of the Central Committee of the Communist Party of Ukraine became very interested in Shevel's proposal. In 1977, Shcherbytskyi officially approved this idea, which was also enthusiastically supported by Borys E. Paton, a head of the Ukrainian Academy of Sciences. In 1977, Shcherbytskyi wrote a special letter to the Central Committee of CPSU in Moscow, proposing to create the Institute of Social and Economic Problems of the Foreign Countries at the Ukrainian Academy of Sciences in Kyiv. In Moscow, only Arbatov supported a creation of the Ukrainian "Americanist" Institute. All his Russian Americanists opposed this idea. Reluctantly, the Soviet leadership in Moscow agreed to approve Shcherbytskyi's proposal, but only under one condition: Moscow ideologists recommended to their Ukrainian colleagues to have "the limited number of local personnel for this new research institution—not more than one hundred researchers." After this, Moscow's approval of the proposal and its approval of Shlepakov as head of this institute, the first official Ukrainian center for American studies (and, overall, for the studies of foreign countries) began functioning in Kyiv as early as October 1978.[25]

During the Cold War, especially in the détente period, institutionalization of various academic centers for American studies in Moscow and Kyiv was used by the officers of the KGB and GRU (military intelligence), the two Soviet intelligence agencies, to create cover positions for themselves, to invite American policymakers and academics to the Soviet Union, and to undertake intelligence-related missions to the United States. As I mentioned before in chapter 1, even the first group of four Soviet students of American studies, who participated in the initial academic exchange with Americans at Columbia University in 1958, included three professional Soviet intelligence officers. American hosts were aware of this mission from Soviet research centers, which sent their representatives to the US "to spy and to interfere with American politics." According to the published "Vasilii Mitrokhin archive files" (the KGB documents, brought to the West by the KGB archivist), the most influential "KGB man" among the Soviet experts in US politics, history, and culture was Georgi Arbatov, an ISKAN director. Despite his public rejection of any connections to the KGB, the "Mitrokhin files" indicate the direct and very close relations of Arbatov with this organization, where he was known under the code name of "Vasili."[26] Arbatov built up an influential circle of high-level contacts in America, and he was regularly required to cultivate these connections. One of the most important of Arbatov's contacts in the 1970s was former Under-Secretary of Defense Cyrus Vance, code-named by the KGB as "Vizir" ("Visier").[27] Arbatov had the KGB representatives in each department of his institute. According to contemporaries, "Many of the Institute's KGB ties are certainly through the Ideology Department, or, more specifically, through Deputy Director [Radomir] Bogdanov who heads the Ideology Department. Bogdanov is a colonel in the KGB and works with the first department at the Institute. He is also in charge of the Institute library." Through the entire 1970s and the 1980s, Arbatov's institute became known as a "major training center" of future Soviet spies, who planned to work in "capitalist America." Other sources also emphasized the important KGB and GRU influence not only through Radomir Bogdanov (deputy director of ISKAN, KGB colonel), but also through Mikhail Milshtein (head of the Political-Military Section of ISKAN, Deputy Chief for Disinformation in the GRU).[28]

The KGB leaders of the first Soviet centers of American studies, such as Sevostianov and Arbatov, established an efficient control over the entire Soviet system of preparation and education of the Soviet experts in American studies not only in Moscow, Russia, but also in Kyiv, Ukraine. At least two generations of Soviet Americanists were trained under close supervision of "the KGB people" such as Sevostianov and Arbatov. Some of their students, also connected to and "approved" by the KGB, became the leaders of the most important schools of Soviet Americanists. Sevostianov's favorite student, Nikolai Sivachev (another "KGB man"), became a head of the American studies center at Moscow State University (MGU) in the 1970s and prepared a group of the KGB-connected students, including the recent chair of American studies center at the Institute of World History, Vladimir Sogrin, and Vladislav Zubok, a former researcher from Arbatov's "spy Institute," now a professor of international history at the London School of Economics. Another younger student of Sevostianov, Valery Tishkov, brought his teacher's KGB connections into the field of Soviet anthropology, becoming a head of the Institute of Ethnography of the USSR Academy of Sciences in 1980. During the same period of time, the KGB academic curators from Moscow, such as Miller from the Institute of Slavic Studies, and Sevostianov from the Institute of World History, promoted a career of Arnold Shlepakov, the founder of Soviet Ukrainian Studies, in Kyiv, Ukraine.

NIKOLAI SIVACHEV, HIS STUDENTS, AND THE THIRD SOVIET CENTER OF AMERICAN STUDIES

One of the most talented students of Sevostianov, who became not only the most influential Americanist historian in the USSR, but also the most effective KGB collaborator in academic exchange programs with the United States was Nikolai Sivachev (1934–1983). Sivachev began his successful academic career as a graduate student from MGU's department of history, participating in US-Soviet student exchange program during 1961–62. The American administrators of this program noted that this Soviet student of US history took classes at Columbia University, "through serious application, made even greater strides in English" and successfully studied the US presidential election of 1936 under the supervision of his adviser, Professor Richard Hofstadter.[29]

This young Soviet Americanist had an unusual biography for such an academic career. Nikolai Sivachev was born on April 26, 1934, in a small remote Mordovian village of Tashkino (central Russia) in the family of poor peasants. After graduating from a local village school with "a distinction," Nikolai entered the Department of History at Moscow State University (MGU) in September of 1951. Being influenced by American feature films he used to watch in his village movie theater in Mordovia during his childhood, Sivachev decided to study the history of American labor and working-class movement in the US. As a typical Soviet provincial student, as a village school graduate, he had one serious problem for achieving his goal of exploring US history—no knowledge of the English language. Therefore, Sivachev spent all his free time during the first two years of his college life studying English, taking the additional (extra) courses of this language, reading available literature in English at the MGU library. As a result of all these efforts, he not only managed to master this foreign language, but after 1953, became a proficient and regular reader of various original American documentary collections devoted to modern US history and American communist periodicals at the reading room of the MGU library. Sivachev's achievements attracted the attention of KGB officers who worked at the USSR Academy of Sciences and at MGU. One of them, Grigorii Sevostianov, who was affiliated with a recently created sector of American countries at the Institute of History, offered this young and talented student "support in his studies of US history" at the end of 1953.[30]

Since that time Sevostianov became Sivachev's official mentor for his studies. Sevostianov recommended him to MGU administration to be admitted by the committee for graduate studies at the MGU Department of History. Eventually, after two years of working as a regular teacher of history at a secondary school in a small provincial town in the region of Cheliabinsk (Urals), following Sevostianov's recommendations, Sivachev entered graduate school at the MGU Department (*fakul'tet*) of History in 1958. As a graduate student of modern and contemporary history of the United States, Sivachev was supported not only by his undergraduate mentor (and the KGB officer) Sevostianov, but also by his new official mentor from MGU faculty, a talented historian, V. M. Khvostov.[31] A combination of academic and KGB support promoted Sivachev's career at MGU. He was one of the first Soviet graduate students of history, officially recommended and approved by Soviet administration for academic exchange with Americans as early as 1960. So, to finish his dissertation about American labor and politics of the New Deal, Sivachev was sent to the US, as an exchange student at Columbia University in the fall of 1961.[32]

This visit to Columbia University in 1961–62 triggered Sivachev's interest in the political history of the New Deal and the social history of US labor. Influenced by his American adviser, conservative American political historian Richard Hofstadter, Sivachev concentrated on history of the political elites in the US during the 1930s. When he returned to Moscow, he added Marxist analysis to his archival findings, defended his Soviet *kandidatskaia* dissertation, and prepared his study of political struggle during the US elections in the 1930s, which was published as a book in 1966.[33] As Yale Richmond, who knew him very well, wrote about Sivachev's first visit to America, "In New York, Sivachev met Eleanor Roosevelt, who when she learned that he was studying the New Deal, provided a room for him at her home, Val-Kill, up the Hudson River, and had a car pick him up to the nearby Roosevelt Library, where he did some of his research."[34]

During this visit in 1961–62, using various American archival collections, Sivachev also collected new material about the American working-class movement during the New Deal reforms in 1933–36. As early September 16, 1964, he finished his new book manuscript, which was discussed and approved for publication by his colleagues from the MGU department of modern and contemporary history.[35] Sivachev's new research work was supported not only by his colleagues, but also by Soviet communist ideologists as "an important historiographical justification" for Soviet criticism of "Chinese Maoist revisionism" and "Maoist ideas about the immediate nuclear attack against the capitalist West." The Soviet ideologists' immediate recommendation was "to publish this study as a book," and "support Sivachev's application for his new research trip to the USA." As Sivachev's colleague from the same department, historian A. D. Kolpakov, noted:

> Sivachev's study is a good illustration of the current situation in the development of the international working-class movement as well. It shows that despite the very bad conditions for progress of the Western labor movement, American working class could effectively influence the progressive development of the society, affect the US government, could improve the social system in the interests of the majority of ordinary American people. . . . These ideas of Sivachev's study clearly reject the Chinese Communist leadership's thesis that the labor movement in the capitalist West was completely rotten and opportunistic, and that communists should stop expecting something positive from the Western working-class movement [and instead communists should concentrate on the nuclear war with the West].[36]

In October of 1966, using his American materials, Sivachev delivered a report to his colleagues about his new research project, which opened a completely new topic for Soviet historiography: "labor legislation in the US." I. Galkin, chair of the department, was so impressed by Sivachev's report that he "immediately proposed to request a recommendation from the Ministry of Higher Education . . . to send Sivachev again for a half a year research trip in America."[37] As a result of this recommendation and support of his KGB supervisors, Sivachev visited the US the second time in November of 1967 as a Soviet official in charge of the Soviet exhibition "Education in the USSR" supported by the official letters of recommendation from the Soviet leadership, including one signed by his official "supervisor," L. Bazhanov, a "KGB man" from the USSR Ministry of Education.[38] During the same time American administration awarded Sivachev with a three-month grant, funding his research at Columbia, Cornell, and George Washington Universities from February to April 1968. Therefore, during his second visit, Sivachev stayed in the US from November of 1967 until the end of April of 1968.[39]

Starting in late 1967, Sivachev visited the United States on a regular basis (five times, using IREX funding). Eventually, he became the most famous and the most respected Soviet academic visitor in America, especially during détente. American scholars contrasted Sivachev as a talented researcher to other Soviet "not very interesting visitors, who were curiosities but not serious scholars." As they reported to IREX, Sivachev "impressed everybody very much with his knowledge of American institutions."[40] After his American visits and intensive archival research, Sivachev prepared two book manuscripts about labor and government relations in US history before and during WWII.⁴¹ He also began writing a new book project about Soviet-US relations during his visit to America in December 1974 through January 1975.

During the 1970s, new centers for American studies were founded at the Department of History of Moscow State University, in Leningrad and other industrial cities of the Soviet Union. According to the Soviet government's decision in 1973–74, the MGU department of history became a center for the establishment of the Fulbright program in the USSR. In 1975, Nikolai Sivachev, from the same department, established the Scholarly Coordinating Council on American Studies at this university. In November 1977, under his leadership a new Soviet center for American studies was organized there, a so-called "laboratory of American studies" affiliated with the MGU department of modern and contemporary history, which began officially functioning in November of 1978.⁴²

By 1975, despite (or probably because of) KGB connections, Nikolai Sivachev became the best representative of Soviet Americanists in all the exchanges programs of the détente era. Sivachev was also a good scholar, a serious historian-researcher, and a very good psychologist who understood very well what the American partners expected from the Soviet guests. In contrast to his image of a "pedantic boring university professor" and "orthodox communist ideologist" for his Soviet students and colleagues, Sivachev projected a very different image of himself for his American colleagues. Some of his MGU students recalled that their instructor impressed them as being "an apparent anti-Semite, anti-intellectual, and even anti-Muscovite, who considered all his Muscovites students to be loafers, 'golden youth' needing re-education through manual labor." Of course, for the American hosts and guests, Sivachev projected a very different personality—of "an open-minded, Westernized, friendly and witty, Soviet intellectual."⁴³ For Americans, he always looked optimistic, smiling, open-minded, humorous, and ready for discussions, trying to avoid any ideological debates and distancing himself from the explicit communist propagandist clichés.⁴⁴ As one American host praised Sivachev's research and communicative skills in 1975,

> Sivachev ... steers away from Sovietologists in general (his field is US internal politics) but has been good with me because I provided him with connections (with VIPs) he couldn't establish otherwise—and took his pictures posing with these VIPs which he values a great deal. He is relatively young, ambitious, extremely hard working, especially for a teaching professor, in collecting archival and bibliographic data; he knows what he wants and has a great deal of determination ... on his part, he was very considerate in not taking too much of my time, and quite informative about general intellectual trends in Moscow. A stout Russian nationalist (although a Mordovian, ethnically), he was a curious contrast with the more ideologically oriented visitors. ... Since his first visit to

the US he has developed rather broad connections (once he was a house guest of Eleanor Roosevelt, and knew my friend Henry A. Wallace) but remained a rather modest sort. There is an authentic strength in this fellow, and he will go far in my judgment.[45]

Using his new American connections during the 1970s, Sivachev obtained a contract with the University of Chicago Press to publish a book in English about the history of US-Soviet relations. So, he contacted Nikolai Yakovlev, another talented Soviet historian-Americanist, *nevyezdnoi*, but very prolific writer, who collaborated with the KGB, and invited Yakovlev to be a coauthor of the American book. Through this contact with Yakovlev, Sivachev received official KGB permission for collaboration with an American publishing house. Then, using IREX funding, Sivachev spent six months in 1978–79 and two months in 1980 reading the proofs of their book and collecting material on American labor-government relations. In 1980, Sivachev not only published the book in the US, but also served as a Visiting Fellow in the Department of Government at Dartmouth College.[46] This book was positively received by his American colleagues. As Elbert B. Smith, a former professor of American history from the University of Maryland and a three-time Fulbright Lecturer in the Soviet Union, told Yale Richmond in October of 1998, that Sivachev and Yakovlev's book was "Marxist and pro-Soviet but not unfriendly to the United States." According to him, Sivachev "liked the United States and was an ameliorating influence on U.S.-Soviet relations."[47] Moreover, as another productive result of his "American visits," Sivachev helped many of his MGU students to establish the necessary connections in America and obtained the official invitations and funding by American hosts. So, Sivachev had supervised a research work of young Americanist Vladimir Sogrin since 1967, assisting him with obtaining the new literature on the history of ideology of political elites in the US. Finally, in 1979, Sivachev directed Sogrin to the topic of the American War of Independence and its ideology. He recommended his former student for IREX funding. As a result of Sivachev's "American connections" and his research visits in the US, Sogrin wrote his pioneering studies in a history of American ideology, which incorporated the original American material, suggested by Sivachev as early as the late 1960s.[48]

Besides Sogrin, another young Americanist, Vladislav Zubok, was also supported and promoted by Sivachev. Vladislav Zubok was a grandson of Lev Zubok, a famous founder of American studies in the Soviet Union.[49] Lev Zubok had a son, Martin, who became a famous sound engineer, working for many years at the Soviet Central (Ostankino) television studio in Moscow. For young Soviet rock music fans, Martin Zubok (1926–2009) became associated with *Magic Lantern*, a legendary Soviet television show of 1976, directed by Evgenii Ginzburg. Martin Zubok helped to mix the videotapes with music from the rock opera *Jesus Christ Superstar* and American movies such as *The Godfather* and *Love Story* for this television show. Vladislav (Vlad) Zubok was born on April 16, 1958, and grew up in the family of this Ostankino's sound engineer, being exposed to a variety of American sound technologies, including his favorite videotapes with Disney cartoon films. Vladislav Zubok still recalled how he, as a child, loved to watch *Snow White and the Seven Dwarfs*, *Bambi*, and *Tom and Jerry* cartoons in his father's television office in Ostankino.[50]

Like many Soviet children of the 1960s and 1970s, Vladislav loved reading the adventure novels about American Indians and American pirates by James Fenimore Cooper and Mayne Reid. He also read Mark Twain's classics and was greatly impressed by science fiction and horror stories by Edgar Allan Poe. He learned by heart the poem "Raven" by Poe during his high school years.[51] Anglo-American rock music and Western films also triggered Vladislav's interest in American culture and history. During the early 1970s he occasionally could get access to the American illustrated magazine *Amerika* in Russian, where one could read Kurt Vonnegut and other authors of contemporary American fiction.[52] Most importantly, little Vladislav learned the story of his grandfather Lev (who died when he was eleven), and was fascinated: having a relative who lived in the United States and returned to Soviet Russia was a rarity in the Soviet Union! Lev's books stood on the shelves in Vladislav's room, and he began to use them as a reference for his school reports. He was also proud that his grandfather was an author of a textbook on world history used in all Soviet schools at the time. And in 1972, Vladislav, with his classmates, visited the US Exhibition in Gorky Park on Research and Development, which had on him an impression comparable to the impact of the 1959 exhibition in Sokolniki on the generation of his parents. American cars, appliances, the Apollo space module, hundreds of high-quality color pictures, and other items opened a window into "another world."[53]

In the summer of 1975, Vladislav Zubok successfully passed his exams and became an undergraduate in history at MGU. His fascination with America was so strong that when the time for specialization came in 1977, he chose to major at the "Laboratory of American Studies." After consultations with Professor Sivachev, the main leader of the laboratory, he began to write a diploma on the domestic politics of Harry S. Truman's administration (1945–1953). Sivachev became his thesis adviser.[54]

Sivachev also played a crucial role in recommending Vladislav Zubok for graduate school at ISKAN in the summer of 1980. This was the dream destination for a young Americanist. In 1983, after his official graduation from ISKAN *aspirantura* (graduate school), through the old Sivachev's connections in the KGB, Zubok was included in the ISKAN personnel as its junior research associate (*mladshii nauchnyi sotrudnik*). Two years after, in 1985, under supervision of Dr. Vladimir Pechatnov (another KGB connection in ISKAN), Zubok defended his *kandidaskaia* (PhD) dissertation at ISKAN, using a new topic of his research, *The Evolution of the Democratic Party and its Executive Elites Before and During the Carter Presidency, 1969–1981*. As all his young colleagues, Zubok planned to begin writing his doctoral dissertation and continue to build his academic career at ISKAN.[55]

But Gorbachev's perestroika changed his academic plans. At the beginning of 1987, an ISKAN deputy-director and KGB officer, Radomir G. Bogdanov, invited Zubok to his office and told him to write a report on the origins of the Cold War. Bogdanov was involved in the work of the Soviet-American historical commission that met in 1979 and then was suspended until 1986. The forthcoming meeting of the commission had a focus on the Cold War.[56] This conversation reshaped Zubok's academic life. From the study of Congressional Records and American domestic politics, Zubok turned his attention to literature about the Cold War. In June 1987, approved by the KGB supervisors, he took part as a junior participant in the meeting of the Soviet-American Commission, met several leading American historians, among them John Lewis Gaddis, William Taubman, Melvyn Leffler, and others. This conference was also supervised by the special sector of the Central Committee of the CPSU, with the "strong presence" of the KGB representatives.[57] Fortuitously by that time, Zubok managed to travel twice outside the Soviet borders: to the GDR in the fall of 1986, and to West Germany in May 1987. He was included in a high-power group of Soviet historians (who were approved by their KGB supervisors), invited to come to the United States in the fall of 1987 at the invitation of USIA, Johnston Foundation, and other American educational institutions, as part of the "perestroika" public diplomacy. The group included Andrei N. Sakharov from the Institute of the USSR History and Aleksandr Chubarian from the Institute of World History, who had their old "KGB connections." This trip began on November 7, 1987, and its itinerary included Washington, D.C., Boston, Chicago, and Dallas, where Soviet visitors attended a conference of American high school teachers. For Zubok, the highlight of the trip was the AAASS Convention in Boston, where he was astounded by the scale of Russian and Soviet studies in the West, and could freely rummage through hundreds of books, including publications of dissidents published in Russian by émigré press.[58]

American Cold War historians also noticed Zubok. He was invited to take part in the special Soviet American conference on the Cold War history (1950–55), hosted by John Lewis Gaddis from Ohio University in Athens, Ohio, in October 1988. Zubok made a great impression on American participants.[59] His paper presentation was a success and helped to build the important future connections of Zubok and ISKAN with American colleagues, which was his important job assignment from the major KGB supervisor of Zubok's institute, KGB colonel Bogdanov.

VALERY TISHKOV AND THE KGB INFLUENCES IN CANADIAN AND ANTHROPOLOGICAL STUDIES

Many of Sivachev's students, like Zubok, became the active participants of academic exchange programs. But, still, KGB officers, like Sevostianov and Bogdanov, controlled the Soviet part of these programs until the end of the USSR. Valery Tishkov, another influential Sevostainov student, became instrumental for KGB influence in the Soviet Academy of Sciences as well. In contrast to many of Sivachev's students, who were born in Moscow and spent all their lives in Moscow, Tishkov was a different type of Soviet intellectual. Tishkov was one of the numerous Soviet provincial intellectuals, who came to Moscow to study and make a career during the Khrushchev Thaw. He was born on November 6, 1941, in the small Russian town of Nizhnie Sergi in the Region of Sverdlovsk (in the Urals), where he grew up in a typical family of Soviet Russian provincial intellectuals. His mother was a teacher at the local elementary school, and his father was a teacher of geography and physical education at the local secondary school in this small Ural industrial town.[60]

While in high school, Valery Tishkov, whose favorite subjects were Russian literature and history, was inspired by his teacher of Russian literature, who advised him to enter the prestigious Moscow State University rather than the local Ural colleges. Thus, after graduating with honors (*s zolotoi medaliu*) from Nizhnie Sergi's high school in 1959, Valery Tishkov moved to Moscow to enroll at the MGU Department of Philology. However, once in Moscow, he realized that academic competition among the entrants into this department was at its highest at MGU in 1959. Therefore, Valery Tishkov changed his mind, and submitted his documents for enrolling in another department, the subject of which he enjoyed studying as well. In the end, Tishkov chose the MGU Department of History. He wanted to study Russian and Soviet history at this department. Moreover, during the third year of his studies, Valery Tishkov decided to select the history of the Communist Party of the Soviet Union (CPSU) as his main specialization at the department.[61]

Many provincial historians, who entered the MGU Department of History in those years, clearly understood that this specialization could help promote their academic and political career, because the history of the CPSU was a required major "ideological" subject taught in every college and university in the Soviet Union. Overall, during Khrushchev's era, the majority of MGU Department of History graduates received "regular job assignments in secondary schools as teachers of history." Nevertheless, a degree that includes the history of the CPSU as "a major specialization" could guarantee a MGU Department of History graduate a "steady and comfortable job as a college professor of CPSU history." This was especially important for a provincial historian such as Tishkov. But unfortunately for him, during the 1962–63 academic year, Tishkov became friends with a few American visiting scholars, who had arrived in the USSR on an academic exchange program and took residence at one of MGU's dormitories. One of these visiting scholars was Martin Malia, a professor of Russian History from the University of California, Berkeley. Malia lent Tishkov "Stalin's political biography" by Isaac Deutscher to read.[62] Tishkov was so impressed by this book, and especially by its detailed description of Stalin's purges and political repressions of the 1930s, that he referenced this material during one of the seminars on CPSU history. A MGU professor, who supervised this class, immediately denounced and reported Tishkov to the department's administration as "a student spreading anti-Soviet rumors among his classmates." To avoid "political persecution" and possible expulsion from MGU, Tishkov switched from the specialization of the history of the CPSU to modern and contemporary history, asking Professor Evgenii Yaz'kov, the deputy chair of the section (*kafedra*) of modern and contemporary history at the Department of History, for permission to "study North American history." At this time, because of Tishkov's frequent and friendly communications with such American MGU visitors, as Malia, Professor Terrence Emmons from Stanford, and Richard Hellie (later a professor of Russian History at the University of Chicago), and because of his reading of American books, such as Stalin's biography by Deutscher, Tishkov became noticed by MGU Americanists, including Yaz'kov, as a "talented student with good spoken and reading skills in English." Therefore, Yaz'kov accepted Tishkov as a new student in his *kafedra* with Tishkov's new specialization in the modern and contemporary history of the US and Canada. Meanwhile, G. N. Sevostianov (a retired KGB officer, turned historian) from the Institute of History of the USSR Academy of Sciences had the practice of supervising (occasionally) various *diploma* research works of the students from MGU's Department of History, who specialized in US contemporary history. Yaz'kov recommended Tishkov to Sevostianov as one of his new talented students "with relatively good English reading skills." As a result of this recommendation, Tishkov became Sevostianov's student, and wrote his undergraduate student diploma work (an equivalent of the American MA thesis) on "The US Position at Potsdam Conference of 1945" under Sevostianov's supervision. According to some contemporaries, Sevostianov's supervision saved Tishkov's academic career and protected him from further harassment by the KGB. Tishkov's classmates denounced and reported him to MGU's administration for "his frequent illegal communications with Americans in MGU's dormitory, and accused Tishkov of drinking American whiskey, smoking Marlboro cigarettes and reading American (forbidden) books." Despite all of these denouncements, Sevostianov's protection guaranteed Tishkov's graduation from MGU safely in 1964. Although Tishkov was a very active member of the Komsomol organization at MGU's Department of History, which recommended him to be included as a member of the special Soviet student exchange group designated for a trip to Canada, the KGB information about his "frequent contacts with Americans" was used by the department's Communist organization as a pretext for denying Tishkov permission to travel abroad in 1964.[63]

Thus, instead of travelling to Canada, Tishkov was compelled to accept his first job assignment in August 1964 in the city of Magadan, in the Soviet Union's Far East, the infamous location of Stalin's labor camps. Despite this "inferior place" for employment, Tishkov was fortunate enough to secure in Magadan a teaching position as a professor of history, rather than the job of an ordinary teacher of history in a provincial Soviet secondary school. Using his good personal connections with the other MGU graduates, who had already secured their teaching positions at the Magadan Pedagogical Institute, Tishkov obtained an official invitation from this institute regarding his job placement there. During 1964–72, Tishkov taught the modern and contemporary history of Europe and America at the Historical-Philological Department of this institute. In 1969, he was even promoted to the position of chair of this department, following the successful defense that same year of his *kandidatskaia* (PhD) dissertation titled "The Historical Preconditions of the Canadian Revolution of 1837" at the Moscow State Pedagogical Institute under the supervision of Aleksei L. Narochnitskii.[64]

Eventually, Tishkov's long-lasting connections with Sevostianov, who "cleared Tishkov's ideological reputation with the KGB," and his fortuitous marriage to a resident of Moscow, not only helped promote his academic career, but also enhanced his legal status for potential travel abroad: he became *vyezdnoi* as early as 1967. During this year, Tishkov traveled abroad for the first time to visit his college friend (from Moscow) in East Germany. After securing KGB clearance, the young historian from Magadan was even included on the official list of the Soviet delegation for the 13th International Congress of Historical Sciences, organized by the International Committee of Historical Sciences in Moscow in August of 1970.[65]

As a result, in 1972, Tishkov left Magadan for good for Moscow, where Sevostianov, using his KGB connections, helped him join the sector of the history of the US and Canada at the Institute of World History. Once in Moscow, Tishkov made a tremendous "leap" in his academic and administrative career. Following Sevostianov's recommendations and KGB support, in 1974, Evgenii M. Zhukov, the director of this institute and the president of the International Committee of Historical Sciences, offered Tishkov the position of secretary of the organizational committee for the preparation of Soviet historians for the upcoming International Congress of Historical Sciences in San Francisco, in the US, in 1975. This position would come to serve as "the key trigger" in Tishkov's administrative career. He was not only included in the official Soviet delegation for this congress, but following his return to Moscow, Tishkov was appointed to the new (and very prestigious and KGB-connected) position of academic secretary of the USSR Academy of Sciences' Department of History (*uchenyi sekretar' otdeleniia istorii Akademii Nauk SSSR*), a responsibility, which he fulfilled until 1981. Meanwhile, he embarked on his new research projects, while traveling (for the first time in his life) to Canada in 1973. During this visit, Tishkov began collecting new material for his research on the early colonial history of Canada, and especially on the history of the Native American tribes of Canada. The major result of this research appeared in the form of Tishkov's *doktorskaia* dissertation titled "The Liberation Movement in Colonial Canada," which he defended at the Institute of World History in 1979.[66] Following the defense of his dissertation and KGB approval, Tishkov was appointed head of the sector of ethnography of the peoples of America at the Institute of Ethnology and Anthropology of the USSR Academy of Sciences in 1981.[67]

Beginning in 1973, and up to perestroika, Tishkov had made thirty official research trips to the United States and Canada. He became the leading Soviet expert in Canadian studies, and the official organizer of the Soviet Studies of Native Americans, particularly in the field of Native American anthropology. Tishkov's direct connections to the KGB and the administration of the USSR Academy of Sciences were instrumental in his obtaining a very prestigious American research grant: the Eisenhower Exchange Fellowship. In 1980, the American administration of this academic exchange program sent an announcement regarding this fellowship to the Soviet administration of the Academy of Sciences. As a result, the academy's presidium approved its only candidate for this grant—Valery Tishkov, the scientific secretary of the USSR Academy of Sciences' Department of History. The Americans' initial, official reaction to Tishkov's candidacy was negative. Only after a long period of negotiations, when the USSR Academy of Sciences rejected to send an alternate candidate, did the Eisenhower Foundation finally accept Tishkov's nomination in the spring of 1980. The direct result of this trip to the US was Tishkov's new book about historians and history writing in the United States, which was published in 1985 in Moscow.[68] At the same time, finally, Tishkov established his professional reputation of not only being an expert in Canadian history, but also of being a specialist in US history. During the 1980s, he became the "official" (approved by Soviet intelligence) Soviet Americanist, who combined not only his knowledge of both US and

Canadian history, but also his expertise in Native American history, ethnography, and anthropology.[69]

The case of Valery Tishkov, a talented and ambitious historian from a Soviet Russian provincial town, was another example of the KGB's and official academic hierarchy's important role in the process of Soviet knowledge production as it pertained specifically to the promotion of the academic career of those Soviet provincial scholars, who specialized in American studies. The most famous case of such collaboration between the KGB and Soviet Americanists with a provincial background was the story of MGU Professor Nikolai Sivachev. Nevertheless, for Soviet *Indianistika* (American Indian studies), the role of Tishkov, who was apparently connected to the KGB through Sevostianov, especially after 1982, became instrumental. Tishkov shaped *Indianistika* into an entirely new academic field in Soviet American studies. At the same time, Tishkov confirmed the strong KGB connections, which traditionally had long existed in the Institute of Ethnography at the USSR Academy of Sciences, being active in various exchange programs not only with US academic institutions, but also with numerous Canadian research centers. Many of Tishkov's colleagues at the institute, including Iosif Grigulevich (Lavretsky) (1913–1988), were professional KGB officers and experienced Soviet spies.[70]

Besides "Moscow School" of Soviet Americanists, during the 1970s, the new school of American studies appeared in Leningrad/St. Petersburg. The leader of this school was Alexander Fursenko (1927–2008). Fursenko was born into the family of a famous Soviet scientist, becoming a member of the Soviet academic elite. After graduating from the department of history of Leningrad State University in 1951, Fursenko entered a graduate school at the Leningrad branch of the Institute of History of the USSR Academy of Sciences. His first contacts with the KGB started in 1954 after his defense of PhD about US expansionism in China. In 1955 Fursenko began his academic career as a researcher at the Leningrad branch of the Institute of History, and in 1959 he had his first official visit to the US, which strengthened his connection with the KGB. After this visit, Fursenko became the new leader of the Soviet American studies in Leningrad in the 1970s; between 1986 and 1990 he built his career not only in his academic institute, but also inside the official hierarchy of the USSR Academy of Sciences. Eventually, Fursenko's KGB connections helped him not only build a very important net of personal contacts inside of American academia, but also promoted the careers of his two sons, who became very close personal friends of Vladimir Putin as well.[71]

YEVGENY PRIMAKOV AND POST-SOVIET INTELLIGENCE CONNECTIONS OF RUSSIAN AND UKRAINIAN SCHOLARS

Both Nikolai Bolkhovitinov and Vadim Koleneko, former Soviet Americanists from the Institute of World History in Moscow, whom I interviewed in May 2008, also emphasized the significant role of the "KGB people" from the Institute of Oriental Studies (*Institut vostokovedeniia*) at the USSR Academy of Sciences in establishing the connections with Western academia. They especially mentioned the KGB connections of that institute's director, Yevgeny M. Primakov (1929–2015). Primakov, who was born in Kyiv to a Jewish-Ukrainian family on October 29, 1929, graduated from the Moscow Institute of Oriental Studies (MGU) in 1953 and finished MGU graduate school (*aspirantura*) in 1956. Then he worked as a journalist in the Middle East and the US until 1970. During this time, he was recruited by the KGB under a code name MAKSIM, and Primakov "had been sent on frequent intelligence missions to the United States and the Middle East." After his return to Moscow, from 1970 to 1977, Primakov served as Deputy Director of the Institute of World Economy and International Relations, and from 1977 to 1985 he served as Director of the Institute of Oriental Studies. During this time, his institute also became a center for educating Soviet spies, and many of Primakov's colleagues also functioned as "the KGB curators" of many academic centers in Soviet republics, including the Institute of History in Kyiv, Soviet Ukraine. Later on, in 1991–1996, Primakov became a director of the KGB First Chief Directorate responsible for foreign intelligence, later renamed as Foreign Intelligence Service of the Russian Federation (*Sluzhba vneshnei razvedki*—SVR).[72]

Still, the most important for establishing KGB connections with Western (especially American) research centers (especially Slavic/Soviet studies centers in the US and Canada) were Soviet Americanists. I had already mentioned the role of Arbatov (KGB code name VASILII) from ISKAN. Three other leaders of the Soviet Americanist centers were either KGB officers or KGB agents. I refer to Grigorii Sevostianov, Soviet intelligence officer, who was a head of such a center at the Institute of World History in Moscow between 1968 and 1988; to Nikolai Sivachev, a KGB agent, a former student of Sevostianov, leader of the similar center at Moscow State University between 1974 and 1982; and to Arnold Shlepakov, a KGB agent, a director of the Americanist center at the Institute of Social and Economic Problems of Foreign Countries in Kyiv between 1978 and 1991. Another prominent "KGB/FSB person" among Soviet and Russian Americanists was Vladimir Sogrin, a Sivachev's student, who became a director of the Center for North American Studies at the Institute of World History in Moscow after 2008. Many of those centers included professional intelligence officers, who were officially retired from their KGB service. Sevostianov's center had at least two of those officers: Vadim A. Koleneko (1943–2011), a specialist in Canadian studies, and Vladimir V. Poznyakov (1946–2021), an expert in Soviet-American intelligence before and during the early Cold War.[73]

One of the founders of Soviet *Amerikanistika* (American studies), Nikolai N. Bolkhovitinov, noted that the functions of Soviet Americanists (experts in US/Canadian politics, economy, history, and culture) included not only collecting and analyzing information about the US and Canada, but also about the American experts in Soviet and Russian studies, and establishing the personal contacts with American "Sovietologists."[74] These "functions were sometime, directly connected to the KGB, involving the special espionage operations against those experts." This "became obvious with the beginning of cultural and academic exchanges between the US and the USSR in 1958 when the first Soviet guests had started visiting America on a regular basis." According to Bolkhovitinov, the KGB "not only supervised academic research" in various institutes of the USSR Academy of Sciences ("especially in Arbatov's Institute in Moscow and Shlepakov's Institute in Kyiv"), but also "used Soviet Americanists, like Nikolai Sivachev, Vadim Koleneko, Vladimir Poznyakov, and Vladimir Sogrin from Moscow and Alexander Fursenko from Leningrad, for the very particular purposes of Soviet intelligence." But the major task for those Soviet guests "was to establish the personal contacts with their American counterparts."[75]

In his analysis of the international connections of the KGB-connected Soviet scholars from Soviet academic institutions, Bolkhovitinov missed the one important role of those people: their KGB supervision of provincial academic institutions, including those in Soviet Ukraine. The KGB-connected scholars from Moscow, such as Ilia Miller, Grigorii Sevostianov, Georgi Arbatov, Nikolai Sivachev, Valery Tishkov, and Yevgeny Primakov, played a role of the KGB curators for scholars from the provincial research centers, such as Ukrainian research institutions, monitoring not only their research, but also their international connections with Western academia. Unfortunately, this tradition of "KGB supervision" and "KGB curators" survived even after the USSR collapse.

As Leonid Leshchenko, a former Soviet Ukrainian Americanist noted, "The KGB and its successor organizations (FSB and SBU) always promoted a career of so-called 'ideologically reliable' scholars, especially in the international organizations, which funded research in humanities and social studies. During the Cold War, there were IREX and Fulbright, during the late 1980s and 1990s there was Soros Foundation in both [post-Soviet] Russia and Ukraine." Those reliable scholars (with their KGB connections) included

Shlepakov and Kulchytsky and their students and/or their children. According to Leshchenko and Bolkhovitinov, those KGB-connected scholars, who became the first exchange scholars during perestroika and the 1990s, included Vladislav Zubok, a student of the KGB officer/scholar Sivachev, and Alexei Miller, Illia Miller's son from Moscow, and Grigoriy Kasianov, a favorite student of the KGB-connected Kulchytsky. It is noteworthy that despite their old KGB connections from the Soviet times, today, such Ukrainian scholars, like Kulchytsky, took a patriotic pro-Ukrainian and anti-Kremlin position, distancing publicly from their Soviet past.[76]

Moreover, during the 1990s, the KGB/FSB/SBU allowed to lead the local (Russian and Ukrainian) offices of the international organizations, such as Carnegie and Soros Foundations, only by those "KGB [and GRU]-checked, reliable and loyal scholars" such as Vladislav Zubok and Dmitrii Trenin (Carnegie Foundation in Moscow), Alexei Miller (Soros Foundation, Moscow), Ivan Kurilla (Soros Foundation, Volgograd State University), and Georgiy Kasianov (Soros Foundation, Kyiv, Ukraine).[77] After the collapse of the USSR, these close personal connections between the Russian and Ukrainian participants of those international organizations, such as Soros (Open Society) Foundation, called in Ukraine "the International Renaissance Foundation," were serving as a common ground for the collaborative projects of the scholars from the former Soviet republics, such as Belarus, Russia, and Ukraine. The most popular form of this collaboration, funded by Soros (Open Society) Foundation, was the Higher Education Support Program with various regional seminars for "excellence in teaching" including regular international summer schools in Ukraine and Russia.[78] Through these summer schools, Georgiy Kasianov, who became a director of the education program of the International Renaissance Foundation in Kyiv, sponsored by philanthropist George Soros, established relations (since 2009) with Alexei Miller and Vladislav Zubok, "FSB-approved Russian participants of those international programs," who represented also various FSB-funded organizations, such as the Russkii Mir Foundation and Valdai Discussion Club.[79]

Paradoxically, the origins of such relations were deeply rooted in the KGB operations against "Soviet main adversary—the United States," which were used by the Soviet intelligence for influencing and infiltrating the Western political, cultural, and educational institutions during the Cold War, especially during the intensification of cultural and academic exchanges between the Soviet Union and the West (and especially during Soviet exchange programs with the United States). The next chapter will analyze how the "KGB people" used and "abused" this system of academic exchange.

NOTES

1. "Ilia Solomonovich Miller (1918–1978)," *Sovetskoe slavianovedenie*, 1978, no. 4, 126–127. See also Tsentral'nyi derzhavnyi arkhiv vyshchykh organiv vlady ta upravlinnia, Kyiv, Ukraine (hereafter—TsDAVOVUU), fond 4621, op. 13, spr. 1277, ark. 2–37. Compare with my interview with Nikolai Bolkhovitinov, Moscow, May 21, 2001.

2. Interview with Bohdan Josypovych K., a retired KGB/SBU officer, February 9, 2019, Kyiv, Ukraine; SBU, f. 16, spr. 1006, ark. 161–167.

3. GRU: *Dela i ljudi* (GRU: The Deeds and the People), edited by V. M. Lurie and V. Ya. Kochik (Moscow: Olma-press, 2003), 423; V. Kochik, *Razvedchiki i rezidenty GRU* (Intelligence Officers and Residents of the GRU) (Moskva: Eksmo, 2004). I also quote from Filip Kovacevic's blog: https://thechekistmonitor.blogspot.com/2021/04/soviet-mil-intel-illegal-litvin-interview.html. See about Vladimir Kazakevich in chapter 1 of this book.

4. Ezra Beudot, "Empire of Liberation: Investigating Soviet Activity in Africa from Khrushchev to Gorbachev," MA Thesis (Carleton University, Ottawa, Canada, 2020), 7, 85; Natalia Telepneva, *Cold War Liberation. The Soviet Union and the Collapse of the Portuguese Empire in Africa, 1961–1975* (Chapel Hill, NC: University of North Carolina Press, 2022).

5. See various publications about Grigulevich, especially about his spying activities in Christopher Andrew and Vasili Mitrokhin, *The Sword and the Shield: The Mitrokhin Archive and the Secret History of the KGB* (New York: Basic Books, 1999), 87, 99–101, 147, 162–163, 300, 357–358, and the recent publication by Andrei Znamenski, "Joseph Grigulevich: A Tale of Identity, Soviet Espionage and Storytelling," *The Soviet and Post-Soviet Review*, vol. 44, no. 3 (2017): 314–341.

6. See Aleksandr Nekrich, *Forsake Fear: Memoirs of an Historian*, translated by Donald Lineburgh (Boston: Unwin Hyman, 1991), 72, and my interviews with Bolkhovitinov and R. Ivanov.

7. See a detailed description in his memoirs: G. N. Sevostianov and V. I. Zhukovskaia, *Za liniei fronta* (Minsk: Belarus, 1980), and the official obituary on the Russian Academy of Sciences' site: http://worldhist.ru/News/356/9367.

8. See his publication where he describes his career in the Far East: G. P. Sevostianov, *Ekspansionistskaia politika SShA na Dal'nem Vostoke, v Kitaie, i Koreie v 1905–1911 gg.* (Moscow: Nauka, 1958). After this book, he stopped writing something original. But as a head of "American" sector since 1967, he had been editing mainly the collective works of his sector's colleagues. See an official Soviet publication, openly praising the professional background of Sevostianov as a Soviet spy/KGB intelligence officer in Byelorussia and the Far East before his academic career in 1950. It was published in a rubric *"Nauchnaia zhizn'* (Scholarly Life)" in *Amerikanskii ezhegodnik* during perestroika. See S. N. Burin, "K 75-letiiu akademika G. N. Sevostianova," *AE* 1990 (Moscow, 1991), 211–215. Compare with another official publication "Novye chleny Akademii nauk SSSR," in *Vestnik AN SSSR* (Moscow, 1988), Vypusk 2, 123–126; and "Grigorii Nikolaievich Sevostianov: [nekrolog]," *Novaia i noveishaia istoria*, 2013, no. 3, 245–248.

9. 'Doklad akademika N. N. Bolkhovitinova,' *Novaia i noveishaia istoria*, 2003, no. 6, 185; 'Yubilei I. A. Beliavskoi,' *Amerikanskii ezhegodnik* [hereafter *AE*] *1995* (Moscow, 1996), 13, 15. In 1970 the sector began publishing its periodical *Amerikanskii ezhegodnik*.

10. See various editions of the memoirs, written by the first director of this institute: G. A. Arbatov, *Zatianuvsheiesia vyzdorovlenie (1953–1985 gg.) Svidetel'stvo sovremennika* (Moscow, 1991), 381–399; Georgi Arbatov, *Chelovek sistemy: Nabliudenia i razmyshlenia ochevidtsa eio raspada* (Moscow, 2002), 132–147; and a chapter "The Institute: How We 'Discovered America'" in English in Georgi Arbatov, *The System: An Insider's Life in Soviet Politics* (New York: Random House, 1992), 295–328. ISKAN had its own monthly magazine *SShA: ekonomika, politika, ideologiia*.

11. See how Arbatov described the role of the revived IMEMO: Arbatov, *Zatianuvsheiesia vyzdorovlenie*, 73–74. Compare with Piotr Cherkasov, *IMEMO. Institut Mirovoi Ekonomiki i Mezhdunarodnych Otnoshenii. Portret na fone epokhi* (Moscow: Ves' mir, 2004), 81–138, 139–200, 201–286.

12. Piotr Arbatov, *The System*, 297.

13. See Arkhiv Rossiiskoi Akademii Nauk [Moscow, Russia], Fond 2021, Institut Soedinennykh Shtatov Ameriki i Kanady (ISKAN) RAN, 1968–1995, Opis 1: Upravlencheskaia dokumentatsia ISKAN (1968–1990), Predislovie, ll. 2–3.

14. Georgi Arbatov, *The System*, 289–290, 292. Arbatov explained that as late as 1968 even he, director of the new USA Institute, still had not a single American acquaintance because "given the restrictions of the times . . . I didn't even have the right to initiate such contacts." See also R. English, *Russia and the Idea of the West: Gorbachev, Intellectuals, and the End of the Cold War* (New York: Columbia University Press, 2000), 148.

15. See his numerous books of memoirs, including one in English, especially, Arbatov, *The System*, 11–294.

16. Arbatov, *The System*, 298; Barbara L. Dash, *A Defector Reports: The Institute of the USA and Canada* (Falls Church, VA: Delphic Associates, 1982), A-10–12, pp. 3–5.

17. See Barbara L. Dash, *A Defector Reports*, 5, 6.

18. Georgi Arbatov, *The System*, 174.

19. Barbara L. Dash, *A Defector Reports*, 11.

20. Ibid., 16–19, and interviews with Nikolai Bolkhovitinov and Vladislav Zubok. See also Barbara L. Dash, *A Defector Reports*, 20–21.

21. Barbara L. Dash, *A Defector Reports*, A-10, 3.

22. Seweryn Bialer, *The Soviet Paradox: External Expansion, Internal Decline* (New York: Alfred A. Knopf, 1986), 294.

23. Arbatov, *The System*, Introduction by Strobe Talbott, p. xvi.

24. Leonid Leshchenko and Ihor Chernikov, "Vsesvitnio vidomyi vitchyznianyi uchenyi: Istoryk-miznarodnyk, organizator nauky i diplomat. Do 80-litia vid dnia narodzhennia akademika NAN Ukrainy Arnol'da Mykolaivycha Shlepakova (1930–1996 rr.)" in *Mizhnarodni zv'iazky Ukrainy: naukovi poshuky i znakhidky. Vypusk 19*, Ed. by S. V. Vidnians'kyi (Kyiv: Institut istorii NAN Ukrainy, 2010), 27–28. A

majority of scholars affiliated with this institute studied various problems of US and Canadian politics.

25. Vitaliy K. Vrublevskiy, *Vladimir Shcherbitskiy: zapiski pomoshchnika: slukhi, legendy, dokumenty* (Kyiv: Dovira, 1993), 180–181. See also documents in Arkhiv Instituta istorii Natsional'noi Akademii nauk Ukrainy (hereafter ANANU), Opys 1-L, Otdel kadrov, spr. 1277, l. 77 (about Shlepakov moving as a director of the new institute), spr. 1198, l. 48 (about Yevtukh joining Shlepakov in this new institute).

26. Christopher Andrew and Vasili Mitrokhin, *The Sword and the Shield*, 211–212, 213.

27. Christopher Andrew and Vasili Mitrokhin, *The Sword and the Shield*, 211–213.

28. Barbara L. Dash, *A Defector Reports*, 20–21; James Sherr, *Soviet Power: The Continuing Challenge* (Palgrave Macmillan UK, 1987), 159, https://doi.org/10.1007/978-1-349-08524-8. Compare with the CIA documents of 1988 about the KGB connections of Bogdanov and his colleagues: https://www.cia.gov/readingroom/docs/CIA-RDP90T00435R000100040012-5.pdf.

29. Library of Congress, Manuscript Collection, IREX Documents (Hereafter—LC. IREX), RC 68, F 36, p. 25.

30. Interview with one of Sivachev's students, Marina Vlasova, March 20, 1991, Moscow.

31. See his biography in K. V. Khvostova, "Khvostov Vladimir Mikhailovich (1905–1972)," *Portrety istorikov: Vremia i sud'by. Vol. 5*, Ed. by G. Sevostianov, (Moscow: Nauka, 2010), 572–583.

32. I quote my interview with Sivachev's student, Marina Vlasova, March 20, 1991, Moscow; and A. S. Manykin and V. V. Sogrin, "Nikolai Vasilievich Sivachev (1934–1983)," *Portrety istorikov: Vremia i sud'by. Vol. 4*, Ed. by G. Sevostianov, (Moscow: Nauka, 2004), 422–436, especially pp. 422, 423, and 424.

33. Nikolai V. Sivachev, *Politicheskaia bor'ba v SShA v seredine 30-kh godov XX v.* (Moscow: MGU, 1966).

34. Yale Richmond, *Cultural Exchange and the Cold War: Raising the Iron Curtain* (University Park, PA: Penn State University Press, 2003), 44. "Sivachev's interest in Roosevelt, Richmond noted, continued after his return in Moscow; and in 1982, when the Soviet Union marked the centennial of Roosevelt's birth with a TV special, Sivachev was the featured speaker." And he explained the reasons for Sivachev's interest in the New Deal: "Sivachev, in later years, confided to American friends that he had been sent to Columbia to learn why the United States, under Franklin D. Roosevelt, had had a New Deal and not a communist revolution. Sivachev learned why and, in doing so, became one of the Soviet Union's leading authorities on Roosevelt and Soviet-American relations." Ibid., 44.

35. Arkhiv MGU, f. 9, op. 8, d. 917, ll. 2, 8. Even the Soviet policy analysts, who were present, praised this manuscript.

36. Arkhiv MGU, f. 9, op. 8, d. 917, l. 8.

37. Arkhiv MGU, f. 9, op. 8, d. 1009, l. 14.

38. See about this in LC. IREX. RC 68, F 36, p. 23, 25, and letter of L. Bazhanov, November 28, 1967. Compare with my interviews with Bolkhovitinov, Yale Richmond, and Donald Raleigh; and Yale Richmond, *Cultural Exchange and the Cold*

War, 43–44. Sivachev's colleagues spread rumors about Sivachev's establishing the official KGB connections during this visit to the US in 1967. (Interview with Robert Ivanov and Igor Dementiev, March 21, 1991, Moscow, IVI, USSR Academy of Sciences).

39. LC. IREX. RC 27, F 16: a file of "Nikolai V. Sivachev, Associate Professor, Chair of Modern and Current History, Department of History, MGU, Assistant Dean, with a topic 'Government and Labor Relations in the USA in World War II' for 3 months beginning February 1, 1968." On January 12, 1968, the officials from Inter-University Committee on Travel Grants sent over a letter about a visit of Sivachev to all schools where he planned to do research. This letter had an introduction as following: "Nikolai Sivachev who is presently in this country with an official Exhibit."

40. LC. IREX. RC 21, F 113 (1972), p.2. In his letter from June 11, 1975, David Cronon, Dean, College of Letters and Science, the University of Wisconsin-Madison, praised Sivachev and his stay, which "was successful in all respects. He was with us for two weeks as a house guest in my home and spent as much time as possible doing research in the libraries of both the University and the State Historical Society of Wisconsin. He also had contacts with some of our faculty members and was entertained socially on a number of occasions. Through the generosity of the University librarian, we were able to provide him with Xerox copies of two dozen PhD dissertations done here in areas of his scholarly interests in American labor history." And he explained his contacts with Moscow guest: "I am making a point to go to the meetings (with Sivachev) because I want to keep up the contacts with Professor Sivachev and other Soviet colleagues whom I got to know during my stay as a Fulbright lecturer at Moscow University last year." See in LC. IREX. RC 21, F 39.

41. Nikolai V. Sivachev, *Pravovoe regulirovanie trudovykh otnoshenii v SSHA* (Moscow: Iuridicheskaia literatura, 1972), idem, *Rabochaia politika pravitel'tva SShA v gody vtoroi mirovoi voiny* (Moscow: MGU, 1974). His major findings were summarized in his last book: idem, *SSHA: Gosudarstvo i rabochii klass: (ot obrazovaniia Soedinennykh Shtatov Ameriki do okonchaniia vtoroi mirovoi voiny)* (Moscow: Mysl, 1982).

42. I. V. Galkin, E. F. Yaz'kov, "Laboratoriia amerikanistiki MGU," *SShA: ekonomika, politika, ideologiia*, 1987, no. 8, 65; A.A. Porshakova, "Laboratoriia istorii SShA v MGU," *AE. 1989*, 256–265. In 1983 after Sivachev's death, Evgenii F. Yaz'kov became a leader of this center: Larisa V. Baibakova, "E.F. Yaz'kov (1923–2009): tvorcheskii put' pedagoga i uchenogo," *Novaia i noveishaia istoria*, 2011, no. 3, 202–220, especially pp. 212–213. See also Yu. N. Rogulev, "Dvenadtsat' let vzaimovygodnogo sotrudnichestva (o professional'nykh sviaziakh istorikov-amerikanistov MGU s amerikanskimi kollegami)," *AE. 1986*, 246–250. Compare with *Pamiati professora N. V. Sivacheva. SShA: Evoliutsia osnovnykh ideino-politicheskikh kontseptsii*, edited by A. S. Manykin (Moscow, 2004), see esp. 5–16.

43. I quote my interview with Marina Vlasova, Moscow, March 20, 1991, and I also refer to my long interview with Vladislav Zubok via phone, December 30, 2012. Vlasova confirmed, witnessing "the obvious expressions of Russian nationalism, anti-Semitism and even misogyny by Sivachev." Sergei Burin also recalled the negative

role of Sivachev in organizing the ideological ostracism of Burin who was caught by an MGU librarian for drawing funny caricatures of Lenin in the end of 1960s. See about this story in detail in Sergei I. Zhuk, "'Academic Détente,'" 306–307.

44. Various people, like his former MGU students Vladislav Zubok and Marina Vlasova, and his American colleague Donald Raleigh, noted this.

45. LC. IREX. RC 21, F 17, Vladimir Petrov's letter of 3 February 1975, p. 2.

46. LC. IREX. RC 180, F 66 (1978–80). Nikolai Sivachev and Nikolai Yakovlev, *Russia and the United States: U.S.-Soviet Relations from the Soviet Point of View* (Chicago, 1980).

47. Yale Richmond, *Cultural Exchange and the Cold War*, 45. See also Donald J. Raleigh, "In Memory of N.V. Sivachev," *Soviet Studies in History*, Spring 1984, vol. 22, no. 4: 3.

48. LC. IREX. RC 187, F 48 (1979). See about a recommendation of Sogrin for MGU graduate program in Arkhiv MGU, f. 9, op. 8, d. 1009, l. 93. Among his books, see V. V. Sogrin, *Istoki sovremennoi burzhuaznoi ideologii v SShA* (Moscow, 1975); idem, *Ideinyie techenia v Amerikanskoi revoliutsii XVIII veka* (Moscow, 1980), and idem, *Osnovateli SShA: Istoricheskie portrety* (Moscow, 1983).

49. See a about Lev I. Zubok in Sergei I. Zhuk "Inventing America on the Borders of Socialist Imagination: Movies and Music from the USA and the Origins of American Studies in the USSR," *REGION: Regional Studies of Russia, Eastern Europe, and Central Asia,* 2013, vol. 2, no. 2: 249–288, especially 264–270.

50. I quote my email correspondence with Vladislav Zubok, December 17, 2010. See also about tremendous popularity of those Soviet television shows, which were prepared with a participation of Martin Zubok, in Sergei I. Zhuk, "'Soviet Young Man': The Personal Diaries and Paradoxical Identities of 'Youth' in Provincial Soviet Ukraine during Late Socialism, 1970–1980s," *The Australian and New Zealand Journal of European Studies*, vol. 5, no. 2 (2013): 34; idem, "Hollywood's Insidious Charms: The Impact of American Cinema and Television on the Soviet Union during the Cold War," *Cold War History*, 2014, vol. 14, no. 4: 612.

51. Correspondence with Vladislav Zubok, December 17, 2010.

52. See about this magazine, whose circulation in the USSR was resumed under Khrushchev in 1956, in Walter L. Hixson, *Parting the Curtain: Propaganda, Culture and the Cold War, 1945–1961* (New York: St. Martin Press, 1998), 117–119, 152.

53. Vlad Zubok's email correspondence, November 4, 2015.

54. His thesis (*diplomnaia rabota*) had a title: *"The Fair Deal of Harry S. Truman, 1946–1949."* Zubok defended his thesis in May of 1980.

55. See about these various editions of the memoirs, written by the first director of ISKAN: G. A. Arbatov, *Zatianuvsheiesia vyzdorovlenie (1953–1985 gg.) Svidetel'stvo sovremennika* (Moscow, 1991), 381–399; Georgi Arbatov, *Chelovek sistemy: Nabliudenia i razmyshlenia ochevidtsa eio raspada* (Moscow, 2002), 132–147; Georgi Arbatov, *Zhizn,' sobytiia, liudi: Avtobiografiia na fone istoricheskikh peremen* (Moscow: Liubimaia Rossiia, 2008), 305–343; idem, *The System: An Insider's Life in Soviet Politics* (New York, 1992), 329–355. Compare with Piotr Cherkasov, *IMEMO. Institut Mirovoi Ekonomiki i Mezhdunarodnych Otnoshenii. Portret na fone epokhi*

(Moscow: Ves' mir, 2004), 531–570, and Robert D. English, *Russia and the Idea of the West*, 193–228.

56. Interview with Vladislav Zubok, January 25, 2011. See about Radomir Bogdanov as a KGB officer in Barbara L. Dash, *A Defector Reports*, 20–21; Christopher Andrew and Vasili Mitrokhin, *The Sword and the Shield*, 211; Yale Richmond, *Cultural Exchange and the Cold War*, 88.

57. George F. Kennan, *Sketches from a Life* (New York: W. W. Norton, 2000 [1st edition: 1989]), 345, 346ff.

58. Interview with Vladislav Zubok, January 25, 2011, and Vladislav Zubok's email correspondence, November 4, 2015.

59. See about this conference in James G. Hershberg, "The End of the Cold War and the Transformation of Cold War History: A Tale of Two Conferences, 1988–1989," *Imposing, Maintaining, and Tearing Open the Iron Curtain: The Cold War and East-Central Europe, 1945–1989*, edited by Mark Kramer and Vít Smetana (Lanham, MD and Boulder, CO: Rowman and Littlefield's Lexington Press, 2014), 533–550. See about Zubok's participation on pp. 537–538, 547, 549.

60. I used materials from Valery Tishkov's official website (hereafter *Biografiia. Valerii Tishkov*) and the chapters from his own memoirs, which he had sent me by email on February 25, 2015: (From unpublished manuscript by V.A. Tishkov 'Antropologiia sebia' [hereafter Tishkov, *Anthropology of Myself*]). I retrieved his information (on March 15, 2015) also from http://www.valerytishkov.ru/cntnt/biografiya/avtobiogra.html#.

61. *Biografiia. Valerii Tishkov*, 3.

62. It was the first edition of Isaac Deutscher, *Stalin: A Political Biography* (New York: Oxford University Press, 1949). See also about Malia's visit to MGU in David C. Engerman, *Know Your Enemy: The Rise and Fall of America's Soviet Experts* (New York: Oxford University Press, 2009), 140.

63. *Biografiia. Valerii Tishkov*, 3–4. Both Nikolai Bolkhovitinov and Sergei Burin (who also was Sevostianov's student) confirmed this story in their interviews. (See my interviews with Sergei N. Burin, January 15, 1995, Moscow, and with Nikolai N. Bolkhovitinov, Moscow, July 10, 2004).

64. Tishkov, *Anthropology of Myself*, pp. 6; ['Glava IV. V Akademii nauk'], 7–14.

65. Aron Gurevich, *Istoria istorika*, 164–166, and Aleksandr Nekrich, *Forsake Fear*, 241–244. The citation is from Sergei Burin's interview, January 18, 1996, Moscow. See also a history of these International Historical Congresses in Karl Dietrich Erdmann, *Toward a Global Community of Historians: The International Historical Congresses and the International Committee of Historical Sciences, 1898–2000*, edited by Jürgen Kocka and Wolfgang J. Mommsen in collaboration with Agnes Blänsdorf, transl. by Alan Nothnagle (New York: Berghahn Books, 2005), 253, 254–256.

66. See his books based on the research for this dissertation: Valery A. Tishkov, *Strana klenovogo lista*; idem, *Osvoboditel'noe dvizhenie v kolonial'noi Kanade*.

67. Tishkov, *Anthropology of Myself* ['Glava IV. V Akademii nauk'], 7–15.

68. Eventually Tishkov used material from this trip for his two books: (1) about US historians—V.A. Tishkov, *Istoriia i istoriki v SShA* (Moscow: Nauka, 1985), and (2) about Native Americans—V. A. Tishkov, V. G. Stel'makh, and S. V. Cheshko, *Tropoiu*

slioz i nadezhd: Kniga o sovremennykh indeitsakh SShA i Kanady (Moscow: Mysl,' 1990).

69. Tishkov, *Anthropology of Myself* ['Glava IV. V Akademii nauk'], 13–14. Both Bolkhovitinov and Burin confirmed this story. I quote Burin's definition: "Tishkov was the official Soviet Americanist."

70. I refer to my old interview with the retired KGB officer/Canadian expert, Vadim Koleneko, May 14, 2008, Moscow. See also Christopher Andrew and Vasili Mitrokhin, op. cit., 87, 99–101, 147, 162–163, 300, 357–358.

71. *New York Times*, July 5, 1959; R. Sh. Ganelin, V. V. Noskov, V. N. Pleshkov, "Fursenko Aleksandr Aleksandrovich (1922–2008)," *Portrety istorikov: Vremia i sud'by*. Vol. 5, edited by G. Sevostianov (Moscow: Nauka, 2010), 555–571. LC. IREX. RC 21, F 109, letter by Theodore Von Laue, May 15, 1973, pp. 1–2.

72. See especially Christopher Andrew and Vasili Mitrokhin, op. cit., 13.

73. Christopher Andrew and Vasili Mitrokhin, *The Sword and the Shield*, 211–213. Vadim Koleneko, a Byelorussian by ethnic origin, had never kept a secret of his KGB background. In a conversation with me, he shared a history of his career (of course, without any details of his operative's action).

74. Interview with Nikolai N. Bolkhovitinov, Moscow, May 21, 2001.

75. Ibid.

76. Interviews with Leonid Leshchenko, June 23, 2012, and June 25, 2013, Kyiv, Ukraine, and with Nikolai N. Bolkhovitinov, Moscow, May 21, 2001; interview with Stepan Ivanovich T., a retired KGB officer, January 30, 2019, Kyiv, Ukraine.

77. I quote my interviews with Leshchenko, June 25, 2013, and Stepan Ivanovich T.

78. In July 2012, Julianne Fuerst and I (as Western scholars) were invited by Georgiy Kasianov and Alexei Miller to teach at one of the Soros-sponsored summer schools in Chernivtsi Region, Ukraine.

79. Both Leshchenko and a former KGB officer Stepan Ivanovich T. confirmed that FSB in Russia approved the Russian candidates to work with such Western foundations, like Soros or Carnegie Foundations. See also those names "approved" by the Russian intelligence on the official sites of Soros Foundation, Valdai Club, etc.: https://www.opensocietyfoundations.org/voices/ukraine-running-place; https://valdaiclub.com/about/experts/370.

Chapter 3

The "KGB People" and Soviet Americanists in International Academic Exchanges

According to the annual KGB reports, the most important goal of the KGB administration was to prepare the well-trained agents for the intelligence work abroad. During one year, 1969, the Ukrainian KGB sent its 23 agents into various international organizations, located in the US; 200 KGB agents traveled to the US as research specialists, collecting the intelligence information there; 40 KGB operatives worked abroad for hiring the foreigners as the future KGB agents; 3 KGB agents had already been "implemented in the US intelligence"; 2 were "implemented in the Zionist and clerical groups" in the US and Israel; and 292 KGB agents were engaged in the counterintelligence operations against the Ukrainian nationalist centers in the US and Canada. Similar numbers were reported almost every year in the 1970s as well. The new goal was to infiltrate various Slavic/Soviet studies centers at Harvard University, Princeton University, Columbia University, and University of Toronto with the scholars, who supported the Soviet policy and "were ready to promote the positive images and ideas of Russian/Soviet history and culture among the American audience." Almost every year during the 1970s, the KGB managed to infiltrate approximately 250–270 of their agents into various diplomatic, academic, media, and business organizations in the US and Canada, creating so-called "sleeping cells" there for the future intelligence work of the KGB and GRU. In the 1970s, most of those trained agents had professional background in the field known as American studies (or *Amerikanistika* in Russian).[1]

All of these KGB operations also connected the academic exchanges between the Soviet and Western scholars with the geopolitical plans of Soviet intelligence to promote the Soviet diplomatic goals, using Western, especially American, academia through the personal contacts of the participants of those exchange programs. As Nikolai Bolkhovitinov, a famous Soviet Americanist, noted in 1992, "To travel abroad, especially to the United States, the main capitalist enemy of the Soviet Union, you had to have the KGB permission to go." And he continued,

> Every Americanist, every expert in American studies, was considered to be an ideological warrior of the communist party, of the Soviet state and of the KGB, especially if this expert was allowed to go to America. So Soviet Americanist had no choice, he or she had to be either KGB officer, or had to collaborate with this organization. As a result of such an approach, "the KGB people" played important leading roles in all Soviet centers for American studies. Overall, for our better understanding the Soviet side of academic exchanges, we need to be aware of the leading roles of such KGB people in the entire history of these exchanges, beginning with the pioneers of these programs in 1958, such participants like a KGB general [Oleg] Kalugin, a participant of these programs in the 1970s Aleksandr Fursenko, and finishing with the participants of the [academic] exchanges during the 1980s, such young scholars like Vyacheslav Nikonov and Andranik Migranian.[2]

According to other eyewitnesses of the contemporary events, "the KGB people" were instrumental not only in shaping the research agenda in various Soviet centers for American studies, such as the Institute of World History (IVI) and ISKAN (Institute of the USA and Canada) in Moscow, but also in influencing the Soviet program of academic exchanges with the United States. As a former ISKAN scholar, Galina Orionova, noted about the KGB connections in ISKAN in 1979: "[ISKAN] Deputy Director Bogdanov and his predecessor [Vasily] Sitnikov were well-known KGB members . . . [A]nyone who served as scientific, or executive secretary for foreign relations (or *prorector po rabote s inostrantsami* [a college dean in charge of the foreigners—SZh.]) [at Soviet academic institutions] can be identified as a KGB member."[3] Many years later, a former Soviet Americanist from Ukraine explained to me that the "KGB assignments were closely connected to the academic assignments during the research trips abroad." Therefore, he argued that serious historians "cannot study a history of Soviet Americanists without their direct 'KGB connections.'"[4]

KGB operations in America always involved those Soviet scholars (mostly Americanists) who participated in various academic exchange programs. Usually, after the first travel abroad and submission of their travel reports, Soviet scholars were invited by the KGB officers (from the so-called 1st department [*otdel*]) for a "special conversation." As some participants of these conversations recalled, Soviet Americanists had to play "various mind games" and follow their "strategies of survival" during these conversations accepting some KGB offers and rejecting the others. The major goal of these games was to maintain good connections with the KGB to guarantee future trips to America. Not everybody could follow the rules of such games. Breaking these rules could affect one's entire academic career and, especially, plans for travel abroad.[5] The most important part of the "strategies of survival" was a correct adherence to all ideological requirements in the travel report by the scholar. This report had to reflect the major research and teaching goals of the travel and describe the major research centers, personal and scholarly contacts abroad, and main activities during the travel. The KGB reports also required a certain description of the political, economic, and ideological (and since the 1970s, cultural) situation in American society. Trying to ignore these rules was considered to be a serious "deviation."[6] A few talented Soviet Americanists, like Nikolai Bolkhovitinov from Moscow or his young colleague from Odesa Vitaly L. Beloborodko, who rejected the recruiting efforts of the KGB, were punished by a ban to travel abroad.[7] Those Soviet Americanists, who were the KGB officers, or who collaborated with this organization, had no problems with getting permission for their international travels from the KGB.

According to IREX files, 480 (80 percent) Soviet participants in academic exchanges program during 1968–1982, who represented a field of "American studies," were the official policy analysts of the Soviet government, and all of them came from the research institutes of the Soviet Academy of Sciences, such as ISKAN and IMEMO, in Moscow. During the same period of time, almost 80 percent (483) of Soviet Americanists who visited the United States, using American research grants, were various official leaders (mostly academic *apparatchiks*) from the Soviet centers for American studies in MGU, ISKAN, IMEMO and IVI. American observers were skeptical about the mission of these research centers and characterized them in the IREX official reports as the "Spy Institutes."[8]

Meanwhile, American hosts, the experts in Russian and Soviet studies, were always interested in collaboration with the Soviet scholars, trying to help them to integrate into the "improvised international community, created by the open opportunities of détente."[9] Sometimes these American hosts even tried to ignore the "spy" background of their Soviet visitors, if they were official bosses from Moscow centers. American scholars flattered these guests in public, hoping to get the official invitations to visit Russia or begin the collaborative research projects with their Soviet visitors. Among various materials, some IREX files contain a very positive and sympathetic portrayal of Grigorii Sevostianov, a professional Soviet spy and intelligence/KGB officer. Sevostianov was involved in the exchange programs from the early beginning of those programs. Since 1963, Sevostianov had been included in the list of candidates for international academic exchange by the Soviet administration. Sevostianov, a professional Soviet intelligence officer, became one of the first pioneers of the exchange programs funded by the "US imperialist funding agency"—the American Council of Learned Societies. Despite their constant complaints about his "bad spoken English," American hosts were "charmed" by Sevostianov's "correct and polite behavior" during his first American visit from January 7 to May 7, 1963:

> Mr. Sevostianov was handicapped by limited oral English comprehension and conversation ability; apparently, however, he read English well enough for his research purposes.... He has done research at the Library of Congress, the Franklin D. Roosevelt Library, and the libraries at Cornell, Harvard, Yale, Stanford, and the University of California at Berkeley. Lectures he gave in Russian on American studies in the Soviet Union at Cornell and on Soviet studies in American history at Yale were well received.[10]

Eventually, through his KGB connections, Sevostianov became head of the first American studies center in Moscow in 1968, "trying to suppress 'any fresh idea' among his Soviet colleagues, punishing those 'liberals,'" like Nikolai Bolkhovitinov, "for an expression of their open-minded and too revisionist views on US history" in Moscow. As head of this center, he became a popular Soviet guest in America. Paradoxically, this "KGB man," and well-known "enemy of American imperialism," known for his "offensive brutal anti-American" publications in the USSR, based mainly on communist propagandist clichés rather than on serious analysis of historical documents, suddenly was introduced by American hosts in 1974 as "a distinguished Russian diplomatic historian" and as "a scholar of excellent background, a man of great integrity and seriousness." Many American colleagues of Sevostianov, such as Norman Saul from the University of Kansas, characterized Sevostianov as "a serious scholar" who "was well versed in American published material relating to his topic, thus enabling him to use research time more profitably."[11] As it turned out, Professor Saul was interested in Sevostianov's immediate support for "expanding scholarly cooperation directly between the University of Kansas and the [Soviet] Academy of Sciences," and "the possibility of joint conferences, joint publications, and teaching and research exchanges."[12]

All American visitors to the USSR, especially the American experts in Russian/Soviet history, culture, and politics, depended on the good relations with the Soviet officials from the "spy institutes" and, eventually, on their official invitations to visit Moscow. That is why the IREX officials always supported and promoted the visits of such famous Soviet academic officials connected to the KGB, like Sevostianov or Georgi Arbatov. It was a principle of "do ut des"—"we give you our permission to visit US and expect you to allow us to visit the USSR to do our research there," or "we do not pay attention to your KGB and Communist connections, and expect (instead) that you would invite us to the Soviet Union any time we need it."[13]

On August 27, 1973, IREX issued a special "Memorandum about Bilateral Travel Grant Request" to sponsor Arbatov's visit on January 9 through February 6, 1974:

> The US Institute (ISKAN) has served as a useful intermediary in channeling visiting US scholars to other institutes within (Soviet) Academy hierarchy, but these visits have to date not provided satisfactory reciprocal opportunities for "Russianists" and Soviet specialists. We should like to discuss with Arbatov an expansion of our range of contacts and the formation of a bi-national agenda commission which would identify areas of mutual and parallel interest in order to facilitate consultation and collaboration.[14]

As a result, on September 13, 1973, Allen Kassof from IREX wrote Arbatov the official invitation from IREX and ACLS to visit the US with his wife, and to deliver a special public lecture (with a promised honorarium) at the University of Michigan, in Ann Arbor. After this successful visit on February 26, 1974, Cynthia Scott, IREX program officer, in her letter to Arbatov, reminded him about the successful results of his application for American funding for his trips, and promised to support all his future visits to America and at the same time promised to bring in Moscow the list with nominations of American scholars for the 1974–1975 academic year, and asked for a meeting with him in ISKAN to discuss this list of the future American visitors in the USSR.[15]

The general evaluations of the visits by Soviet Americanists to the US and discussions about pros and cons of this exchange program were the major themes of IREX correspondence during the 1970s. The main idea of these documents was to justify the rationale for the exchange with the Soviet scholars. In some reports, IREX officials were sincerely surprised with the rare cases of professionalism and academic honesty of Soviet Americanists.[16] A good summary of the American hosts' reaction to Soviet guests was expressed in some correspondence in 1976, by Eugene B. Skolnikoff, the Director of the Center for International Studies at Massachusetts Institute of Technology (hereafter MIT), who wrote to Julia Holm from IREX,

> [the Soviets] seemed to come with a very specific objective of learning about certain techniques in political science and were relatively little interested in discussing anything else at all. Moreover, I did not have the impression that they were well-grounded in those techniques themselves, though I cannot speak with certainty on that point. The impression certainly was that they were there to get information rather than to have broader discussions. It was not clear to me either that they were sufficiently well-versed in the techniques they wanted to learn

about to be able to assimilate very much of the information they seemed to be after. I might add that my own recent experiences with Russian visitors have been so consistently unsatisfactory, and I have picked up enough similar comments from others, that I find myself increasingly less interested in receiving or meeting with Russian visitors unless I know them well and know that I can have a reasonable exchange of information with them. When Dr. Arbatov visited MIT recently for a small luncheon, I made this point very strongly to him and indicated that from my perspective US-Soviet academic exchanges would deteriorate very rapidly if the Russians continued to carry out their side as seems to have been developing in the last couple of years. He said he "got the message" and would carry it back but offered no other commentary.[17]

A month later, Julia Holm answered Skolnikoff, explaining that,

[O]f seven letters I received back (about Soviet visitors), five were positive. Those five letters came from professors who do not frequently receive Soviet scholars and thus might have more patience and lower expectations than scholars like yourself who see a regular parade of Soviets. There is also a feeling in much of the correspondence that [academic apparatchiks] serve as laboratory specimens—"so this is how a *shishka* acts, talks, and dresses in the mid-70s . . ."—but not as intellectual counterparts. . . . Unfortunately, the evaluations that came back this year [about Soviet visitors] were alarmingly poor—the majority of the Soviet scientists were quite obviously here as a reward and not to do research. . . . I mention this because the problem of—let me be frank—hacks coming guised as scholars, plagues all three exchanges I run.[18]

In general, American hosts were very skeptical about intellectual potential and scholarly contributions of the Soviet Americanists who visited their country. Until the mid-1970s, they called these Soviet visits "a kind of academic tourism," and they expected that more serious Soviet researchers eventually would come to visit as well. Overall, they were not interested in Soviet Americanists coming to American universities. As one expert in East Asian studies from Harvard University complained to IREX in June of 1975:

The Academy of Sciences of the USSR has sent us a succession of people who ask questions but have nothing to offer. They are not historians, but seem to be intelligence specialists, and are not of intellectual interest to us. Meanwhile, our proposal that an historian of interest to us should visit Harvard from their Institute of Oriental Culture of the Academy of Sciences has been bypassed and disregarded for three years past. If the Soviets expect intellectual interchange with us, they should send people competent for the purpose.[19]

Unfortunately, the majority of Soviet visitors were academic or college apparatchiks rather than serious researchers. IREX reports left many portrayals of such Soviet functionaries. All of them contain the similar characteristics:

1. Bombastic, 2. Arrogant, 3. Impolite (arrives without announcement to meet people), 4. Doesn't pay hotel bill, 5. Doesn't arrive for appointments made for him, 6. Speaking out of order, 7. Rejected a [American host's] complaint that information in data sheets was not correct, 8. Rejected a complaint that Soviets ask for too much money, 9. Rejected complaints that Soviets participants only learn, bring little of value to American universities.[20]

More than 60 percent of all IREX reports during the Brezhnev era had direct complaints about bad English language and research skills of Soviet students of American studies. Usually, American hosts could praise (in 40 percent of IREX files) Soviet Americanists, specialists in US economy, politics, diplomacy, and culture from ISKAN and IMEMO, but very rarely Soviet historians, whom they "found [sometime] charming people," but [they] could not "see that visits [of Soviet historians] accomplished any intellectual purpose," because Soviet guests "prosecuted no significant research here [in America]."[21] Even Aleksandr Fursenko, a Soviet historian, the most respected by his American colleagues, was criticized in the IREX reports for the same reason. Thus, in his letter from November 15, 1979, Professor Arthur Schlesinger Jr. from the City University of New York wrote to IREX, answering an inquiry regarding the visit of Fursenko and his research topic about "Evolution of US politics in the 1970s," and complained at the end,

> I have seen him on his previous trips and suppose I will see him again this time. But I cannot forbear passing on to you my strong impression that these meetings are a total waste of time. Fursenko, though a nice fellow, is not a historian. He is a Soviet propagandist, totally impervious to evidence at odds with his stereotypes, and it is a misuse of money to send him (or for that matter any other Soviet "historian" of contemporary affairs) around the United States.[22]

Despite their constant complaints about "the ideological bias" and "preconceived notions" of Soviet visitors, American hosts always emphasized the political and cultural significance of these exchanges. On January 24, 1975, Marshall Shulman from Columbia University, in his letter to IREX, positively evaluated visits of two scholars, Yuri Mel'nikov, a sector head at the Institute of the International Workers' Movement, USSR Academy of Sciences, and Vladimir Zolotukhin from ISKAN:

> I consider both visits to have been useful. As it happened, I met with both men in Moscow afterwards, and both expressed warm appreciation for their reception here, and said that the trip had been valuable for them. I have no doubt

that their desire to reciprocate made my own trip more productive. I have known Dr. Mel'nikov for many years. He is a thoughtful man, and a serious scholar. He has made several trips to the United States, and they are reflected in the differentiations he makes in his writings. . . . Dr. Zolotukhin is the head of a section in the Institute of the USA, and he arranged for me to meet with members of his section in Moscow to discuss the role of the US Congress in the determination of foreign policy. From the discussion, I derived some valuable insights into their perceptions of US political life. The quality of his observations also reflected the value of his experiences in the United States. It is my belief that it is in the United States interest to have Soviet analysts of the US as knowledgeable as possible, to reduce the risk of dangerous miscalculations and unnecessary misunderstandings.[23]

According to the official American documents, the American hosts clearly understood the role of those Soviet Americanists from ISKAN, IMEMO, and other Moscow and Kyiv centers, who were the Soviet policy analysts and the official advisers of the Soviet leadership. For the IREX administration and US State Department, those Soviet "power people," like Arbatov, were the important connections to the Soviet political leaders. During the 1970s, a majority of IREX exchanges, involving Soviet Americanists (almost 80 percent), funded the Soviet policy analysts with discussions of arms control and other diplomatic issues in the US-Soviet relations. Moreover, the IREX administration supported those Soviet research projects, which could provide Soviet leadership with precious information about the situation in US politics, economy, society, and culture, with the goal "to reduce the risk of Soviet dangerous miscalculations" in the "growing arms race."[24]

According to the Soviet policy analysts, who were the active participants in the IREX programs, they tried to bring this message of "their American hosts" to Leonid Brezhnev and other Soviet leaders. Through their personal ties to leadership, Americanists from IMEMO and ISKAN gave Brezhnev realistic recommendations about a careful and reasonable politics of reducing the risks of arms race. Unfortunately, after 1979, "Their efforts to convince Brezhnev [to listen to their analysis after their visits to America] came to naught due to the latter's near-total mental incapacity and the attendant devolution of power to Defense Minister Dmitri Ustinov and the military."[25]

A minority of Soviet Americanists (less than 20 percent), participants in the IREX programs, were the Soviet experts in US history. American hosts also financially supported this category of Soviet visitors. According to IREX reports, "This exchange of scholars, if it can be carried on more broadly, would be a great asset in building better [and closer cultural and intellectual] relations between the United States and Russia."[26] The IREX administration tried to support not only the research projects of the Soviet historians, but also their academic connections to their American colleagues, the American experts in Russian studies—"Russianists" and "Sovietologists." From a technical point of view, establishing such connections was important for helping the Soviet visitors with their adjustment to American realities. American Sovietologists, who knew Russian language and culture, became the first natural "interpreters" of American life for the Soviet guests, experts in US history. As a result, Soviet Americanists had more friendly relations with American Sovietologists than with the local US historians.[27] Moreover, later on, the Soviet visitors became instrumental in obtaining the official invitations to the USSR for their former American hosts. It was the official policy of IREX administration "to encourage the involvement of both Soviet and American scholars in the international, mutually beneficial, academic projects." This policy worked, and all Soviet Americanists, participants in the academic exchanges program, tried to "organize the official invitation for their former American hosts."[28]

Knowing about Arbatov's connections with the Soviet leadership, the administration of both IREX and ACLS tried to use them in order to promote their program of academic exchanges.[29] Since 1974, Arbatov had visited the US on a regular basis. American officials, who knew about Arbatov's useful connections in Soviet academic hierarchy, always supported his nominations for various official positions in the system of Soviet-American academic and scholar exchanges. Therefore, after the sudden death of Nikolai Inozemtsev, an IMEMO director, who was a Soviet head of the ACLS-Soviet Academy of Sciences Commission on the Humanities and Social Sciences, in August of 1982, the Soviet administration elected Arbatov to replace his colleague as a Soviet representative in this commission. Americans, who were interested in maintaining useful connections with the ISKAN director, unanimously supported his nomination.[30]

The American administration of both ACLS and IREX tried to use their personal relations with Soviet academic apparatchiks, like Sevostianov and Arbatov, to engage in personal dialogues with various American funding sources, so-called "patrons" of social sciences and humanities, such as the National Science Foundation, the Pentagon, and the Ford Foundation.[31] The most interesting description of such personal contacts with Arbatov, and simultaneous engagement in these contacts of various American funding agencies, was made by John W. Ward, an ACLS director, in his letter of April 13, 1984. Before he signed the Fifth Protocol of ACLS-Soviet Academy of Sciences Commission on the Humanities and Social Sciences, Ward invited the representatives of IREX and the Ford, the Rockefeller, and Andrew W. Mellon Foundations for a dinner with Arbatov:

On Sunday, May 6 [1984], my wife Barbara and I are having a private dinner party for Mr. Georgi Arbatov . . . You may know Georgi Arbatov's book, The

Soviet Viewpoint, which is an extended interview by Willem Oltmans, the Dutch journalist. Mr. Arbatov is the major spokesman for the Soviet regime vis-à-vis the West. He is a member of the Presidium of the Communist Party and twice recipient of the order of Lenin. He is, in other words, a powerful person in the present Soviet world. I spent the better part of four days in Moscow with Georgi Arbatov and found him tough, well informed, and thoroughly engaging. He is in the United States as the leader of a delegation of the Soviet Academy of Sciences to negotiate a protocol on scholarly and academic exchange between our two countries. . . . Since [the Ford Foundation] supports the work of IREX, we thought a small measure of our appreciation would be to invite you [Ford Foundation's representative] to share an evening with Georgi Arbatov. Conversely, I want to show him the warm, personal attention he showed my wife and me when we were his guests in the USSR.[32]

But the most important of Arbatov's role was creation of and supervision over the group of unique Soviet experts in American studies at ISKAN, who became the real "cultural mediators" between American and Soviet scholars. As Raymond Garthoff described this,

American academic and other visitors [to ISKAN] were not disciplined or instructed to carry an official "American line," but the variance in American viewpoints helped to create a more healthy awareness by Soviet "Americanists" of pluralism in American life, and in the long run a more accurate picture of America in Moscow was in our interest. Moreover, while Arbatov (who had ties to the KGB) and his institute served Soviet propaganda interests, through their publications as well as their contacts, they also gave increasingly realistic internal assessments of U.S. policy to the Soviet leadership as a result of their own growing sophistication. It was by no means a one-way street, and I believe on balance it was in the interests of better understanding and relations between the two countries.[33]

According to both American and Soviet sources, the most popular among US scholars was not Arbatov, nor another official Americanist, but one Soviet historian, directly connected to the KGB, Nikolai Sivachev. His English was fluent, and knowledge of US history was "very good." Sivachev also attracted American scholars' attention because of his instrumental and leading role in the creation of the Soviet center of American studies at MGU and of the Fulbright Program in Moscow.[34] According to the Soviet government's decision in 1973–74, supported by another IREX grantee and a MGU rector, Rem Khokhlov, the MGU department of history became a center for the establishment of the Fulbright program in the USSR.[35] In 1975, Nikolai Sivachev, from the same department, established the Scholarly Coordinating Council on American Studies at MGU. In November 1978, under his leadership, a new Soviet center for American studies was organized there, a so-called "laboratory of American studies" affiliated with the department of modern and contemporary history.³⁶ As a result of such a role, Sivachev became the most important link for many American scholars, who were interested in visiting Moscow as early as the end of the 1960s and the beginning of the 1970s. Eventually, Sivachev combined the role of a good researcher and an efficient organizer of academic exchange programs between the Soviet Union and the United States.³⁷ Moreover, he became a pioneer of implementing computer technology for MGU humanities and social sciences, using his own American experience and bringing to MGU the new American computers and other technological innovations as well.³⁸

The major goal of the Soviet Americanist-scholars' visits to the United States was also establishing connections with and influencing American scholars from the various centers for Slavic/Soviet studies. Different Soviet participants of the US-Soviet academic exchange programs, such as Nikolai Bolkhovitinov, who tried to distance himself from the KGB, Leonid Leshchenko, who admitted the fact of his collaboration with the KGB, and Vadim Kolenko, a retired KGB officer from Bolkhovitinov's sector of American studies in Moscow, emphasized that all KGB officers from the first department of their institutions gave the Soviet candidates for the trip to America special instructions on how to contact American and Canadian Slavists/Sovietologists and how to promote the Soviet diplomatic and academic interests inside American and Canadian centers for Slavic and Soviet studies. Paradoxically, Soviet scholars, oriented by their KGB supervisors for anti-American and pro-Soviet propagandist actions, eventually (through their personal contacts with the Americans) developed the positive attitudes toward "the capitalist America." Such ambivalent attitudes affected all KGB people's actions in the United States and Canada. Overall, the longer Soviet Americanists stayed in US, the more positive impressions of America they developed and brought back to the USSR. They improved their English language speaking ability and communicative skills and gained professional experience as the experts in US history, politics, and culture, "not only working at the American archives and libraries, but also participating in everyday life of ordinary Americans, going shopping, watching 'sitcom' series on American television, and the new Hollywood blockbusters in American movie theaters." After frequent visits to US and long stays there in the 1970s, many Soviet Americanists recalled how they "developed great admiration for the West, for the United States ... respect for the country, its strength, its people."³⁹ All Soviet Americanists noted how important personal contacts with Americans were for their own "discovery" of America and the construction of their mental images of American society and culture. Both Bolkhovitinov and Fursenko acknowledged that living with Americans, in their homes, in the student dorms, influenced them more than just their business and academic relations with their American colleagues.

Soviet guests were impressed not only with good conditions of life and research in America, but also with optimism, energy, and individual initiative of ordinary Americans. Both their reports to their Soviet administration and the reports of their American hosts reflected this positive reaction. Aleksandr Fursenko, a Leningrad historian, confessed later, he "fell in love immediately with America, especially with New York City, the first time [he] visited the US in 1959, which was obvious in [his] official report to the international department."[40] As a young Soviet expert on US modern history, Fursenko was included in the Soviet delegation of consultants, who presented the official Soviet exhibition "The Achievements of Science, Technology and Culture in the USSR" in New York during June-July 1959.[41] Since this first visit, Fursenko had always stressed in his official reports the positive influences of his American visits on his academic and personal life. Even in 1969, when his official visit, funded by ACLS, was interrupted by his sudden serious sickness (he caught Hong Kong flu in the US), Fursenko still praised America. His American hosts also noted his fascination with American life.[42] On May 15, 1973, Theodore Von Laue, a chair of the history department at Clark University in Massachusetts, wrote that Fursenko was overwhelmed with a collection of the American Antiquarian Society and spent his time for researching, Xeroxing, etc. He gave a detailed description not only of the busy research schedule of the Soviet Americanist, but also of Fursenko's other activities:

> He also gave a talk to my Soviet History class and a scholarly lecture comparing the American and the French revolutions. In his talk to my students, he spoke quite freely and most helpfully from my point of view, about his life in the Soviet Union, his family, his material condition, his attitude toward Stalin. My students were quite moved at times and increasingly cordial. They had never encountered a member of the CPSU and the Soviet Academy of Sciences: they found him a very human and attractive person. I also took him to a session of the Connecticut Valley African Colloquium at Wesleyan University in Middletown, Conn., where I happened to read a paper, and subsequently to our farmhouse in West Dover, Vt., where we spent a weekend (with snow). With our help, he also recovered a bit from a strenuous first month in New York City, going (with us) on a side trip to Sturbridge Village.[43]

But, according to his American hosts, the most important part of Fursenko's visit included his personal contacts with Americans, his stay in American homes, and sincere honest conversations with Americans not only about politics and diplomacy, but also about family, culture, and various problems of everyday life. Theodore Von Laue explained the significance of these personal contacts that laid the foundation for the "real academic détente" between the scholars of the Soviet Union and the United States:

> The greatest mutual benefit, I would judge, came from Mr. Fursenko's stay at my house. We have known each other for 16 years and corresponded on professional matters. He knows that I know something of the hidden aspects of Soviet life and treat them with some compassion; he knows I will not be critical of his country. He also appreciated being taken into my family and receive an inside view of American society, without embellishment or ostentation. He in turn freely shared with us his family problems (though my wife did not convert him to women's lib). At any rate, we managed to establish and to deepen a basic human trust between us which transcends all differences of nationality and ideology. He is a sincere person, genuinely interested in understanding American realities without ideological blinders, though a patriotic citizen of the Soviet Union and conforming to its politics. He considers it his mission to bring American realities closer to the Soviet public, rejoicing over the current détente in Soviet-American relations. One of my students, critical of the Americanization of the world as he observed it in West Africa, actually found him much too subservient to American taste and fashion.[44]

But at the same time, after personal conversations with Soviet Americanists, such as Fursenko, American hosts noted an expression of "Russian nationalism" with authoritarian "Stalinist" mentality and of the special "exclusive" cultural mission, among Soviet visitors to the US. Von Laue described this manifestation of Fursenko's Russian "Stalinist" identity as following:

> I found him [Fursenko] occasionally too Russian, almost Stalinist, too abrupt in his manners sometimes, too harsh in his judgments, too convinced of his mission and importance, too inconsiderate and inflexible, even arrogant when his work was at stake, impatient, yet trying very hard to be thoughtful.[45]

Overall, many American hosts praised Fursenko's American visits as beneficial for a positive mutual perception of Soviet-American academic exchanges, noting in 1973 that "the informal reports [about Fursenko's visits] were all favorable. . . . The fact is that Dr. Fursenko had been in the United States before, spoke English well, and was outgoing in his relations with others all helped in making his visit a very considerable success."[46]

Such positive mutual moments in the "construction" of American hosts and Soviet guests co-existed with the negative issues in an everyday practice of these exchanges. Both academic exchanges and Soviet participation in various Western organizations and academic venues brought a number of the KGB agents to the "capitalist West" (especially to America and Western Europe). At the same time, various Soviet tourist groups included numerous

KGB agents (included Fursenko himself), who participated in KGB operations, targeting Western academics, journalists, and various political figures.

CONCLUSION: LEGACY OF SOVIET AMERICANISTS IN PROMOTION OF PRO-SOVIET CONNECTIONS AND PRO-RUSSIAN INTERESTS IN AMERICAN ACADEMIA

From the early beginning, the academic exchanges between the United States and the USSR were used for infiltration by the "KGB people." American officials from ACLS and IREX tried to avoid asking questions about the KGB connections of their Soviet guests, being afraid that such questions could disrupt the entire programs of Soviet-American academic exchanges. They considered such questions to be the prerogative of the FBI. In December of 2014, Allen H. Kassof from IREX explained to me this attitude, arguing that "IREX was a non-governmental organization that had no capacity to determine who among the Soviet exchange scholars was associated with the KGB." But at the same time, American hosts knew about such KGB connections: "As students of the Soviet system, however, we assumed that most if not all of the participants would, at the very least, be debriefed, and that some must have had had active connections, but we had no way of knowing who they were or whether they had been sent to the United States with assignments."[47]

The "KGB people" included a wide variety of the experts, from the ranked KGB officers to various scholars and scientists (including Soviet Americanists), who collaborated with the KGB and provided those "directing organs" not only with intelligence information and necessary "informal" contacts in academic and diplomatic circles, but also with very important expertise in such different fields of knowledge as the functions of the US Department of State, movie and television industries, computer science, or banking system.[48] Many Soviet participants recalled how their KGB supervisors requested them to provide information about different functions of US banks "to use this experience for organization of the Soviet foreign banks, working abroad."[49]

The KGB people (both KGB officers and its agents) became instrumental in organizing all major Soviet centers of American studies: G. Sevostianov in the Institute of History in Moscow in 1953; G. Arbatov in ISKAN in Moscow in 1967; N. Sivachev—in MGU in Moscow in 1975–78; and A. Shlepakov in Kyiv, in Ukraine, in 1978. Besides policing the Soviet academia and ideologically supervising their colleagues and students, the KGB people became "mediators" between the Soviet and American societies. But the most important effect of the exchange program on Soviet Americanists was the development even among the "KGB people" of a psychological phenomenon, which some contemporaries called "a fondness of America and its people." As Mikhail Gorbachev's interpreter explained this phenomenon, "Most [Soviet] experts on the United States, regardless of differences of view on particular issues, seemed genuinely to like America and the Americans."[50]

At the same time, some contemporaries noted that strong KGB connections made the Soviet field of American studies completely dependent on the state's decisions, destroying intellectual autonomy and creativity of Soviet Americanists. As cases of the famous organizers of the Soviet centers for American studies demonstrated, their "fondness of America" had certain limits and was distorted by their loyal service for their state. Chronologically, the role of the KGB people in Soviet American studies changed dramatically. During the first stage of academic exchanges, after 1958, real spies like Kalugin, dominated and controlled the Soviet pool of participants. Brezhnev's détente of the 1970s and a necessity of establishing of the "efficient" relations with the United States led to a diversification of the KGB functions among Soviet scholars. Besides the traditional espionage, "the KGB people" began collecting and analyzing the information about US history, politics, culture, economy, and technology, which could be used and implemented in Soviet domestic politics and consumption. During this stage, the KGB engaged and supported the research of the most talented Americanists, such as Nikolai Sivachev, promoting their career. The last stage in the history of academic exchanges, after 1979, until perestroika, demonstrated the flexibility of "the KGB people" in Soviet academia, who not only adjusted to the Western "innovations" living abroad, but also tried to bring those new "American" concepts and practices into the Soviet reality, maintaining their ideological and financial control over Soviet consumption of the Western ideas and practices. Scholars, like Georgi Arbatov and Nikolai Sivachev, whose careers were supported by the KGB, were used by this organization for creating a more liberal and "Westernized" image of Soviet academia during the intensive political and cultural dialogue with the United States in the 1980s.

In a longer historical perspective, Soviet participation in academic exchange programs with America was successful. Soviet Americanists began their own participation in creation of international community of scholars, becoming partners in academic exchange with their American colleagues. They established good relations not only with American experts in US history, politics, and culture, but also with American specialists in Russian/Soviet studies. To some extent, participation of Soviet Americanists in this international community would not only shape the development of American studies in the USSR, but also influence Russian studies in America. After visiting America, Soviet Americanists became hosts for American guests, experts in Russian studies, building strong personal connections with them—Bolkhovitinov with Norman Saul, Sivachev with Donald Raleigh, Vladimir Sogrin with Saul and

Alfred Rieber, etc. Eventually, through these personal connections, Soviet Americanists and their American colleagues created the important academic international network, which involved their students as well, and which survived the collapse of the Soviet Union in 1991. Paradoxically, as a result of expanding this network during the 1990s, not only American Sovietologists benefited from these connections, but the entire field of Russian studies in America became influenced by former Soviet Americanists, students of Arbatov, Bolkhovitinov, Sivachev, and Fursenko. Using this network, these former Soviet scholars, like Vladislav Zubok (an expert in Carter's presidential campaign), Sergei Plekhanov (a scholar of American political science), Andrei Znamenski (a specialist in history and anthropology of American Indians), and myself (an expert in social history of colonial New York and Pennsylvania) moved to North America and now teach Russian history and politics there. At the same time, after replacing Nikolai Bolkhovitinov in 2002 as a new chair of the Center for North American Studies at the Institute of World History in Moscow, Vladimir Sogrin re-established the center's relations with the Russian intelligence, continuing the traditions of Sogrin's teacher, Grigorii Sevostianov, a KGB/FSB officer, who was leader of that center before Bolkhovitinov.[51]

Paradoxically, the US officials, who were responsible for Soviet-US exchange programs, tried to support not only the research projects of the Soviet Americanists (majority of whom were KGB people), but also their academic connections to their American colleagues, the American experts in Russian studies. From a technical point of view, establishing such connections was important for helping the Soviet visitors with their adjustment to American realities.

As chapter 5 of this book demonstrates, in Canada, Ukrainian Americanists, such as Arnold Shlepakov and his students from Soviet Ukraine, were the most active Soviet connections of the centers of Ukrainian studies, such as in Edmonton and Toronto, to the KGB operations. Soviet Americanists and their KGB supervisors began their own participation in the creation of an international community of scholars, becoming partners in academic exchange with their American colleagues. After the collapse of the USSR, former Soviet Americanists in Russia still maintained strong personal connections with their American colleagues. Two American historians who were linked to Vladimir Sogrin had stayed at his Moscow apartment, and were helped by him during their research in Moscow. One of them was a "Slavist," Alfred Rieber. Another was "Americanist" Norman Saul. Norman Saul was personally connected to an infamous KGB person from the Institute of World History, Vladimir Poznyakov, providing him with a personal invitation to visit the University of Kansas.[52] Eventually, through these personal connections, Soviet Americanists, including the KGB agents (like Poznyakov), and their

American colleagues created the important academic international network, which involved their students as well, survived the collapse of the Soviet Union in 1991, and still exists in Western academia, promoting Russian academic imperialism, Russian cultural values, and Russian political interests.[53]

NOTES

1. SBU, f. 16, op. 1, spr. 993, ark. 115–117.
2. Interview with Nikolai Bolkhovitinov, December 15, 1992, Moscow.
3. Barbara L. Dash, *A Defector Reports: The Institute of the USA and Canada* (Falls Church, VA: Delphic Associates, 1982), 98, 99. See about the role of KGB in a creation of the Soviet centers for American studies in Arkhiv Rossiiskoi Akademii Nauk [Moscow, Russia], Fond 1900, Institut vseobshchei istorii IVI) Akademii nauk sssr, 1969–1985, Opis 1: Upravlencheskaia dokumentatsiia ivi, especially, d. 241: protokoly zasedanii direktsii instituta (for October–December 1968), ll. 1–8, and d. 632: protokoly zasedanii sektora istorii SShA i Kanady (for September-December 1968), ll. 1–27; Fond 2021, Institut Soedinennykh Shtatov Ameriki i Kanady (ISKAN) RAN, 1968–1995, Opis 1: Upravlencheskaia dokumentatsia iskan (1968–1990), especially d. 809 (1968), ll. 1–92; d. 221 (1969–71), ll. 1–122; d. 241: Protokoly zasedanii direktsii instituta (za 1971–73), ll. 1–44. See also about ISKAN "KGB men" in Christopher Andrew and Vasili Mitrokhin, *The Sword and the Shield: The Mitrokhin Archive and the Secret History of the KGB* (New York: Basic Books, 1999), 211–212.
4. Interview with Leonid Leshchenko, June 25, 2013, Kyiv, Ukraine.
5. I use phrases from my interview with Marina Vlasova and Aleksandr Fursenko, March 19, 1991, Moscow. See also Nekrich's memoirs about travels abroad of Soviet Americanists from his Institute of History, and especially about the case of Lev Slezkine, who was denied to travel abroad: Aleksandr Nekrich, *Forsake Fear: Memoirs of an Historian* (Boston, 1991), 135, 201. Even the people who were close to the KGB, like Arbatov, had problematic relations with this organization, and sometimes experienced real persecution by the KGB officers. See G. A. Arbatov, *Zatianuvsheiesia vyzdorovlenie (1953–1985 gg.) Svidetel'stro sovremennika* (Moscow, 1991), 269, 272–274.
6. See a typical academic travel report by O. S. Soroko-Tsiupa, an MGU Professor of Canadian History, in Arkhiv MGU, f. 9, op. 8, d. 1011, ll. 11–12, about his travel to Toronto, Canada, during September 1966–June 1967. Compare with ANANU, sprava 1277, ll. 53–54, 64, and sprava 1198, ll. 31–34.
7. Library of Congress Manuscript collection, IREX files (Hereafter LC. IREX). RC 94, F 28, file of Vitaly Beloborodko.
8. LC. IREX. RC 237, F 13 (1977). See an IREX paper dated September 20, 1977, with handwritten description of ISKAN as *"a Spy Institute."* As David Goldfrank from Georgetown University recalled, the entire situation with Soviet-American exchanges reminded him of the Radio Erevan joke he heard 40 years ago. "Vopros: Are our academic exchanges with the United States reciprocal and equitable?

Otvet: Yes, our academic exchanges with the United States are reciprocal and equitable. They send us scholars, and we treat them like spies; we send them spies, and they treat us like scholars." Cited from Goldfrank's email message to me, August 29, 2013.

9. As Norman Saul mentioned earlier, in 1975, "academic détente was part of [Soviet Americanists'] mission to this country." See in LC. IREX. RC 228, F 18, p. 2.

10. LC MC, ACLS, II: 789, "Interim Report on 1961–63 . . . , Soviet scholars," p. 4. "Grigorii M. Sevostianov, Senior Scholarly Worker, Institute of History, Academy of Sciences. Dr. Sevostianov's research topic was 'History of the Foreign Policy and Diplomacy of the USA in Modern Times.' His program included visits at the Library of Congress, the Franklin D. Roosevelt Library in Hyde Park, Cornell, Harvard, Yale, Stanford, and the University of California at Berkeley. He delivered lectures at Cornell and Yale Universities. . . . " See ibid., II: 791, "Report on Educational Exchange Project Carried by the ACLS under Grant No. SCC-30047," p. 4.

11. LC. IREX. RC 21, F 17 (1974–75), and LC. IREX. RC 228, F 18, citation from a letter by Allen Kassof, December 26, 1974. Compare with my interviews with Nikolai Bolkhovitinov, Robert Ivanov, Aleksandr Fursenko, and Aron Ya. Gurevich (March 19, 1991) and their very negative relations to the "KGB general" Sevostianov; they characterized Sevostianov as "the worst enemy of American people" as the "Soviet hawk of the Cold War."

12. LC. IREX. RC 228, F 18, p. 2: "After consultations with faculty and administration and subsequent conversations with Dr. Sevostianov in Washington by myself . . . , it was decided to extend a proposal for a joint Soviet-American conference on World War II to be held in Lawrence in the fall of 1976, including a joint publication of papers. The State Department and American Historical Association were also consulted in regard to this project, which was presented to Dr. Sevostianov by Professor John T. Alexander in Moscow in May."

13. These phrases were mentioned by Marina Vlasova, compare with interview with Donald Raleigh, May 16, 2012.

14. LC. IREX. RC 161, F 25, IREX Memorandum, August 27, 1973, and letter of Cynthia Scott, February 26, 1974.

15. Ibid.

16. LC. IREX. RC 187, F 13: Sergei Plekhanov's file, praising his erudition.

17. LC. IREX. RC 228, F 45, letter by Eugene B. Skolnikoff, June 22, 1976, pp. 1–2.

18. LC. IREX. RC 228, F 45, letter by Julia Holm, July 14, 1976, pp. 1–2. Another problem, which IREX officials began complaining about after 1975 was the KGB trying to stop the serious researchers from going to US: "Support for dissidents among American scientists is growing steadily and I am very curious to see if their actions might not positively affect the quality of scholars coming here."

19. LC. IREX. RC 228, F 54, letter by John K. Fairbank, June 27, 1975. On May 12, 1975, IREX Memorandum recommended to finance (3–4 weeks) visit of talented Soviet sociologist, "which would promise to lead us beyond the kind of academic tourism which [existed in early years]." See in LC. IREX. RC 161, F 29.

20. LC. IREX. RC 91, F 1 (1963–1968). See Folder: "Trip to USA of P.I. Shitov, from Department of Foreign Relations, Ministry of Higher Education, March (4–27) 1968." He went to visit colleges and universities in US where Soviet students stayed. See a special handwritten note with the complaints about Shitov's visit from IREX representatives.

21. LC. IREX. RC 21, F 68, letter by Donald Fleming from Charles Warren Center at Harvard, April 6, 1976, about a visit by Igor Dementiev. The similar unenthusiastic report about E. Yaz'kov's visit is placed in the same folder under F 85.

22. LC. IREX. RC 187, F 25, letter by Arthur Schlesinger Jr., New York, November 15, 1979.

23. LC. IREX. RC 228, F 17, letter by Marshall Shulman, January 24, 1975.

24. Look though the entire IREX file for the Year 1975 with recommendations to provide the Soviet analysts with all necessary information about the US economy. LC. IREX. RC 228, F 17. I quote a phrase "Soviet power people," from my interview with late Richard Stites, November 18, 2008, Philadelphia.

25. See Georgi Arbatov, *The System: An Insider's Life in Soviet Politics* (New York: Random House, 1992), 202, and Robert D. English, *Russia and the Idea of the West: Gorbachev, Intellectuals, and the End of the Cold War* (New York: Columbia University Press, 2000), 163–164, 165.

26. LC. IREX. RC 31, F 26, p. 2.

27. Both Sevostianov and Bolkhovitinov (from IVI) became close friends of the American expert in the Russian history, Norman Saul. Sivachev (from MGU) became a friend of American historian of Soviet Russia Donald Raleigh. Sivachev's student, Vladimir Sogrin (from IVI), still is a good friend of Norman Saul and has close friendly connections with Alfred Rieber, an American historian of imperial Russia.

28. Interview with Yale Richmond, May 9, 2012.

29. LC. IREX. RC 161, F 25, IREX Memorandum, August 27, 1973, and letter of Cynthia Scott, February 26, 1974.

30. See about death of Inozemtsev and his role in Piotr Cherkasov, *IMEMO. Institut Mirovoi Ekonomiki i Mezhdunarodnych Otnoshenii. Portret na fone epokhi* (Moscow: Ves' mir, 2004), 483–509. Compare with the official documents in LC MC, ACLS, ii: 661, "The Fifth Protocol and Attachments of ACLS-Soviet Academy of Sciences Commission on the Humanities and Social Sciences" (Moscow, 1984), pp. 1–5. All American politicians, who were involved in the diplomatic negotiations with the Soviet Union, appreciated the psychological and diplomatic skills of Arbatov in developing the US-Soviet relations. See in Henry Kissinger, *The White House Years* (Boston: Little, Brown, 1979), 112; and Zbigniew Brzezinski, *Power and Principle: Memoirs of the National Security Adviser, 1977–1981* (New York: Farrar, Straus & Giroux, 1985), 153ff.

31. I also use a good study of these patrons in Mark Solovey, *Shaky Foundations: The Politics–Patronage–Social Science Nexus in Cold War America* (New Brunswick, NJ, and London: Rutgers University Press, 2013).

32. LC MC, ACLS, ii: 661, "The Fifth Protocol and Attachments of ACLS-Soviet Academy of Sciences Commission on the Humanities and Social Sciences" (Moscow,

1984), p. 5. It is quotation from Ward's letter to the Ford Foundation. Similar letters were sent to other agencies.

33. Raymond L. Garthoff, *A Journey Through the Cold War: A Memoir of Containment and Co- existence* (Washington, D.C.: Brookings Institution, 2001), 344. Compare also with James Voorhees, *Dialogue Sustained: The Multilevel Peace Process and the Dartmouth Conference* (Washington, D.C.: US Institute of Peace Press, 2002), 71.

34. According to Bolkhovitinov, Ivanov, Gurevich, Burin, and Dementiev, these Sivachev's initiatives were other proofs of his close relations with the KGB.

35. LC. IREX. RC 161, F 44 (1975–76). Compare with Yale Richmond, *Cultural Exchange and the Cold War: Raising the Iron Curtain* (University Park: Penn State University Press, 2003), 40–43.

36. A.A. Porshakova, "Laboratoria istorii SShA v mgu," *ae. 1989*, 256–265. In 1983 after Sivachev's death, Evgenii F. Yaz'kov became a leader of this center. See also Yu. N. Rogulev, "Dvenadtsat' let vzaimovygodnogo sotrudnichestva (o professional'nykh sviaziakh istorikov-amerikanistov mgu s amerikanskimi kollegami)," *ae. 1986*, 246–250. Compare with *Pamiati professora N.V. Sivacheva. SShA: Evoliutsia osnovnykh ideino-politicheskikh kontseptsii*, edited by A.S. Manykin (Moscow, 2004), see esp. pp. 5–16.

37. Both Yale Richmond and Donald Raleigh confirmed this in their conversations with me. See also E.F. Yaz'kov, "N.V. Sivachev i razvitie shkoly nauchnykh issledovanii i prepodavaniia istorii Soedinennykh Shtatov Ameriki v Moskovskom universitete," and William A. James, "Rabotaia s Nikolaiem Sivachevym po programme Fulbraita," in *Pamiati professora N.V. Sivacheva*, 5–16, and 17–30. See also the details of his biography in a chapter 2 of this book.

38. A.S. Manykin and V.V. Sogrin, "Nikolai Vasilievich Sivachev," 427. Sivachev personal initiative produced the first at MGU Department of History's office of "technical means of education"—*kabinet technicheskikh sredstv obucheniia.*

39. I quoted my interview with Robert F. Ivanov, Moscow, June 25, 1991, and English, op. cit., 150. Another Soviet Americanist who became a diplomat noted, "You start to resemble the people, the country, where you work, and this was especially so for those who worked on the USA. It took a higher level of professionalism and culture, and such experience changes your outlook." Ibid., 298.

40. Interview with Aleksandr Fursenko, March 21, 1991, Moscow, IVI.

41. *New York Times*, July 5, 1959; R. Sh. Ganelin, V. V. Noskov, V. N. Pleshkov, 'Fursenko Aleksandr Aleksandrovich (1922–2008),' *Portrety istorikov: Vremia i sud'by*. Vol. 5, edited by G. Sevostianov (Moscow: Nauka, 2010), 555–571, citation is from p. 561.

42. Interview with Aleksandr Fursenko, March 21, 1991, Moscow, IVI.

43. LC. IREX. RC 21, F 109, letter by Theodore Von Laue, May 15, 1973, p. 1.

44. Ibid.

45. Ibid., pp. 1–2. And he finished his letter with a phrase, "Poor man: his visit in the U.S. was so hectic, too much to be observed and digested! I wonder how he feels now, back in Leningrad, with all his presents and his memories."

46. LC. IREX. RC 21, F 109, letter (May 15, 1973) by Norton Ginsburg, Dean of the Center for the Study of Democratic Institutions in Santa Barbara, California.
47. See my email correspondence with Allen H. Kassof, December 13, 2014.
48. See about the advising role of Soviet Americanists in development of Soviet visual media in Sergei Zhuk, "Hollywood's Insidious Charms: The Impact of American Cinema and Television on the Soviet Union during the Cold War," *Cold War History*, 2014, vol. 14, no. 4 (2014): 593–617.
49. Interview with Nikolai Bolkhovitinov, March 23, 1991, Moscow. According to former Soviet KGB officers, who participated in these exchange programs, this information about banking and financial service in the West would be used for future financial operations in post-Soviet Russia and Ukraine. See Oleg Kalugin, *Spymaster: My Thirty-Two Years in Intelligence and Espionage Against the West* (New York: Basic Books, 2004), 424.
50. Pavel Palazchenko, *My Years with Gorbachev and Shevardnadze: The Memoir of a Soviet Interpreter* (University Park, Pa.: The Pennsylvania State University Press, 1997), p. 95. See also Yale Richmond, *Cultural Exchange*, 91. Compare with another description of such a phenomenon in Allen H. Kassof, "Scholarly Exchanges and the Collapse of Communism," *The Soviet and Post-Soviet Review*, vol. 22, no. 3 (1995): 270.
51. Interview with Nikolai Bolkhovitinov, July 18, 2004, Moscow. See also chapter 2 of this book.
52. Even former KGB officer Vadim Koleneko was sincerely surprised that American scholars could officially invite "an openly anti-American and pro-Soviet KGB person, like Poznyakov" to the United States. I quote my interview with Koleneko at the Institute of World History, in Moscow, Russia, on May 24, 2001.
53. Interview with Yale Richmond, May 9, 2012; and interview with Nikolai Bolkhovitinov, June 2, 2005.

Chapter 4

The KGB Spies, Infiltration into American Society, and KGB "Sleeper Cells/Illegals"

A retired Ukrainian KGB officer, who worked undercover in the West in the 1970s, noted in a conversation with me in January 2019,

> People now forgot that our major goal working in the West, especially in America, was not just spying and stealing new technologies there, but influencing the public opinion, using media, politicians, and also various universities' educational centers (including Slavic centers) in pro-Soviet direction, promoting the main Soviet geopolitical interests. Pursuing this goal, Soviet intelligence officers, working overseas, tried to infiltrate and sponsor various peace, trade union and communist movements. Western academia (especially in the English-speaking countries, such as the US, Canada, and the UK), was very useful and efficient channel for promoting pro-Soviet notions and images by so-called "Soviet sympathizers." Such KGB actions started the period of the "spy wars" between American and Soviet intelligence in the early 1960s, which had continued through the 1980s. This tradition of Soviet intelligence operations, targeting Western educational institutions, survived the collapse of the Soviet Union, and is still obvious in the domination of so-called KGB mindset over the Russian cultural diplomacy, which promotes Russian cultural and academic interests in the West, especially in America and England, infiltrating various universities and colleges there with the Russian agents, and supporting pro-Russian (usually leftist and anti-imperialist) American scholars to become the new faculty members in Western colleges.[1]

As some observers noted, today the FSB, the Russian successor of the KGB, still preserved its old mindset, "in which [now] Russian nationalism supplanted communism and in which spies had a duty to preserve the state to protect the motherland [of Russia]."[2]

In 2019, this former Soviet intelligence officer referred to the so-called spy wars, which began with a KGB reaction to the American U-2 spy scandal, when in May 1960 the Soviets shot down the American U-2 spy plane and captured its pilot, Francis Gary Powers.[3] Another KGB reaction, contributing to the spread of these spy wars, was connected to the series of public revelations by American media in May 1960 about the Soviet spying activities inside of the US of 12 Soviet secret agents of the KGB (including the recently arrested in New York KGB colonel Rudolf Abel).[4]

The KGB administration in Soviet Ukraine was especially worried about the case of Vadym Kiriliuk, who represented the official Ukrainian delegation at the General Assembly of the United Nations in New York City. This case also revealed how the KGB targeted not only the Ukrainian diaspora, but also the American institutions of higher education. Vadym Oleksandrovych Kiriliuk was born in 1928 in the Ukrainian city of Vinnytsia. After his graduation from the law department of Kyiv State University, he joined the KGB and moved to Moscow. Before September 1955, Kiriliuk was working as a KGB junior security officer. From 1955 to 1957, he studied at the special KGB school in Moscow. After his graduation from this KGB school, Kiriliuk worked at the First Main Directorate of the KGB, which oversaw foreign operations and intelligence activities abroad. According to the Directorate's order, in 1958 Kiriliuk was included in the official delegation of Soviet Ukraine, which participated in the work of the General Assembly of the United Nations Organization (UNO) in New York City. While living in the US, Kiriliuk was hired by the Ministry of Foreign Affairs of Soviet Ukraine to represent it in the Secretariat of the UNO, where he had worked until January 1960. One of Kiriliuk's assignments was to promote Soviet ideological and cultural interests among "American educators," especially at the centers of Soviet studies at Columbia, Harvard, and Georgetown Universities. Using various pro-Communist and Afro-American groups among the students and faculty of those schools, the KGB agents, directed by Kiriliuk, not only monitored political preferences of the American faculty there, but also tried to "push those preferences in the pro-Soviet and pro-Russian directions, discrediting both Jewish Zionists and Ukrainian nationalists."[5]

According to the KGB report, "in April 1959, Iosif Zatirka, a US citizen of the Ukrainian origin, visited the Soviet Embassy in Mexico and offered the secret written information about the US and agreed to help [the KGB with the classified information] in the US. Due to the fact that Zatirka gave the precious information, which presented the [strategic] interest [to the USSR], the KGB residents in the USA decided that Kiriliuk [who was fluent in Ukrainian] would continue to work with him inside the US under a nickname of George."[6] As it turned out, after the first meetings with Kiriliuk/George, Zatirka "encountered some problems performing the KGB assignments," he "got scared, and then later denounced" Kiriliuk ("as a KGB spy") to the American police. As a result, following Zatirka's denunciation of Kiriliuk, the American government sent a special note of complaint to the General Secretary of the UNO about Kiriliuk's spying activities. Using his family emergency as a pretext to retire from an official position at the UNO, Kiriliuk managed to escape safely from New York City to the USSR in January 1960.[7]

But his behavior created a scandal, compromising the UNO membership of Soviet Ukraine and its official delegation at the United Nations in the US. Former KGB officers, who still remember the situation in the 1960s, noted that this "Kiriliuk's case" inspired a series of the active measures against "the CIA agents" inside Soviet Ukraine. According to those officers, the wave of "spy scare" of the 1960s in the USSR, and especially in Soviet Ukraine, was the KGB's "peculiar" response to the "public exposure of the Soviet spies" inside the US, such as "Kiriliuk's case." At the same time, "Kiriliuk's case" was a lesson to the KGB administration to be careful, influencing "American academia" and dealing with the "Ukrainian diaspora."[8] Moreover, "Kiriliuk's case" and the previous FBI arrest of KGB Colonel Rudolf Abel in 1957 exposed another old channel of Soviet intelligence against the United States—the existence of Soviet agents posing as Americans, living among Americans, who were called "the illegals," "the sleepers," or "the sleeper cells." These agents lived as Americans or Canadians under assumed names, like Abel, and developed their personal contacts, like Kiriliuk, inside the American Ukrainian community of New York. These sleeper agents also became connected to American and Canadian colleges and think tanks, infiltrating them and performing other "special operations" of the Soviet, and now Russian, intelligence.[9]

According to those who studied the KGB secret operations, "deep-cover agents who lived abroad under false identities" were known as "illegals." Traditional spies work under diplomatic cover in a foreign country, "posing as something like a second counselor for trade at the embassy. If such a spy is caught, they have diplomatic immunity and can only be expelled. Other spies work under nondiplomatic cover, as, say, a businessman. They have no diplomatic immunity." In the Russian terminology, they are "illegal." Many countries undertake this kind of spying, but the KGB administration takes it a step further:

> A deep-cover Russian illegal can be not just operating under cover of a different occupation but can take on an entirely different nationality. The Russian will not—to all appearances—be Russian but instead be German or Canadian or even American. They can spend decades undercover in a different country, burrowing deep into their target society—sleepers. Some will live and die in a foreign land, buried in a graveyard under a name that was never truly their own.

Illegals are the pride of Soviet and Russian intelligence—having assets deep inside enemy territory provided a sense of power and reassurance and an edge over their adversaries.[10]

Since 1922, Soviet intelligence had used the practice of "sleeper cells" in their fight against capitalist America. One of the earliest cases of such Soviet spying activities was related to the Zalman Litvin (1908–1993), who created such a sleeper cell with his wife in the US.[11] Litvin was an officer of Soviet military intelligence (GRU), who was the head of the Soviet spy ring on the US West Coast from 1938 to 1945, operating under the cover name of "Mulat," or "Mulatto."[12] In early 1938, Litvin arrived in Los Angeles with a Canadian passport in the name of Ignatii Samuel Witchak; there, he enrolled in the Department of Political Science at the University of Southern California as a non-credit student. He was diligent in his studies and, within a year, managed to become a regular student. In the same year, he fulfilled his initial intelligence assignment, having built his residency group in the US. Litvin used his time at the university not only as a cover and for his studies, but also for spotting potential recruits for Soviet intelligence. As he would later write in his notes for an unpublished memoir, he took an active part in seminar classes: "It was there, in the presentations by the students, that their political views were revealed. I listened to such presentations with great attention and made my conclusions about whom I should try to get close to, and who might be of help in solving my tasks." Litvin graduated from the University of Southern California, earned a master's degree in political science a year later, and became an instructor in the same department. Gradually, he managed to build a group of "pro-Soviet symphasizers," which numbered 10 agents, US citizens. All of them worked on an ideological basis (being pro-Communist), without any financial compensation. Following the Nazi invasion of the Soviet Union in June 1941, Litvin's assignment changed: now he had to obtain political and technical information on areas such as aircraft engineering, radio engineering, shipbuilding, and weapons manufacturing from the United States. Simultaneously, he continued teaching constitutional and international law and the history of modern civilization—and went about preparing his PhD thesis. However, following the defection in Canada of one Soviet intelligence officer, Litvin's cover was blown, and he was placed under heavy FBI surveillance. After a few weeks in hiding, during which he moved from place to place to escape surveillance, he was secretly transported to the Soviet Union. In March 1946, his wife and their American-born son were also rescued and transported to the Soviet Union.[13]

Meanwhile, Soviet intelligence elaborated its operations against their official allies, the US and the UK during WWII, using a strategy of the spies' "sleepers."[14] The similar operations of Soviet spy infiltration in the

US continued during the Cold War after WWII as well. Soviet "illegals" posing as Americans became the most active part of Soviet intelligence operations, which united efforts of the KGB and GRU on the American soil. Khrushchev's "opening" of Soviet society to a dialogue with capitalist countries and a new Soviet international diplomacy of peaceful co-existence created the new channels for the KGB operations abroad. As early as December 1961, the KGB recommended to their operatives "to explore possibilities and recruit as KGB agents those Soviet experts, who go to the international exhibits and fairs; about recruiting the Soviet citizens (the experts in various fields of interest, who often went abroad and who were fluent in foreign languages, especially in English) as the KGB agents; and about possibilities of recruiting the foreign citizens during communications with Soviet experts at various Soviet exhibits in foreign countries, and infiltrating those agents in various American educational and cultural institutions."[15] Starting in the 1960s, the KGB operatives tried to train numerous married couples posing as Americans in the US and Canada not only for collecting the strategic information, but also "for influencing the American public, especially young college students, to develop and maintain their interest in Soviet culture, technology and history."[16]

According to the KGB documents, as early as 1959, using the possibilities of various cultural, academic, and touristic exchanges with the West, Soviet intelligence began the new strategy and tactics "for infiltration of the KGB agents into various political, cultural, educational and academic institutions in America to promote positive and attractive image of the Soviet life and politics for the ordinary people in the West."[17] Throughout the entire 1970s and the 1980s, this strategy of "KGB infiltration into capitalist American society" led to the creation of various "sleeper cells" of the KGB agents in Canada and the United States.[18]

After 1958, the KGB began its new campaign for modernization of its intelligence infrastructure and a "network of spies" in the West. On June 27, 1959, the KGB administration submitted special recommendations to the regional branches of the KGB about "initiating the search for the candidates for a replacement of a position of an adviser for science and technology" (for intelligence assignments) at the Soviet embassies in the US, England, Canada, and other "capitalist countries." The major requirement of those recommendations was that the possible candidates "should know foreign languages (especially English) and be the experts in one of the fields such as chemistry, oil industry, automatics, radio electronics, analytical instrumentation, electric industry, and had a practical experience serving as a director of an industrial plant or as a chief constructor of the constructing department at such a plant, and had at least a Ph.D. (*kandidatskaia stepen'*) in science, and, finally, had a wide erudition and a broad technological and cultural knowledge."[19] Inside Ukraine, the KGB recommended for those operatives, who were selected for intelligence work inside the US, to make contacts with "the possible old spies-agents who used to work in capitalist countries and now settled in Ukraine," and try to develop various forms of "their own active measures" and "to investigate" those spies' possible contacts in the West. At the same time, the KGB administration complained about "the foreign language illiteracy" of the freshly recruited young KGB officers for the work in the US and emphasized the necessity of recruiting real experts in foreign languages, such as English, German, French, Spanish, and Arabic, as the future KGB agents, "especially for sending them in the international organizations in New York City, Geneva and Vienna."[20]

As a result of these efforts, the KGB administrations started the recruiting campaigns among the faculty and graduate students at the Ukrainian colleges to send them abroad to the US as a part of the exchange program group in 1960 and formed a group of forty-eight candidates for this operation. Moreover, the KGB tried to enforce their counterintelligence measures against the possible American anti-Soviet actions. According to the KGB information, received in April 1960, the US, West German, and other foreign intelligence services tried to recruit Soviet citizens abroad and persuade them to stay in the West. To resist these actions, the KGB administration ordered to send the specially trained agents from the faculty and students at Soviet Ukrainian colleges in the groups of the recommended and selected people (with an obligatory knowledge of at least two foreign languages) for the intelligence work in the capitalist countries. As a result, in Kyiv, a special school was organized for the training of the recruited agents from the faculty and students to prepare them for intelligence and counterintelligence work, especially in the US. During the first official program of exchange with the US in 1960, seven specially trained Ukrainian agents were recommended for the travel to the US: three graduate students and four faculty members. This became a long tradition of the Kyiv office of the KGB: only the recruited KGB agents participated in all academic exchange programs of Soviet Ukraine with the United States. The KGB engaged the official Ukrainian venues, responsible for cultural and academic exchanges with the Ukrainian diaspora, such as the Society for Cultural Relations with Ukrainians Abroad and its newspaper *Visti z Ukrainy* and its radio station, in their spying activities against American and Canadian educators of Ukrainian origin. Such practices existed in Soviet Ukraine until the beginning of the 1990s.[21]

The peak of infiltration of the KGB agents in "American cultural and educational institutions" and in the "special" touristic groups composed by the Society for Cultural Relations with Ukrainians Abroad for its official visits in the US and Canada was during the détente of the 1970s. Almost every year, the KGB reported to the Ukrainian communist party leadership about "their adding of one or two KGB officers to such tourist trips" to America. Usually, a high-ranked officer, like in May of 1974, a colonel of the KGB, Aleksandr A. Diachenko (under the name of Demidenko), was included in such a group as a supervisor and "controller" of the Soviet tourists' contacts with the Ukrainian diaspora in America.[22] Even in 1983, among 288 official members of delegations from Soviet Ukraine visiting the US and Canada, there were thirty-five agents of the KGB and 10 KGB operatives. One of their assignments was establishing connections with "American and Canadian educators, members of the college faculty and their students." From August to September 1983, during the concert tour in Canada of the vocal-instrumental ensemble Chervona Ruta, the KGB used four participants of this group as their agents Ivanov, Vissarion, Krisitinov, and Kas'ianovskii, not only for "protecting the Soviet musicians from the provocative actions of the adversary, but also for connecting the local young audience in America, targeting especially college students in the USA and Canada." Some of these agents contacted those American Ukrainian students, who were interested in establishing relations with Soviet Ukraine.[23]

Other channels for the KGB operations were various international organizations, where Soviet Ukraine participated. On February 23, 1962, the KGB administration in Kyiv discussed the opportunity of how to use international organizations, especially in the US, where Soviet Ukraine was a member, as a venue for intelligence work and spying for the benefit of the KGB.[24] As KGB analysts reported, "There were thirty-seven such organizations, among which the most important for intelligence work and KGB operations were the United Nations Organization (hereafter—UNO) in New York City, UNESCO in Paris, France, European Section of the UNO, the Economic Commission of UNO for Europe, and the World Organization of Labor in Geneva, Switzerland, and the International Atomic Energy Agency [MAGATE in Russian abbreviation—SZh.] in Vienna, Austria. The new expanding quotas of a representation for those organizations from Soviet Ukraine gave [the KGB] opportunity to infiltrate these organizations with the KGB agents, representing Ukraine."[25] The KGB operatives, who worked in New York City, provided the detailed analysis of a history and structure of the UNO, paying "a special attention to the office of chancellery (*kantseliariia*) of UNO General Secretary and its office of human resources (*upravlenie kadrov*)." According to their reports, "in the last department there was a unique concentration of the personal files of various UNO officials from other nations and the UNO personnel, which would allow [under the certain circumstances] to a KGB candidate to study the possibility of using those files' information" for the future KGB special operations.[26]

The KGB supervisors submitted detailed instructions to their agents on how various departments of the organizations such as UNESCO and the

UNO "allowed numerous possibilities for espionage through various contacts, etc."[27] According to the KGB analysis, the United Nations Organization "offered [to the KGB agents] a unique opportunity of establishing the contacts with the representatives of governments and the business circles of the main adversary, and for an acquaintance with economy of those nations."[28] Another useful venue for the KGB espionage was the World Organization of Labor, which "gave [to the KGB agents] a plenty of opportunities to use it for establishing the personal connections with the state, business and trade union circles of our main adversary; [and the KGB agents] had to try to promote themselves to the leading positions and the offices of this organization as the official representatives of Soviet Ukraine."[29] The KGB administration also provided their operatives with detailed instructions on how to work and build their careers inside those organizations.[30] As these instructions specified, "The major task of all assignments for the KGB agents in all those organizations [was] a study (*izuchenie*) of representatives of the states of our main adversary [the US, Canada, UK etc.]."[31] They recommended use of various parties with drinking and receptions in these organizations to establish personal connections with important people, etc. This document emphasized, "There [was] a unique relaxing atmosphere for the citizens of the USA and UK, without a control from their governments, so they [the official representatives of those nations] could be more open for the contacts with the Soviet citizens."[32] The KGB administration especially suggested using the Christmas holidays (in December) and Easter holidays (in April) "for establishing more intimate contacts" with the representatives of "the main adversary." One of the main assignments for the KGB agents was to promote the "ideas of Soviet internationalism" during their contacts with their Western colleagues, resisting the influence of "Ukrainian nationalism and Jewish Zionism." As former Ukrainian KGB officers, participants of those contacts in UNO in New York City, joked about such assignments, "It was more about promotion of various forms of Russian imperialism and Russian cultural interests rather than support of the interests of non-Russian republics of the USSR."[33]

The KGB also tried to change the entire strategy of preparation of the special operations against the US in 1959–1962. The KGB administration in Kyiv recommended to the regional KGB offices "to improve work for preparing and training the best candidates in various spheres: journalism, humanities and science—to serve as the secret agents of the KGB against the main adversary."[34] Eventually, throughout the entire 1970s and 1980s, the KGB developed two of their very important offices, which they incorporated into all educational institutions in all republics of the USSR. One was a so-called "first department," which had a general KGB monitoring function, including "recruiting the future KGB agents from the faculty and students" and supervising various travels abroad, requiring the candidates to perform KGB assignments from the candidates for travel. Another was the office of the dean for the foreign students and visitors (*prorector po rabote s inostrantsami*), which supervised all foreign students, who were enrolled in the educational institution, and foreign visitors and guest scholars. The heads of both offices were the KGB nomenclature with special KGB clearance. Those two offices survived the collapse of the USSR and still exist under different names in post-Soviet colleges and universities. Eventually, many young former Soviet deans for the foreign students became active participants in the exchange programs with America, such as Ivan Kurilla, a young professor of US history from Volgograd State University in Russian Federation, who served in this position of *prorector po rabote s inostrantsami* in his post-Soviet Russian university during 2002–2003.[35]

Still, the most important target of Soviet intelligence was to infiltrate the Soviet agents into various institutions of American political, economic, academic, and media life, using those agents as "sleeper cells" for the future intelligence work of the KGB and GRU. American counterintelligence agents tried to stop such activities. The most famous and successful counterintelligence operation was the story of another Soviet KGB sleeper agent, Jack Barsky, who was apprehended by the FBI. Jack Philip Barsky (born as Albrecht Dittrich in East Germany) was planted as a sleeper agent in the United States by the Soviet KGB. He was an active sleeper agent between 1978 and 1988. He was located by US authorities in 1994 and then arrested in 1997. Barsky quickly confessed after being arrested and became a useful source of information about Soviet and Russian spying techniques. For many years, Barsky's case became another proof of the old legacy of the KGB sleeper agents, who were active in America. As it turned out, a special Directorate S of the KGB, responsible for sending the "illegals" to the West during the Cold War, was transformed in post-Soviet Russia into a special agency of Russia's Foreign Intelligence Service (SVR, *sluzhba vneshnei razvedki* in Russian).[36]

Through the entire existence of Soviet/Russian "sleeper cells" in America, the leadership of the Soviet/Russian intelligence emphasized the major goal of their agents: "You were sent to USA for long-term service trip. Your education, bank accounts, car, house etc.—all these serve one goal: fulfil your main mission, i.e., to search and develop ties in policymaking circles in US and send intel [intelligence reports] to C[enter]."[37] The KGB "sleeper" agents in the US not only developed ties with American politicians, but also targeted the "historically black colleges and universities" especially in the Washington, D.C., area, such as Howard University. They tried to find "the most radicalized" Afro-American students, who supported the Black Panthers movement, and used them for various pro-Soviet actions, including the "anti-Vietnam war demonstrations" with participation of the students from Howard University during the 1970s. The most successful operations by the KGB sleeper agents on Howard University's campus were devoted to various actions against the American Ukrainian meetings and demonstrations in Washington, D.C. Usually, "the KGB agitators" engaged Howard University's students in these actions by disseminating leaflets and various literature about "the racist" and "fascist" origins of the Ukrainian diaspora in America, "ideologically discrediting" and portraying all American Ukrainians as "the militant anti-Afro-American and Neo-Nazi group," which was "a real threat to all Afro-Americans and Jews" in the United States. In some cases, the KGB managed to involve the Black Panthers and Communist followers from Howard University to disrupt and disperse the American Ukrainians' demonstrations in downtown D.C. The most famous attempt to provoke a physical conflict between Howard University's students, engaged by the KGB, and American Ukrainians in downtown Washington, D.C., was prevented by the local police on September 16, 1984. The KGB agents tried to discredit the anti-Soviet actions of the American Ukrainian activists at the Taras Shevchenko monument in Washington, D.C., on September 16, 1984, to mark the twentieth anniversary of its official opening in the US against "the forceful Russification of Ukraine." American Ukrainians planned to even attract the Afro-American students from Howard University, spreading among them information about friendship between a Ukrainian poet Taras Shevchenko (1814–1861), and American black actor Ira Aldridge (1807–1867). Eventually, the KGB succeeded in disruption of those plans using disinformation about the so-called fascist and racist nature of "Ukrainian nationalists," spreading various leaflets and pamphlets about the Ukrainian "white racists" among the black college students in their dorms. As a result of this KGB operation, the Black Panthers became involved in this conflict with the alleged Ukrainian racists and fascists in America.[38]

Still, Soviet/Russian sleeper agents in America were mostly used for getting "strategic information" about the US international position and the American attitudes toward the USSR/Russia. As Moscow Center requested from their agents (so-called "illegals") to get more information on: "[C]urrent international affairs vital for R[ussia] highlighting US approach and providing us comments made by local experts (political, economic) scientist's community. Try to single out tidbits unknown publicly but revealed in private by sources close to State department, Government, major think tanks."[39]

Suddenly, this legacy of the old Soviet intelligence operations against the "capitalist America," which was initiated as early as 1922, and became a prominent feature of the KGB "active measures" in the 1980s, survived the collapse of the USSR and created serious problems for the FBI in the 2000s. Officially, the US Department of Justice called the Russian spy ring in the US the "Illegals Program." The spies were trained in Russia and then sent to the

US (often through Canada, where they could create a more believable history) in order to gain access to intelligence from high-ranking officials in government and academia. As journalists noted, in 2000 the American "FBI learned of ten Russian agents operating undercover inside the US. Some of them had been there for years. These sleeper agents (or 'illegals') were trained officers sent to the US to blend in, become American, and live what appeared to be normal lives." Those Soviet/Russian "illegals" took classes at various American colleges as undergraduate and graduate students, then they became teachers and researchers at various Canadian and US think tank research centers, contributing to strengthening of the "pro-Soviet and pro-Russian" position of Western academia.[40]

As KGB reports emphasized, "sleeper agents" had to target especially American universities and colleges to "recruit" the students and faculty members for the needs of Soviet intelligence.[41] According to the recent study by Gordon Corera, "In the early eighties, the KGB planned to expand to six illegal 'residencies' (meaning agents or couples) in place [in America]. Each was supposed to recruit three or four sources in the White House, State Department, Pentagon, and also think tanks and universities—these included the Hudson Institute, Rand Corporation, Columbia University's School of International Relations, and Georgetown's Center for Strategic Studies. Moscow also wanted active recruitment of students at Columbia, New York, and Georgetown Universities."[42]

One couple of Russian "illegals," who lived in New Jersey, focused especially on the local colleges in New York City. Eventually they concentrated on Columbia University. One of those agents, Cynthia Murphy (Lydia Guryeva), began studying at Columbia in 2008 for an Executive MBA, and her Moscow supervisors requested from her to collect information on her American classmates. Cynthia was asked "to dig up" personal data of students. Moscow Center was especially "interested in students who had applied for a job at the CIA or who might do so in the future."[43] As FBI agents found out, Moscow required from Murphy to "strengthen ties [with] classmates [at Columbia] on daily basis incl. professors who can help in job search and who will have (or already have) access to secret info." Moscow Center requested from Cynthia Murphy to report the detailed personal data of the Columbia students, especially "character traits," with "preliminary conclusions about their potential (vulnerability) to be recruited by Service."[44] As Gordon Corera explained,

> This is classic agent-spotting working. Anyone who looked good at Columbia would be run through the system back in Moscow to see if they were worth pursuing and having a file built up. . . . [For Russians it was important] to identify recruits [among Columbia students] who might end up going undercover and begin a file on them. They could either be spotted abroad or perhaps a personal

weakness could be uncovered that might lead to recruiting a mole . . . within the agency. The ideal [for Russians] was a penetration agent—recruiting someone young and then directing them inside.[45]

On June 27, 2010, as a result of a multi-year FBI investigation called *Operation Ghost Stories*, ten KGB agents, eight of them living as married couples, were arrested in the US. One married couple of those KGB agents attracted the attention of the Western and Russian media, especially when they began publishing their memoirs and giving public interviews after their return to Russia.[46]

They were (according to their falsified birth certificates) a Canadian couple, Donald Heathfield and Tracey Lee Ann Foley, who in fact turned out to be the KGB "sleeper agents" Andrei Bezrukov and Elena Vavilova, who lived in Canada since 1992, and in the USA since 1999, working for the Russian intelligence as "a sleeper cell" of the Russian spies (they used Canadian identities stolen for them by the KGB). Andrei Bezrukov was born on August 30, 1960, in Kansk, Krasnoiarsk Region of Siberia. From 1978 to 1983, he studied history at Tomsk State University. Elena Vavilova was born on November 16, 1962, in the Russian city of Tomsk. From 1970 to 1980 she went to a school with intensive study of the German language. In 1980 she enrolled to study history at Tomsk State University. After her third year of university, she married Andrei Bezrukov, a fellow student, and together with him moved to Moscow to begin their training as intelligence officers studying the French and English languages. Elena eventually graduated from Tomsk University in 1985 via a distance learning program. Since the late 1980s, for almost twenty-five years Elena and Andrei worked as deep-cover intelligence officers in France, Belgium, Switzerland, and finally in Canada under the assumed names.[47] While in Canada, Heathfield (Bezrukov) took classes at York University from 1992 to 1995, graduating with a bachelor's degree in international economics; in 1997 he graduated from the technical university in Paris, France, with a master's degree in international business. After moving to the United States, in 1999 he took classes at Harvard University, graduating in 2000 from its John F. Kennedy School of Government with a master's degree in public administration. While living in Toronto with Bezrukov, Vavilova gave birth to two sons, Timothy and Alexander, and took classes and graduated from McGill University, in Montreal. In 1999, the family settled in Cambridge, Massachusetts. Vavilova worked as a real estate agent first at Channing Real Estate and later for another real estate company, Redfin. Meanwhile, her husband worked from 2006 to 2010 as a partner in a consulting company named Global Partners Inc., and for another company named Future Map, specializing in government and corporate strategic forecasting and planning systems. Using their connections in Boston and

Washington, D.C., these KGB agents tried to establish personal connections not only with American politicians, but also with the important think tanks, getting strategic military and technological information from those American sources and transferring it to Moscow. As Bezrukov explained the major goal of "the illegals" in his public interview: "The highest class of intelligence is to understand what your opponent will be thinking about tomorrow, and not what he was thinking about yesterday."[48]

After their arrest, Bezrukov and Vavilova, with eight other Russian intelligence "sleeper" agents in the US were exchanged with four Russian citizens, who were American and British spies, on July 9, 2010, in Vienna, Austria. Moreover, in 2011, the FBI released dozens of video clips and documents from *Operation Ghost Stories* that revealed new information about the Russian operatives who had been caught posing as ordinary Americans the year before.[49] All those FBI documents (now available to the public) demonstrated that the traditional KGB operations targeting Western academia survived the USSR collapse and still exist in the story of the Russian sleeper cells, such as Bezrukov and Vavilova. This sensational story attracted the attention of international press and became an inspiration for the American TV show *The Americans*.[50]

CONCLUSION: AMERICAN TV SHOW ABOUT THE RUSSIAN SLEEPERS AND RUSSIAN CULTURAL IMPERIALISM

Paradoxically, the "spy" TV series *The Americans*, which fascinated millions of Americans since January 2013, became strangely connected to another phenomenon—Russian cultural imperialism.[51] During my interview session in 2019, former Soviet intelligence officers in Kyiv were the first people who told me about this connection between Russian cultural imperialism and fascination with the portrayal of Russian spies, "who were called 'the illegals,' 'the sleepers,' or 'the sleeper cells' by the American media and by American television, which created the idealized image of such Soviet/Russian spies in the popular US television series, that we watched it here in post-Soviet space as well."[52] The American TV show, which those retired officers referred to, was *The Americans*. One of those officers told me in January of 2019, "If you (as a historian) want to know how [a Russian President] Putin began his 'hybrid' war against Ukraine in 2014, you MUST watch those American TV series about Russian agents and analyze their mind-set, comparing it to the real events behind this American television show."[53] At the same time, this retired KGB officer noted a psychological danger of massive fascination with the Russian undercover agents portrayed in *The Americans*: "Do not forget how dangerous those people, like Putin, are today. Now, using the 'hybrid war' methods, those Russian brutal successors of Soviet 'sleeper' spies are winning over '[too much] politically correct and civilized' American politicians."[54]

Various stories about Soviet and Russian spies in America (especially during the Cold War, 1945–1991) were already covered by numerous American movies and television shows.[55] Some of those stories were about Soviet KGB sleepers in America, like the story of KGB colonel Rudolf Abel, arrested in 1957 in New York City.[56] The most recent popular film about KGB "sleeper agent" Abel was Steven Spielberg's movie, from 2015, *Bridge of Spies*.[57]

But two years earlier, millions of Americans had already learned about this problem of Russian sleeper agents in America, who lived like "the ordinary Americans," by watching *The Americans*.[58] A former CIA officer, Joe Weisberg, and his friend Joel Fields wrote a story for this show and became its executive producers.[59] This television show was broadcast on FOX television network from January 30, 2013, to May 30, 2018.[60] The major characters of this show were the members of a KGB "sleeper cell," two Soviet Russian intelligence officers Elizabeth (Keri Russell) and Philip Jennings (Matthew Rhys), pretending to be the American married couple, who reside in Falls Church, Virginia, a suburban area near Washington, D.C., with their American-born children. This show started at the peak of the Cold War after the inauguration of Ronald Reagan in January 1981 and finished in December 1987, a few days before the Soviet Union and the United States signed the Intermediate-Range Nuclear Force Treaty, during the beginning of the improvement of the US-Soviet relations. The story of the KGB spies is shown in the interaction of the Washington FBI office and the KGB spy station (*rezidentura*) in the capital city of the United States. The major player in this television show is the Jennings' neighbor, an FBI agent working as a counterintelligence officer, Stan Beeman (Noah Emmerich). The intelligence dialogue between the KGB agents and an FBI agent shaped the entire intrigue of this television series.[61]

This TV series was received very well, not only by millions of viewers all over the world, but also by the press.[62] Even the Russian intelligence officers, whose real-life stories were used in this TV show, praised it. One of them (Bezrukov) noted,

> The result [of watching the series] is quite close to reality, though without the killings and the wigs. The creators of the series were able to show the atmosphere, and the inner feelings of illegals, and the difficulties, including personal ones, that one has to face, and the personality that it required to do such work. Many moments are conveyed accurately, honestly, and professionally. My wife and I did not expect that the American creators of the series would be willing

and able to show the characters of the spies so deeply and unbiasedly, even with sympathy.[63]

His wife, a colonel of FSB (Vavilova), confirmed her approval of this TV show as well:

> The producers have captured well the atmosphere of the eighties. The illegals have a human side with believable emotions and problems of their daily life. However, violence and disguise are never part of the professional work. This way the spies would have not been able to last for a long time. I believe those scenes were necessary to keep the attention of the viewers. . . . I can hardly believe the real illegals could have met their handler inside the US and they would have immediately moved to another house after discovering that an FBI agent lives just across. But again, real life and movies are not the same thing.[64]

Overall, according to Vavilova and Bezrukov's interviews, the TV series correctly portrayed the operations of the KGB/FSB sleeper agents: their collection of the strategic information, influencing American politicians and educators, and connecting with the radical left groups, including pro-Communist Afro-Americans. But at the same time, even those Russian intelligence officers emphasized an "unusual" fascination with the Russian "illegals" shown in *The Americans* among both American and post-Soviet (especially Russian) TV viewers. At one press conference, their son Alexander Vavilov noted that both he and his parents were fans of the FX adaptation of their lives. "My parents said they enjoyed watching it because it at least portrayed the sense of patriotism and the sense of connection. It's a good show," he shared with the Associated Press.[65]

Meanwhile, Ukrainian intelligence officers warned that such an international fascination with this American TV show fits Putin's propaganda in both Russia and in the West, and his "cult of the Russian intelligence service." Moreover, with the Russian war against Ukraine, this cult serves the mobilization of all Russian intelligence against the "the anti-Russian West."[66] Even the former characters of the American TV series, Vavilova and Bezrukov, became actively engaged in the anti-American and anti-Ukrainian propagandist campaigns in Russia today. Their recent publications serve this propagandist effort of Putin's regime very well. A striking feature of Vavilova's novel/memoir, where she described a story behind *The Americans*, is an obvious critical attitude toward post-Soviet Ukrainians. In this book, the Russian spies, the members of the KGB/FSB sleeper cell, regularly reported on the US-Ukrainian relations to their Moscow supervisors ("a Center"). Vaviolva's novel described in detail how, in 2003, the Russian spies, using their connections with US military officers while playing golf together, collected the intelligence information about a group of the Ukrainian "special guests," who spent time in the US attending the classes at Georgetown University in Washington, D.C. It turned out that those "visitors from Ukraine" were the specially trained Ukrainian intelligence and military officers, who participated in developing the US-Ukrainian "strategy of the national security of Ukraine." Russian spies immediately informed their center about Ukraine's plans to join NATO, and how the Americans would support these plans against the geopolitical interests of Russia.[67] This anti-Ukrainian approach is obvious in other parts of Vavilova's book. Even describing an assistance to her husband in the American prison by its inmates in 2010, Vavilova emphasized, in a negative way, the main "mafiosi" prisoner type, who helped her husband, portraying this mafiosi prisoner as a "corrupt Ukrainian bandit," who was (as it turned out) a recent emigrant from Ukraine. This trend of vilifying and demonizing the Ukrainians became the main feature of this Russian intelligence officer's book.[68]

Unfortunately, such an anti-Ukrainian and anti-American bias now prevails among most of the FSB/SRV/GRU officers, and it is a main feature of the collective mentality for the entire intelligence community in Russia today. In this geopolitical context, paradoxically, the Cold War TV mini-series, such as *The Americans*, could be used for the promotion of the idealized, heroic images of Russian intelligence officers, like Putin, who were fighting with so-called American anti-Russian conspiracy, "defending Mother Russia against US imperialism."[69] At the same time, the Russian intelligence is still successful in their operations against the Americans. Using the new Russian money of post-Soviet oligarchs, the FSB is buying not only American academics, but also FBI agents, including their counterintelligence officers. Such cases of "American corruption" inside of the FBI are used as anti-American propaganda for contrasting the heroic patriotic Russian intelligence officers to the "corrupt Americans."[70]

In the next chapters, this book will demonstrate how so-called cultural and academic Russian imperialism became interwoven in the special operations by Soviet and Russian intelligence, targeting Western academia and the Western public, especially in the United States and Canada. This kind of imperialism ignored an independence of Ukraine, imposed the Russian-centered interpretations of the past and the present, and promoted pro-Russian views not only in the universities of the US and Canada, but also in the respectable American think tanks.

NOTES

1. Interview with Stepan Ivanovich T., a retired KGB officer, January 30, 2019, Kyiv, Ukraine.

2. Gordon Corera, *Russians Among Us: Sleeper Cells, Ghost Stories, and the Hunt for Putin's Spies* (New York: William Morrow Paperbacks, 2021), 22.

3. Christopher Andrew and Vasili Mitrokhin, *The Sword and the Shield: The Mitrokhin Archive and the Secret History of the KGB* (New York: Basic Books, 1999), 174.

4. See about Rudolf Abel (Vilyam Willie Fisher) in Christopher Andrew and Vasili Mitrokhin, *The Sword and the Shield*, 146–148, 156–157ff. Compare with a scandal of GRU Colonel Oleg Pentkovsky, who worked for MI6 and CIA, in op. cit., 182, 183.

5. Galuzevyi Derzhavnyi Archiv Sluzhby Bezpeky Ukrainy (The Branch State Archive of the Security Service of Ukraine [SBU]), (Hereafter SBU), f. 16, op. 1, spr. 1218, ark. 265.

6. SBU, f. 16, op. 1, spr. 944, ark. 98–101. Citation from ark. 100.

7. Compare with Pierre J. Huss and George Carpozi, *Red Spies in the UN* (New York: Coward-McCann, 1965), 136–140.

8. See my interviews with the KGB retired officers Stepan Ivanovich T. in Kyiv and Igor T. in Dnipropetrovsk.

9. I quote Stepan Ivanovich T.

10. Gordon Corera, *Russians Among Us*, 15.

11. I am especially grateful to Filip Kovacevic, who directed me to these sources. See the English translation of the interview of the first Soviet "illegal" in America, Zalman Litvin, a year before his death in the material, which Filip Kovacevic posted: The Chekist Monitor: Interview of Soviet Military Intelligence Illegal Zalman Litvin (1992): https://thechekistmonitor.blogspot.com.

12. Myron Momryk, "Ignacy Witczak's Passport, Soviet Espionage and the Origins of the Cold War in Canada," *Polish American Studies*, vol. 68, no. 2 (Autumn 2011), 67–84.

13. What follows is based on Filip Kovacevic website material and books: Robert J. Lamphere and Tom Shachtman, *The FBI-KGB War: A Special Agent's Story* (New York: Random House, 1986), pp. 34–36; Mike Gruntman, *Enemy amongst Trojans: A Soviet Spy at USC* (Los Angeles: Figueroa Press, 2010). See chapter 2 about Litvin's academic career in Moscow after his fleeing from the US.

14. See especially John Earl Haynes, Harvey Klehr, and Alexander Vassiliev, *Spies: The Rise and Fall of the KGB in America* (New Haven: Yale University Press, 2009).

15. SBU, f. 16, op. 1, spr. 937, ark. 244–247.

16. Ibid., 248–249.

17. SBU, f. 16, op. 1, spr. 927, ark. 48–49.

18. Ibid., 62–65.

19. Ibid., 126–127.

20. Ibid., 167, 168.

21. SBU, f. 16, op. 1, spr. 932, ark. 147–152. See about the Ukrainian official venues, used by the KGB in ibid., spr. 937, ark. 242–243. Among the first recruits of the KGB for exchange programs with the US and Canada were such scholars as "Pavel Arsentievich Lavrov, born in 1903, a chair of history of the Ukrainian SSR, Kyiv

State University," and Arnold Shlepakov, a historian-Americanist from the Institute of History, the Ukrainian SSR Academy of Sciences. See ibid., spr. 932, ark. 149. All former KGB officers whom I interviewed about this confirmed an existence of this old practice.

22. SBU, f. 16, op. 1, spr. 1089, ark. 251–256.
23. SBU, f. 16, op. 1, spr.1217, ar. 160, 161.
24. SBU, f. 16, op. 1, spr. 938, ark. 92–109.
25. Ibid., 92–93.
26. Ibid., 94–95. In the Russian original it sounded like this: "*eto dalo by nashemu agentu vozmozhnost' navedeniia navodok na ob'ektov i ikh pervichnogo izucheniia.*"
27. Ibid. 95–97, 97–98.
28. Ibid. 99–100.
29. Ibid., 100–102.
30. Ibid., 102–104.
31. Ibid., 105.
32. Ibid., 106.
33. Ibid., 107. See also my interviews with the KGB retired officers Stepan Ivanovich T. in Kyiv and Igor T. in Dnipropetrovsk.
34. SBU, f. 16, op. 1, spr. 938, 108.
35. Ibid., 136–139. See my interviews with the KGB retired officers Stepan Ivanovich T. in Kyiv and Igor T. in Dnipropetrovsk. See about other functions of the KGB in SBU, f. 16, op. 1, spr. 939 (March 1963), ark. 31–32, 34–38, 40–46, 48, 49–50. In his official c.v., Kurilla called this position "Vice Rector for International Programs." See https://eu-spb.academia.edu/IvanKurilla/CurriculumVitae.
36. See a book of Barsky's memoirs: Jack Barsky with Cindy Coloma, *Deep Undercover: My Secret Life and Tangled Allegiances as a KGB Spy in America* (Carol Stream, IL: Tyndale Momentum, 2017).
37. I quoted a secret Moscow message for Russian illegals from Gordon Corera, op. cit., 216.
38. Interview with Stepan Ivanovich T., a retired KGB officer, Kyiv, February 12, 2019. The best description of such KGB operations involving Howard University's students is in SBU, f. 16, op.1, spr. 1218, ark. 265.
39. Quoted by Gordon Corera, *Russians Among Us*, 217.
40. Among many studies of the Russian sleeper cells, see especially Gordon Corera, *Russians Among Us*, 6, 14, 66–67, 73, 218–219.
41. SBU, f. 16, op. 1, spr. 993, ark. 115–117.
42. Gordon Corera, *Russians Among Us*, 406.
43. Ibid., 218.
44. Ibid., 219.
45. Ibid., 219, 218.
46. I refer especially to Yelena Vavilova and Andrei Bronnikov, *Zhenshchina, kotoraia umeiet khranit' tainy* [A Woman Who Can Keep Her Secrets] (Moscow: Eksmo, 2022).
47. See especially about their life in Europe and Canada before the collapse of the USSR in Yelena Vavilova and Andrei Bronnikov, *Zhenshchina*, 15–22, 30–142.

48. Compare with a phrase, quoted in Gordon Corera, *Russians Among Us*, 128.
49. See https://www.fbi.gov/news/stories/operation-ghost-stories-inside-the-russian-spy-case. I use this FBI information for a description of Bezrukov/Vavilova adventures.
50. See Yelena Vavilova, op. cit., 191–251. For numerous interviews, newspaper articles, and blog posts about this case, see Gordon Corera, *Russians Among Us*.
51. Among numerous articles about this TV series, see especially Joshua Rothman, "The Cruel Irony of 'The Americans,'" *The New Yorker*, March 16, 2016. See https://www.newyorker.com/culture/culture-desk/the-cruel-irony-of-the-americans.
52. I quote my numerous interviews about the "illegals" with Stepan Ivanovich T.; Bohdan Josypovych K., a retired KGB/SBU officer, February 9, 2019, Kyiv, Ukraine; Igor T., a retired KGB officer, May 15, 1991, Dnipropetrovsk, Ukraine; Ivan Grigorovich K., a retired KGB officer, February 3, 2019, Kyiv, Ukraine; Leonid K., a retired KGB officer, March 3, 2019, Kyiv, Ukraine.
53. Stepan Ivanovich T. Both Russians and Ukrainians watched this show on television, using various internet providers.
54. Stepan Ivanovich T. Another officer noted this as well. See my interview with Leonid K. as well.
55. Some of them are about Soviet sleeper spies such as *Telefon* (1977), or *Red Sparrow* (2018). See about the last film in Gordon Corera, *Russians Among Us*, 145–146.
56. See about Rudolf Abel (Vilyam Willie Fisher) in Christopher Andrew and Vasili Mitrokhin, *The Sword and the Shield*, 146–148, 156–157ff.
57. See Richard Brody, "Spielberg's Airtight 'Bridge of Spies,'" *The New Yorker,* October 22, 2015, https://www.newyorker.com/culture/richard-brody/spielbergs-airtight-bridge-of-spies.
58. Among numerous articles about this TV series, see Joshua Rothman, "The Cruel Irony of 'The Americans.'"
59. Laura M. Holson, "The Dark Stuff, Distilled," *New York Times*, March 29, 2013.
60. See https://www.thedailybeast.com/obsessed/why-the-americans-creators-joel-fields-and-joe-weisberg-wanted-to-probe-a-serial-killer-in-the-patient.
61. See https://2009-2017.state.gov/t/avc/trty/102360.htm.
62. See among numerous reviews, especially this one "about the best show on TV returns in *The Americans*": https://www.rogerebert.com/streaming/the-best-show-on-tv-returns-in-the-americans.
63. See an original interview at https://www.kommersant.ru/doc/2781713. See a translation in English of this interview in Gordon Corera, op. cit., 310–311.
64. Ibid., 311.
65. See https://www.distractify.com/p/is-the-americans-based-on-a-true-story#:~:text=Who%20are%20Elena%20Vavilova%20and,enrolled%20at%20Tomsk%20State%20University.
66. I quote Stepan Ivanovich T., a retired KGB officer, Kyiv, February 12, 2019.
67. Yelena Vavilova, op.cit., 262–265.
68. Ibid., 336–337.

69. See about this in detail in my book: Sergei I. Zhuk, *KGB Operations against the USA and Canada in Soviet Ukraine, 1953–1991* (London and New York: Routledge, 2022), especially pp. 241–245.

70. I refer to the FBI scandal of 2023: During 2021–2023, Charles McGonigal, a former counterintelligence leader in the FBI's New York field, worked for the Russian oligarch Oleg Deripaska. See in Aaron Katersky, "Ex-FBI counterintelligence chief Charles McGonigal sentenced for 50 months in prison for working with Russian oligarch," December 14, 2023, abcnews.go.com

Chapter 5

The KGB, Ukrainian Diaspora in America, and Academic Exchanges

The KGB always targeted the national diasporas in America.[1] As former KGB general Oleg Kalugin noted, the most important for the KGB was the Ukrainian diaspora in America (in both the US and Canada), and the KGB "had a good network of agents among the Ukrainian émigrés, particularly in Canada, where several million Ukrainians had settled."[2] The KGB "carried on a low-level campaign to infiltrate numerous anti-Soviet émigré organizations, as well as so-called centers of ideological diversion. Virtually, all of the large national groups in the Soviet Union—Ukrainians, Armenians, Lithuanians, Latvians, and Estonians—had vocal émigré organizations abroad that fought for independence of their countrymen at home." And he continued,

> [Our] job in KGB foreign counterintelligence was to insinuate agents into these groups who would keep abreast of émigré activities, let us know which leaders were likely targets for recruitment, and, if possible, soften the anti-Soviet thrust of these usually rabid anti-Communist organizations. Our ultimate goal in working with these groups was to find agents who might eventually go to work for Western intelligence and security services.[3]

Soviet intelligence tried to influence and divide American Ukrainians, using various "useful assets (or useful idiots)" (pro-Soviet individuals) among them and infiltrating the KGB agents into the American Ukrainian organizations, including various Ukrainian research centers in both the US and Canada as well. According to former KGB officers,

> The KGB engaged the American and Canadian Communists on regular basis in their operations, knowing that a majority of the Canadian Communists were the ethnic Ukrainians. At the same time, the Soviet intelligence tried to influence the pro-Soviet dimensions of various American academic debates about Soviet Ukraine, its past and present, and infiltrate the Ukrainian research institutions in

America, using both American/Canadian communists and the KGB agents for those special operations.[4]

ARNOLD SHLEPAKOV, THE KGB, UKRAINIAN AMERICAN STUDIES, AND UKRAINIAN DIASPORA

All former KGB officers, whom I interviewed in Ukraine in 2019, also emphasized another important aspect of the KGB operations against the Ukrainian diaspora abroad—involvement of the Soviet Ukrainian scholars in a process of "academic dialogue" with American Ukrainians, especially during the academic exchanges with Western academia. As one intelligence officer from Kyiv noted, "Specially trained scholars from Soviet Ukraine served as a connecting link between Soviet and American Ukrainians. We called them our 'curators' [*kuratory*] for the Ukrainians abroad. As far as I can recall, the most effective and popular among the American Ukrainians were two of them—a journalist Vitaly Korotich and a historian Arnold Shlepakov."[5] Such "KGB people from Soviet Ukrainian academic and cultural establishment" were always involved in a variety of exchange programs of Ukraine with the US and Canada.

The most prominent KGB-connected figure in these exchange programs, a so-called Soviet "curator" of the Ukrainian diaspora in "capitalist America," was Arnold Shlepakov (1930–1996), a founding father of the Ukrainian American Studies, who served as the major connection between American/Canadian left Ukrainians, such as Peter Krawchuk, to the official academic hierarchy in Soviet Ukraine through the entire period of the late socialism, after Stalin.[6]

"I came from a typical privileged family of the Soviet intellectuals," admitted Arnold Shlepakov as he described his social and cultural background in 1991. "As far as I can recall," he continued, "I had never experienced any economic problems or financial difficulties while growing as a child or college student in Soviet Ukraine during the late 1940s and early 1950s." In reality, he did experience some difficulties in his childhood, because he grew up during World War II, which affected his life as well. Arnold Shlepakov was born on June 16, 1930, in the city of Vinnytsia into the family of Soviet Ukrainian intellectuals (or *sluzhashchikh*, as he wrote in his autobiography in 1978).[7] His father, Mykola S. Shlepakov, was a prominent Ukrainian philosopher, who became a professor of philosophy at Kharkiv State University in 1930. Arnold Shlepakov grew up in the city of Kharkiv and attended the local elementary school there for three years until June 1941, when WWII reached Soviet Ukraine. The Shlepakov family fled the war, headed east, and settled in the city of Kzyl-Orda in Kazakhstan, where Arnold attended classes at the local middle school for two years. In 1944, his family returned to Kharkiv, which had recently been liberated by the Red Army from Nazi occupation. Shortly afterward, Arnold's father was invited to teach as a professor of philosophy at Kyiv State University, where he was promoted to chair of the history of philosophy that same year. As a result of this career promotion, the Shlepakov family's financial situation improved dramatically. "By the beginning of 1946, after our move to Kyiv," Shlepakov recalled later, "we were living much better and more comfortably. My mother, a philologist, quit her job and now spent all her time helping me with my studies. Two servants were hired to help us in our spacious apartment, provided by the city's authorities for our family."[8]

In 1947, Arnold Shlepakov graduated from Kyiv High School No. 147 with honors (featuring the golden medal award), as well as with the first genuine experience of engagement in Soviet youth politics. For almost two years, following the suggestions of his father, Arnold was well-known as the most capable of Komsomol activists, who eventually was elected secretary of his school's Komsomol organization. As he explained, by 1947,

I had already dreamed of becoming a diplomat because I saw how our neighbors, professional diplomats, who worked for the USSR Ministry of Foreign Affairs, lived comfortably and travelled around the world. Moreover, these neighbors often visited our apartment, had dinners with us, brought us new American music records, and told interesting stories about their travels and adventures abroad. During this time, I was fascinated with the United States and American popular culture. Together with my friends we watched American motion pictures such as movies about Tarzan, an ape-man, and listened to American jazz. Under the influence of American pop music, I even began learning English instead of the obligatory German in the official Soviet curriculum in 1946–47. I dreamed of travelling to America to see with my own eyes the country, which had become the symbol of real modernity (*sovremennosti*) and inspiration for all humankind. But our neighbors emphasized that I had to have a "clean personal ideological record" of my life, to be a Komsomol activist and collaborate with the KGB. Such an experience would help me, they said, to be admitted to the department of foreign relations at Kyiv State University [hereafter KDU], and, eventually, to fulfill my dream and visit America.[9]

During that same year, under the inspiration of the conversations he had with his neighbors, Shlepakov submitted his documents to the KDU department of foreign relations, passed the entrance exams with "A's" and entered Kyiv University as an undergraduate student. According to Shlepakov, it was a period of the rise of the real and mass interest in American studies, in everything related to the United States. For this reason, Shlepakov and many of his classmates at the department, such as Semion Appatov and Leonid

Leshchenko, the future Soviet Ukrainian Americanists, began learning English and taking courses on US history and politics at the KDU department of foreign relations during the late 1940s. Following the suggestions of his neighbors-diplomats, Shlepakov not only studied the English language and the history of foreign countries and diplomacy, but also demonstrated his political activism by becoming secretary of the department's Komsomol organization and head of the department's student scholarship society. According to his classmates, during his student years Arnold Shlepakov exemplified the typical representative of the "Soviet privileged class, always well-dressed and always avoiding any student assignments at the department that involved any kind of physical labor."[10] As one of his close friends revealed later, "Many of Shlepakov's classmates were envious of his privileged social status, of his family, and of his connections with the university's administration."[11] His colleague, Leonid Leshchenko, recalled that to him Shlepakov "looked like an Americanized *styliaga*, meticulously dressed with his fashionable hair style." But despite his image of the Americanized *styliaga*, Shlepakov always demonstrated publicly his Soviet patriotism, "loyalty to the Soviet political system," and his preparedness to "serve Communist course."[12] In December 1950, Arnold Shlepakov (still an undergraduate student!) joined the Communist Party's organization at the department of foreign relations.[13] As his former colleagues noted, this was a unique case in the history of Soviet academia: "It was a very rare occasion when an undergraduate student without any 'proletarian background,' being just a child of Soviet intellectuals, became a member of the Communist Party at the university!" One of them added that Shlepakov's case was indicative of "the existence of his very strong KGB connections as well [at this time]."[14]

As a result of his political activism (particularly of his membership in Communist Party) and successful studies in history and diplomacy, Shlepakov not only graduated from Kyiv University with honors as a "historian and expert in foreign relations with good knowledge of English language" in 1952, but he was also officially recommended by his department for graduate studies at the Institute of History of the Ukrainian SSR Academy of Sciences that same year. Eventually, Shlepakov succeeded as a graduate student at this academic institute and in 1955 defended his *kandidatskaia* (PhD) dissertation with the "politically correct" title of "The Reunification of the Ukrainian People in One United Ukrainian Soviet State—the Outstanding Victory of the USSR's Foreign Policy."[15]

At the Institute of History in Kyiv, during his graduate studies in the 1950s, Arnold Shlepakov's mentor was the famous Soviet diplomat and scholar of diplomatic history, directly connected to the KGB, Dr. Oleksii D. Voina, who suggested that for his dissertation Shlepakov use various official letters of those Canadian Ukrainians, who supported the reunification of all

Ukrainian lands into one Soviet Ukrainian state following World War II. In 1953, Voina sent his student to the archival collection of the Ukrainian SSR Ministry of Foreign Affairs. Eventually, this visit to the Ministry of Foreign Affairs required the young Shlepakov's "clearance" by the KGB. As some of his colleagues assumed, this research activity in the ministry's documentary collections in 1953–1955 led not only to the establishment of Shlepakov's strong personal connections with the KGB, but also to his rising interest in the history of Ukrainian emigration to the United States and Canada. After the KGB's official approval of Shlepakov as an "ideologically reliable student of Soviet foreign policy," Oleksii Voina recommended Shlepakov to work with those Canadian Ukrainians who visited Soviet Ukraine. (According to the official requirements, to meet a foreigner, Shlepakov had to be officially approved by the KGB.[16])

In 1956, Canadian Communist of Ukrainian origin, Peter (Petro) Krawchuk visited Kyiv and brought to Voina his book manuscript about the history of Ukrainian emigration in Canada.[17] Voina read the manuscript and recommended it for publication. Moreover, Voina introduced Krawchuk to two young talented historians from the Institute of History: Fedir Shevchenko and Arnold Shlepakov, who agreed to edit Krawchuk's text for publication in the Ukrainian language by the Soviet Ukrainian Publishing House. The Soviet administration assigned two official Soviet editors of this manuscript who were the old professors from the same institute in Kyiv: Fedir Los' and Luka Kyzia, but the actual editing was done primarily by Shevchenko and Shlepakov. This was the beginning of important contacts with foreigners for the young Shlepakov. Beginning in 1956, he had established strong personal connections with the Canadian citizen Peter Krawchuk, and began corresponding regularly not only with Krawchuk, but also with other Ukrainian Canadians.[18] Shlepakov was actively engaged in the activities of the Ukrainian Society for Cultural Relations with Abroad (*Ukrains'ke tovarystvo kul'turnogo zv'iazku z zakordonom*). As a representative of the Ukrainian Academy of Sciences, this young scholar participated in all of the meetings, which included American and Canadian guests.[19]

Moreover, Shlepakov became Krawchuk's very close friend, exchanging books with him, and helping this Canadian guest every time he visited Ukraine. Very often, Shlepakov tapped Krawchuk as a precious source of information about Canada and the history of the working-class movement in North America. Between 1956 and 1972, Shlepakov sent Krawchuk at least five letters annually. As a member of the editorial boards of major Ukrainian periodicals such as *Ukrains'kyi istorychnyi zhurnal* and *Vsesvit*, Shlepakov also invited Krawchuk to publish his materials about Ukrainian Canadians in these Soviet Ukrainian magazines.[20] In 1961, Shlepakov played an important role in assisting Krawchuk to make arrangements during his family's visit to Ukraine regarding the enrollment of Krawchuk's daughter, Larisa, in Kyiv State University as an undergraduate student. In fact, Mykola (Nikolai in Russian) Pidhornyi, the first secretary of the Central Committee of the Communist Party of Ukraine, assisted Larisa Krawchuk in becoming a KDU student. But Shlepakov attempted to demonstrate to Krawchuk his usefulness as well.[21]

Another "unexpected" result of Shlepakov's personal contacts with Krawchuk involved the "rediscovery" of his own (i.e., Shlepakov's) Ukrainian national identity. As Shlepakov later explained, "Krawchuk could not speak Russian fluently; therefore, any Soviet official mediator between him and the Soviet bureaucracy had to speak Ukrainian with him, and to have good Ukrainian speaking skills." Thus, Shlepakov (as one such "mediator") not only improved his own Ukrainian linguistic skills, but also realized that his good knowledge of Ukrainian language and culture became instrumental for promoting his own career in Soviet academia. And he joked,

> Paradoxically, my communicational efforts with our Ukrainian Canadian guests led to the shaping, first of all, of my new identity as a Ukrainian intellectual rather than the identity of Soviet intellectual, who lived in Ukraine. Eventually, all this experience pushed me in the direction of reading more about my own Ukrainian history and culture (including the history of Ukrainian Canadians). The more I read about Ukrainians in America, the more I felt respect toward the Ukrainian nation, which contributed to the flourishing of North American civilization in both Canada and the United States.[22]

As a result of all these communicational efforts, by 1961, thanks to Krawchuk's contacts and the books sent from Canada by Krawchuk, Shlepakov had accumulated a significant amount of material for his new research topic on the Ukrainian farmers' and workers' immigration to the United States and Canada. Eventually, Shlepakov published this material in the form of a book, based mostly on secondary published sources from the US and Canada, provided to him by his Canadian colleagues such as Krawchuk. It is noteworthy that Shlepakov's first monograph on the first Ukrainian emigrants to Canada was written in good Ukrainian language; he later presented a copy of his book as a gift to the Ukrainian Canadian Krawchuk, the latter being a representative of the very "Ukrainian labor migration" described in Shlepakov's monograph.[23]

After 1966, Shlepakov became somewhat of an "academic" celebrity due to his skyrocketing career in traditional academic scholarship and Soviet diplomacy as well. He was appointed an official adviser to both the Ukrainian SSR Ministry of Foreign Affairs and the International Department of the Ukrainian SSR Academy of Sciences. The KGB began requesting his recommendations for the list of candidates whose future travel plans would include the US and Canada. As early as the spring of 1965, responding to the request of KGB officials from the first (international) department of the Institute of History, Shlepakov provided a positive recommendation and approval for the vice president of the KDU (*prorektor z naukovii roboty*), Dr. A.Z. Zhmudskii, and the chair of the KDU Department of Geography, Professor A. M. Marinich, to visit the University of Alberta in Edmonton, Canada, from April 28 to May 12, 1966.[24]

From November 1966 until May 1967, Shlepakov traveled throughout France and Switzerland as an official representative of Soviet Ukraine under UNESCO funding. As part of his travels to attend a UNESCO conference in Paris, Shlepakov actively participated in the international discussion regarding necessary reforms in the system of science and college education in developing nations. Beginning in September 1970, for three years in a row, Shlepakov was a member of the official Soviet Ukrainian delegation to the sessions of the General Assembly of the United Nations in New York City. He became the "real star" of the Soviet Ukrainian "academic diplomacy."[25]

Shlepakov always denied his connections to the KGB. Although in some of his trips to the US, Shlepakov collected "the strategic information from the available American publications in social science," and he reported this information to the first (KGB) department of his institute during the late 1960s and early 1970s.[26] One such report about "four studies of the American scholars on the theory of the planning management and the perspective forecasting of the scientific-technical progress, which were related to the US military-industrial complex and to the state strategic doctrine, regarding the scientific and technological future of the USA" was even incorporated in the official KGB letter to the Ukrainian Communist leadership on May 18, 1972.[27] Still, Shlepakov publicly tried to distance himself from the KGB and "its people."[28]

However, some of his close friends noticed strange changes in Shlepakov's personality during this period of time. He became more secretive and moodier. During the 1960s, in private conversations with his close friends, Shlepakov used to boast about the new "forbidden" pamphlets of the Soviet dissidents or the "forbidden" books from the West, which he would receive by means of his Canadian or American colleagues. After 1970, Shlepakov ceased boasting about such literature and began avoiding "dangerous conversations involving criticism of Soviet politics and communist ideology." Leonid Leshchenko connected these changes in Shlepakov's behavior to certain scandals in his private life, which were used by the KGB for manipulating and influencing Shlepakov. On the one hand, "during the 1970s, Shlepakov became more active in organizing various conferences and collective publications, involving all of his long-time friends and colleagues in these projects, but on the other hand with the skyrocketing ascent of his public academic career, he gradually turned into a typical Soviet academic bureaucrat, distancing himself from these same long-term friends."[29]

As early as 1969, Shlepakov was elected Chair of the Department of Modern and Contemporary History of Foreign Countries at the Institute of History and as a corresponding member of the Academy of Sciences of the Ukrainian SSR that same year. In 1970, he became a full professor of world history. In essence, Shlepakov not only supervised the studies of the history of foreign countries at the institute (until 1978), but also played an important role in its administration, fulfilling the role of deputy director of the Institute of History during 1971–1974.[30]

By the 1980s, Shlepakov stopped producing anything original in American studies. Similar to many Soviet "official" Americanists (including G. Arbatov and G. Sevostianov in Moscow), he became mainly an "official academic" organizer of various forms of "institutionalization" of American studies in Kyiv. Shlepakov continued to publish, but mostly as an editor of various collective monographs, occasionally contributing one or two chapters to such publications.[31] He served as an editor of every major academic and popular publication in Soviet Ukraine, focusing on the history and culture of the "capitalist Western countries." More specifically, Shlepakov would lend his editorial expertise to a broad spectrum of publications and topics ranging from various purely academic editions about the international solidarity of the working class in the struggle against fascism, to themes of national relations in the United States and Canada, in such Ukrainian magazines as *Ukrainskyi istorychnyi zhurnal*, *Vsesvit*, and *Visnyk* of the Ukrainian Academy of Sciences. Shlepakov was also a major organizer of all official receptions for the delegations of foreign scholars and scientists in the Ukrainian Academy of Sciences in Kyiv.[32]

Eventually, Shlepakov's "organizing genius" contributed to the creation of a new research institute, devoted to the special study of foreign (mainly capitalist) countries of the world. As Shlepakov recalled he "always dreamed of creating something similar to Inozemtsev's IMEMO but in Kyiv, in Ukraine."[33] That is how he proposed to transform the "overgrown department of modern and contemporary history at the Institute of History" into a new separate academic institution, which officially began functioning under Shlepakov's leadership in October 1978. It was located in downtown Kyiv, and the Soviet administration approved its official title, proposed by Shlepakov—the Institute of Social and Economic Problems of Foreign Countries (ISEPZK—in Ukrainian abbreviation). Shlepakov also initiated the publication of his institute's periodical *The World Abroad: Social-Political and Economic Problems*, in which he published materials devoted to

American studies, sometimes including the participation of scholars from the United States as well.[34]

During the existence of "Shlepakov's Institute" (as ISEPZK was known in Kyiv and Moscow), its director assembled talented Ukrainian scholars committed toward researching important issues on international politics, diplomacy, and American studies. Eventually, by the end of the 1980s (in addition to the traditional ideological anti-Western themes), the institute's personnel concentrated on such research topics as "the international divisions of labor and structures of the world's economic relations; national problems in Western Europe and the Americas; immigrational processes and the status of immigrants; economic and scientific-technological aspects of the protection of nature and other ecological issues; the West's relations with the developing countries of the Middle East."[35] However, the most important and unique research topic that Shlepakov proposed to his colleagues at ISEPZK was the study of the Ukrainian diaspora throughout the entire world, and especially in North America. As Shlepakov used to joke,

> Our Institute in Kyiv was a true pioneer in Soviet academia regarding the study of various aspects of the Ukrainian immigration to Canada and the United States; we found our unique academic niche in the Soviet study of America because we knew our Ukrainian language and culture and we could communicate with American and Canadian Ukrainians in our own native language. None of the Russian Americanists in Moscow or Leningrad could speak our language; therefore, they lost the academic competition of establishing the important contacts with Americans or Canadians of Ukrainian origin. And we, the Ukrainian Americanists in Kyiv, won this competition against Muscovites.[36]

As his close friends later underscored, through his institute, Shlepakov consolidated the most talented Ukrainian scholars with different research interests in one group of genuine experts in immigration and national processes in the industrial Western countries, especially in North America. Leonid Leshchenko noted, "Shlepakov created, from all of us, the first (and the most respected) school of Ukrainian Americanists in the Soviet Union." During the 1980s, Leonid Leshchenko and his younger colleagues, such as Volodymyr B. Yevtukh, began their original research on the United States and Canada, under the inspiration and support of Shlepakov. Until 1991,[37] "Shlepakov's Institute" functioned as the leading Soviet center for the study of American/Canadian Ukrainians, which was a new and flourishing field in American studies in the USSR. In October 1985, Shlepakov and his institute supported Krawchuk's initiative to organize the Canadian Society for Ukrainian Labor Research in Toronto. Shlepakov not only delivered a special address to the first meeting of this Society, but also brought a promise of the official Soviet funding for the international research about "the Ukrainian working immigration" in Canada.[38]

Despite all of Shlepakov's activities in the promotion of American studies in Soviet Ukraine and Ukrainian studies in Canada, many contemporaries, including his Kyiv and Moscow colleagues, noticed "how cautious and conservative" he had become in his analysis of American politics, ideology, and culture after 1979. As Bolkhovitinov observed, "After accepting the position of director of his new institute," Shlepakov changed for the worse, "openly demonstrating anti-Americanism even in very intimate conversations with his colleagues." To some extent, Shlepakov's many years of collaboration with the KGB and his connections with the Soviet academic leadership shaped his identity and worldview.[39] As Sergei Burin noted, "In the 1980s, Shlepakov suddenly had a different personality—that of an ideological reactionary; I could not recognize him anymore." Even the more ideologically cautious and conformist Moscow Americanists, such as Robert Ivanov and Igor Dementiev, complained about "the overly aggressive anti-Americanism" that was expressed in public by Shlepakov.[40]

Shlepakov also took a very cautious and conservative ideological position regarding perestroika when Mikhail Gorbachev began his reforms in 1986. As director of a very important "Cold War institution" in Soviet Ukraine, Shlepakov was afraid that the "improvement of Soviet-American relations" would lead to the "dismantling of ISEPZK in Kyiv and ISKAN in Moscow" and to "ideological confusion in Soviet society and, eventually, to economic and political chaos." In August 1991, he believed that Gorbachev and Yeltsin "were shitting through (*prosyraiut* in Russian) the great country of the Soviet Union." To some extent, he also criticized the Moscow Americanists, and Gorbachev's consultants, including such experts as Arbatov, whose "consulting misled and disoriented the Soviet leadership, and eventually, contributed to the failure of Soviet diplomacy in its competition with the United States." I still recall his last phrase from our last conversation in Kyiv: "Arbatov and Gorbachev surrendered our motherland—the Soviet Union—to the Americans!"[41]

Manipulating Shlepakov's "dependence on the directive organs" and his ideological conservatism, the KGB used him for various international ideological campaigns "against the bourgeois falsifiers of history" in the West. The most shameful among such campaigns at the beginning of perestroika was devoted to the official Soviet denial of materials about the Holodomor, the artificial famine in Soviet Ukraine during the period of collectivization in 1929–1933, as presented in Robert Conquest's book of 1986, and interpreted by Soviet ideologists as "a complete falsification."[42] The KGB began tracing the plans about a publication of this book as early as June 1981. The KGB administration initiated a series of propagandist actions, which would include the public declarations about this book by famous historians of Soviet Ukraine, such as Shlepakov.[43] According to his close friends, "Under strong pressure from the KGB, Shlepakov, who had never read Conquest's book and had never been an expert on the history of Stalin's collectivization, agreed to sign a special Soviet letter of recommendation in the form of petition to the Communist Party of Canada criticizing Conquest's study while at the same time approving the publication in Canada of a book, which would reject a plausibility of all the facts about the Holodomor, as presented in Conquest's study."[44] Eventually, such a "pro-Stalin" book, supported by Shlepakov, was published in Canada in 1987.[45]

A Canadian friend of Shlepakov's, Petro Krawchuk, recalled in his memoirs how he was shocked to see, in Toronto, a photocopy of the "Soviet recommendation letter" regarding the publication of an anti-Conquest book personally signed by Shlepakov.[46] One year before his death, in 1996, Krawchuk recalled this story:

> As recently as 1987, after *glasnost* and *perestroika* were introduced by Mikhail Gorbachev, when the Communist Party of Canada asked for a truthful explanation of the 1932–1933 famine, it received denials from Moscow. Then the Communist Party of Canada insisted that the Kobzar Publishing Company publish the book "Fraud, Famine and Fascism," by Douglas Tuttle, which denies that the 1932–33 famine in Ukraine was artificially organized by the Stalin regime. The book was recommended for publication by Yuriy Kondufor, director of the Institute of History in the Academy of Sciences of Ukraine, by Academician Arnold Shlepakov, director of the Institute of Social and Economic Problems of Foreign Countries, and by Vasyl Yurchuk, director of the Institute of Party History. The book eventually was published but not by the Kobzar Publishing Company, even though it was pressured very hard to do so.[47]

Shlepakov never accepted criticism addressed at him about his participation in such campaigns. Until June 1991, he served as director of his institute. During perestroika, Shlepakov was still an active official of the Presidium of the Ukrainian Academy of Sciences, teaching various courses on diplomacy and American history at Kyiv State University, and editing a number of collective monographs of his colleagues. However, after 1991, Shlepakov ceased producing original research work. His close friends recalled that during the last years of his life Shlepakov never demonstrated publicly his frustration about the collapse of the Soviet Union and the end of his leadership in ISEPZK, which by the end of 1991 was restructured and renamed the Institute of World Economy and International Relations of the National Academy of Sciences of Ukraine. But Leonid Leshchenko noticed that Shlepakov began drinking heavily again, and in confidential conversations he used to repeat only one phrase: "After 1991 Soviet American Studies died completely."

Leshchenko thought that the end of Shlepakov's Institute in its original format in June 1991 contributed not only to his emotional shock, but also to Shlepakov's gradual mental demise and his unexpected death in 1996.[48]

According to his close colleague and friend Leonid Leshchenko, after 1964, the year of his first visit to the capitalist America, until perestroika in the 1980s, Arnold Shlepakov played the major instrumental role in the "unofficial channel of connections" between Peter Krawchuk and the KGB headquarters in Kyiv, Soviet Ukraine. All Ukrainian colleagues knew about "the special personal relations" between Krawchuk and Shlepakov, who became a "frequent guest" of Krawchuk's house in Toronto.[49] Paradoxically, Krawchuk mentioned Shlepakov's name only a few times in his memoirs. At the same time, his family archive in Toronto contains many of Shlepakov's personal letters to Krawchuk, starting with their correspondence in 1957.[50] Moreover, in 1991, Arnold Shlepakov in his conversation with the author of this text, boasted about Krawchuk's dependence on the financial support from both the Soviet government and the KGB, which Shlepakov provided through his personal connections in Kyiv.[51]

VITALY KOROTICH AND KGB ATTEMPTS TO INFLUENCE UKRAINIAN DIASPORA IN AMERICA

A story of the relations between the Ukrainian Canadian Communist Peter Krawchuk and Soviet Ukrainian scholars, such as Arnold Shlepakov, revealed to be just another KGB effort to control and manipulate the Ukrainian diaspora in Northern America, using not only Canadian communists but also their connections to the intellectuals in Soviet Ukraine. The major goal of the special operations, or active measures of the KGB in Northern America, was to discredit and "weaken" the "Ukrainian anti-Soviet nationalists" there. Peter Krawchuk and other American/Canadian Ukrainian communists became useful tools for those KGB operations.

The KGB also used the officials (many of them KGB officers) of the Soviet embassies in the US and Canada to influence the American/Canadian left in "the desired direction."[52] After 1968, every year the Soviet representatives had a special meeting at the Soviet embassy in Canada to give the instructions to the Ukrainian Canadian Communists on how to behave in the Canadian public life and how to understand and interpret the realities of life in Soviet Ukraine for the Canadian public. The KGB used the Soviet embassies in both Canada and the United States for such "special meetings" with the American "progressives" and "sympathizers" of the USSR and Soviet communism for not only collecting the important information about the situation in both countries, but also for instructing and influencing ("advising") pro-Soviet

Americans "in a direction of organizing and promoting of the massive American support for the Soviet domestic and international policy."[53]

As the KGB agents reported, the demographic composition of the recent, after WWII, Ukrainian diaspora in America could also be used for influencing those "American Ukrainians in pro-Soviet direction." Many of them were "former displaced persons, who collaborated with the German Fascist occupants and fled to America from retribution." But at the same time, a "considerable number of people" among those Ukrainian emigrants were "the former members of Soviet military troops, held in captivity during the war; and Soviet citizens, brought by force by Germans to work in Germany, and being under influence of hostile propaganda, were afraid to return to their Motherland." The absolute majority of them were "loyal to the USSR, many of them and their children had not accepted the US citizenship yet, and they wanted to return to the Motherland which they missed and recalled with warmth." But, they were afraid of persecution by the Soviet administration. "More educated wanted the Soviet authority to define their status and their rights as deported people, and they should have legal guarantee for their return." Therefore, the KGB administration recommended the Soviet diplomats in the US and Canada "to target such American Ukrainians" in their "diplomatic actions on the American soil, trying to attract them on the Soviet side."[54]

The KGB administration also recommended using popular Soviet Ukrainian writers, such as "a young and talented Vitaly Korotich," for cultural diplomacy of the Soviet Ukrainian government in "capitalist America" "for a creation of the positive humane image" of Soviet Ukraine. Korotich, who became a famous figure in the West as a symbol of perestroika when he was appointed as editor-in-chief of the magazine *Ogonyok* in Moscow in 1986, had made a career as an Ukrainian poet and writer after his graduation from the medical school in Kyiv in 1959. In 1966–1967, Korotich was appointed editor-in-chief of the Ukrainian popular magazine *Ranok*. In February of 1965, Korotich visited Canada as "a UNESCO *stipendiat* (grant holder)" and immediately attracted attention of the local Ukrainian community in Toronto as a representative of the progressively minded Soviet Ukrainian young intellectuals, known as "*shestydesiatnyky*." Peter Krawchuk met Korotich in Toronto and became "his good friend." As Krawchuk recalled, Korotich "told that in Ukraine there was a lot of negative going on, but he expressed his belief in the [moral] strength of [Ukrainian] people: consciousness was growing, especially among the brave youth, which was afraid of nothing."[55] Korotich's reputation of an "opened minded and democratically oriented" person made him popular not only among the politically left American Ukrainians, but also among the moderate representatives of the Ukrainian diaspora.[56]

After these contacts with the left Canadian Ukrainians, such as Krawchuk, the KGB began supporting Korotich as their "useful asset" in promoting Soviet cultural diplomacy in North America. As early as July 1968, the KGB recommended Soviet leadership in Kyiv, supporting a diplomatic career of Korotich:

> During his visit to Canada and the USA as a UNESCO stipend receiver a writer Korotich Vitaly Alekseievich established the wide contacts among progressive and so-called neutral part of Ukrainian emigration, had numerous meetings with participants of different Ukrainian nationalist organizations and publications, which he used for propaganda of achievements of Soviet Ukraine in sphere of culture and organizing of the profitable ideological influence (*okazaniia na nikh vygodnogo ideologicheskogo vliianiia*) in them. . . . For an activation of work of [the Permanent Mission of Soviet Ukraine at the United Nations Organization (UNO)] among local population [especially among the American Ukrainians] and foreign representatives (*prestavitel'stv*) it is useful to send Korotich in Permanent Mission of Ukraine at UNO. . . . This would give an opportunity the [Soviet] Government to more actively establish the necessary contacts among journalists, diplomats and public figures (*obshchestvennykh deiatelei*) of the USA, to set a regular publication of press-releases and other propagandist documents, which could be prepared by the Ministry of Foreign Affairs of the Ukrainian SSR, RATAU [Soviet Ukraine's press agency.—SZh.] and other interested institutions and organizations, and in this way to strengthen abroad the achievements of the Soviet Union and Ukrainian SSR. . . . Working in the Government, Korotich V. A. could be also very useful in exploring widely the Ukrainian emigration and giving practical assistance to the Ukrainian progressive newspapers and journals in the USA and Canada.[57]

Unfortunately for Korotich's diplomatic career, his "too close" relations with American Ukrainians (even on the political left, like Krawchuk) were considered to be suspicious by the KGB. Eventually, the KGB administration in Kyiv collected the information, which discredited Korotich as "a greedy, corrupt and westernized person," who frequently changed his opinion, joining the Ukrainian nationalists, "demonstrating his ideological unreliability." As a result, the communist leadership of Soviet Ukraine, under pressure from the KGB headquarters, which provided the compromising material on Korotich, not only stopped his diplomatic career, but removed his name from the list of the possible editors-in-chief of *Vsesvit* journal in 1971.[58]

As one KGB officer, a contemporary of these events, joked,

> Even the most talented Soviet Ukrainian intellectuals, the useful assets of the KGB, such as Vitaly Korotich, lost their careers in Soviet cultural diplomacy among Ukrainian Americans and were eventually discredited and compromised by their too friendly relations with Canadian Left and such Ukrainian

Canadian Communists, like Krawchuk. Even Canadian Ukrainian Communists were too nationalistic for the KGB administration in Kyiv. So, everybody in Soviet Ukraine, like Korotich, who contacted them too often, became suspected as well.[59]

During this period of time, the special KGB instructions always reminded about the threat from US intelligence officers, who "used the Ukrainian American diaspora, targeting the Soviet Ukrainian tourists," visiting the US and Canada. They emphasized that "the [American] adversary continued to direct his efforts on the individual study, ideological indoctrination, creation of the compromising situations, regarding the Soviet citizens as target for recruiting some of them by the [US] intelligence, to an inclination to non-return in the USSR, getting the intelligence information from them by various means."[60] The US and Canadian intelligence used the "specially trained and prepared representatives of the Ukrainian emigration for the ideological indoctrination and hostile influence on the Soviet citizens from Ukraine."[61] That is why, to fight these "counterintelligence efforts" and protect "the ideological security" of Soviet Ukrainians traveling in North America, the KGB cultivated the group of the so-called "Soviet sympathizers" and "Left politicians," such as Peter Krawchuk, among American Ukrainians and stimulated the intensive contacts with them through "the KGB people" among Soviet Ukrainian intellectuals, such as Arnold Shlepakov or Vitaly Korotich.[62]

The KGB even targeted those representatives of the American Ukrainian diaspora, who participated in the academic exchange between the United States and Soviet Ukraine in the 1970s. They especially became interested in a young American Ukrainian graduate from the University of Michigan, John-Paul Himka (born in 1949). The first official complaint from the KGB about "the spying activities" of the young American exchange scholar (*stazhor* in Russian) was filed on April 2, 1976. It was about "a *stazhor* associated with Kyiv State University (KDU)," "an American of the Ukrainian origin John Himka, suspected in involvement with the USA intelligence," who tried to get access to "the archives and libraries of the Ukrainian Academy of Sciences, of the Institutes of Literature, and History, and of KDU."[63]

As the KGB agents noted, John-Paul "Himka, who had [supposedly] the links to the CIA officers, not only looked for establishing connections" with anti-Soviet dissidents, but also requested access to "the special archival and librarian funds" of Kyiv University and the Institute of History of the Academy of Sciences of the Ukrainian SSR (which was denied by the KGB).[64] In 1976, the KGB agents, following Himka's research about the left, communist groups in Galicia, decided that this "emphasis" on the "Ukrainian nationalistic" social-democrats was directly related to the CIA efforts to undermine the international nature of socialism in Soviet Ukraine.⁶⁵ At the same time, as a former KGB officer explained, his colleagues knew about the leftist, pro-communist views of Himka, which they reported to the political leadership in Kyiv. As a result, the Soviet officials, who monitored the American/Canadian candidates for academic exchanges, preferred such young leftist scholars like Himka, rather than those American scholars like Frank Sysyn, whose research was "too ideologically dangerous—with nationalistic or religious bias," and whose applications for Soviet visa were, eventually, denied by the Soviet administration.⁶⁶

As the former KGB officers explained, they collected the special files of documents about Himka, trying to discredit, blackmail, "compromise him," and use him in the future as a "useful asset" for KGB operations against the CIA in the United States. They changed their plans and stopped monitoring him, when they realized that Himka, after a defense of his American PhD dissertation, moved to Canada in 1977 to teach at the University of Alberta. This was the typical approach toward the American Ukrainian participants of the exchange programs. During the 1970s, the KGB supervisors preferred to work with those Ukrainian Americans, who represented the United States, rather than Canada.⁶⁷

THE KGB, CENTERS OF UKRAINIAN STUDIES, AND POLITICS IN AMERICA

At the same time, the KGB officials noted and tried to monitor the rise of various centers of Ukrainian studies in "capitalist America." Special attention was directed to the founding in January 1968 of Harvard Ukrainian Research Institute and to its first director Omeljan Pritsak (1919–2006), who, according to the KGB information, had collaborated with Nazis during WWII, and had connections with US intelligence as well. The KGB noted the organization of the similar center at Columbia University; the American Ukrainians collected more than $300,000 for those centers at Harvard and Columbia University. Through the entire 1970s and the 1980s, the KGB tried to discredit Ukrainian scholars of all those centers, presenting them as Nazi collaborators and American spies.⁶⁸

As early as 1957, Soviet intelligence noted the first attempts of Ukrainian Americans to fund the special center for Ukrainian studies at the most prestigious university in the US. According to the KGB reports, the Federation of Ukraine Student Organizations of America (SUSTA: S*oyuz Ukrayinskykh Studentskykh Tovarystv Ameryky*) decided to establish a chair of Ukrainian studies at Harvard University. As the official site of the Harvard Ukrainian Research Institute explained,

While supporting the students' goal of preserving Ukraine's unique culture and history in a time of aggressive Soviet suppression, Harvard Professor Omeljan Pritsak insisted on a much larger project: establishing an academic center of Ukrainian studies. He proposed not one but three chairs in Ukrainian studies (history, language, and literature) and asserted the need for a broader program that included opportunities for scholarly research, a publications program, support of library collections, and a venue for scholarly presentation and discussion. This broadening of SUSTA's initiative would eventually come to fruition at Harvard through three chairs in Ukrainian studies and the Ukrainian Research Institute. After the successful fundraising campaign carried out by the Ukrainian Studies Chair Fund (later known as the Ukrainian Studies Fund (USF))—led by Stephan Chemych and largely supported by the Ukrainian diaspora community—met the financial requirements of Harvard to endow a chair, Ukrainian studies were officially established at the University in 1968 with the creation of the Mykhailo S. Hrushevs'ky Chair in Ukrainian History. The remaining two chairs (in literature and language) were endowed by 1973, a year that also saw the foundation of HURI [Harvard Ukrainian Research Institute].[69]

According to the KGB analysts in Kyiv, the first director of HURI, Omeljan Pritsak, came to the US from Germany and began teaching at the University of Washington in Seattle in 1961. Only in 1964 was Pritsak invited to teach at Harvard.[70] As the contemporaries noted, "convinced that only a permanent center combining both teaching and research possibilities at a leading university could ensure a rational scholarly framework, in 1967 Professor Pritsak proposed a bold plan to the Ukrainian community" to create a research institute at Harvard University.[71]

Meanwhile, members of the Ukrainian diaspora had already been conducting a fund drive for some ten years to create such a Ukrainian center. Fundraising efforts were redoubled, and negotiations with Harvard University resulted in an agreement in 1968 that the proposed center would be established there.[72] Even before HURI was officially established, many of the programs it facilitates today were begun by Pritsak and other scholars involved in the nascent Ukrainian studies project. The weekly Seminar in Ukrainian studies began in 1970, creating an opportunity for scholarly exchange that continues to this day. The Harvard Ukrainian Summer Institute (HUSI) began in 1971, offering students and other individuals to take courses in Ukrainian language, history, literature, and culture as part of the Harvard Summer School. Eventually, Harvard Ukrainian Research Institute was established in June 1973 on the recommendation of the university's ad hoc Committee on Ukrainian Studies. This committee, which included professors Omeljan Pritsak, Ihor Shevchenko, Richard Pipes, Horace Lunt, Wiktor Weintraub, and Edward Keenan, had been appointed in 1968 by the dean of the Faculty of Arts and Sciences to formulate and supervise a program for Ukrainian studies at Harvard. The founding of HURI followed the endowment of chairs in Ukrainian history (1968), Ukrainian literature (1973), and Ukrainian language (1973) and the introduction of courses in Ukrainian studies in several Harvard departments. In 1974, the ad hoc committee became the Standing Committee on Ukrainian Studies, an event that marked the completion of the formal structure of Ukrainian studies at Harvard.[73]

The KGB tried to discredit any attempt of serious research in the Ukrainian studies by American and Canadian scholars, especially by those who had a Ukrainian ethnic background at the Harvard Institute. The KGB agents collected the information about Pritsak, and KGB analysts realized that the HURI director was not *"banderovets"* and the first negative reaction of the Soviet intelligence about "the fascist connections" and anti-Russian feelings of Pritsak were an obvious exaggeration of the available biographical information.[74] As former KGB officers from Kyiv noted,

> As early as 1958, the KGB operatives in Poland had already double checked a biography of German scholar Omeljan Pritsak, who was originally a professor at the University of Hamburg. The universities of Cracow and Warsaw invited Pritsak to teach as a visiting professor in "socialist Poland" in 1959, and Soviet intelligence officers had to check Pritsak's background. As it turned out, Pritsak graduated as a historian from "Soviet" Lviv University in 1940, then became of a post-graduate student of the famous Ukrainian Arabist and Turkologist [A.] Kryms'kyi in Kyiv University, served four months in Soviet Army in 1940. When Nazi troops occupied Kyiv in 1941, young graduate student Pritsak was sent to Germany as an *Ostarbeiter* by the German administration. In 1943 one German scholar Arabist, who knew Pritsak's scholarly potential, helped him to resume his post-graduate studies at the University of Berlin. Eventually, after the war, Pritsak defended his doctoral dissertation in West Germany and became a famous specialist in Turkology and Altaic studies. Moreover, Pritsak distanced himself from the Ukrainian nationalists, who settled in Germany, and he never criticized Soviet Ukraine in public. For Soviet intelligence, people, like Pritsak, became "useful tools" in fighting the radical Ukrainian nationalists, so-called *"banderovtsy,"* inside the Ukrainian diaspora in the West.[75]

Through the entire 1960s and the 1980s, The KGB agents focused on strengthening the split between the radical Ukrainian nationalists (*banderovtsy* in the KGB documents) and a more moderate part of the Ukrainian diaspora in America. These agents supported and helped to publicize all over America, a moderate "pro-Soviet" position of the Ukrainian American intellectuals, such as Omeljan Pritsak, a director of the Harvard Ukrainian Research Institute, Bohdan Krawchenko, one of the leaders of the Canadian Institute of the Ukrainian Studies, and Yu. Darevich, a Physics Professor at the University of Toronto, and Yu. Gaetskii, a Professor of History at the University of Chicago. According to the KGB reports, these Ukrainian Americans "rejected to participate in the political actions of *banderovtsy*," "opposed their attitudes directed on boycott of the scientific and cultural connections with Soviet Ukraine." "In contrast to *banderovtsy*," they "demanded directing the activities of the Ukrainian emigration to a preservation of the Ukrainian language, culture, and strengthening its cultural role in the social life of the country of their residence."[76]

At the same time, the KGB agents engaged the American and Canadian Communists of Ukrainian origin in the KGB operations against the local Slavic/Soviet studies centers, promoting various pro-Soviet academic topics for discussions. As I had already mentioned, since 1968, on a regular basis, the Soviet Embassies in the US and Canada had special "instruction meetings" for local American communists, directing them on how to participate in various academic discussions in the Slavic/Soviet studies centers at the American universities. Soviet KGB curators also closely monitored the evolution of the Canadian Institute of Ukrainian Studies, which started in 1976 in Edmonton, at the University of Alberta, which was spreading its office to the University of Toronto as well. Later, the KGB analysts paid their special attention to the Centre for Ukrainian Canadian Studies, which was founded in 1981 at the University of Manitoba.[77]

As the KGB operatives emphasized, overall, despite offering some scholarships to Soviet Ukrainian dissidents by HURI and other Ukrainian research centers in America, the leaders of those centers, like Pritsak, avoided the open anti-Soviet declarations and their personal participation in the political anti-Soviet campaigns, which targeted Soviet Ukraine.[78] Even the associates of HURI on their website noted a "cautious" political approach toward Soviet Ukraine by such Ukrainian centers like HURI during the Cold War:

> In the 1970s and 1980s, HURI was able to appoint Soviet dissidents: historian Valentyn Moroz, writer and editor Nadia Svitlychna, and Volodymyr Mezentsev. Restricted by the political situation with the Soviet Union during these decades, HURI's support for fellows and visiting scholars focused on Polish-Ukrainian studies and the experience of Jews in Ukraine.[79]

The KGB experts, who monitored evolution of various Ukrainian studies centers at Columbia University in the US and in Edmonton, Toronto, and Manitoba in Canada during the late 1970s and the 1980s, noted how those centers tried to distance themselves from political debates, criticizing Soviet Ukraine "but being careful not to cross the line of the ideological and political confrontation." Despite the KGB attempts to use Jewish diaspora against Ukrainian diaspora in America in the major KGB operations there, especially during various KGB operations against American Ukrainians, who were presented in Soviet propaganda as "bourgeois nationalists, anti-Semites and fascist collaborators," even KGB operatives, who participated in those operations, had to acknowledge the "relatively friendly" approach of the Ukrainian studies centers in America toward Soviet Ukraine, and those centers' attempts to build "a dialogue between Ukrainian and Jewish diasporas" in the United States.[80]

Still, for the KGB, the most important task was to follow the politics, especially political elections, in both the US and Canada, which involved the representatives of the Ukrainian diaspora in America and to try to "create a political influence for pro-Soviet candidates." On July 15, 1968, the KGB agents in Canada informed their administration in Kyiv that they "focused their operation on the elections of members of the Canadian parliament," when seven Canadian Ukrainians were in the list of possible candidates. These agents "checked the background and ideological positions of each of those candidates," and promised to "monitor thoroughly all of them to use them in the future in the interests of Soviet Ukraine." The KGB agents reported to their Kyiv administration that they "became especially interested in influencing" the Ukrainian Canadian businessman Mark G. Smerchanski (1914–1989), from the Liberal Party of Canada, Province Manitoba, "who was loyal to Soviet Ukraine, and assisted materially" the Ukrainian Canadian Congress and Ukrainian Orthodox Church. Smerchanski visited the USSR in 1967, and the KGB noticed his "good behavior without any public demonstration of the anti-Soviet feelings." They noted that "he expressed his strong interest in maintaining good trade relations between Canada and the Soviet Union."[81]

Since 1968, the KGB representatives had continued their monitoring of all elections in both Canada and the US, trying to influence the "pro-Soviet inclined politicians" and promote their political careers all the time.[82] During the summer of 1972, the KGB agents in Canada promoted in American and Canadian mass media information about the Canadian Prime Minister Pierre Trudeau's comparison of the Ukrainian nationalists with the French separatists in the Province of Quebec. Through the entire 1970s, any "bad and negative description of the Ukrainian diaspora in America" by Canadian politicians was disseminated by the KGB representatives in various American media with the purpose of discrediting "anti-Soviet inclinations" of American Ukrainians.[83]

The KGB managed to recruit and infiltrate numerous agents (eight in only one year in 1973) in various Ukrainian Canadian organizations, "the Ukrainian nationalistic newspapers," and Canadian universities in the cities of Winnipeg, Montreal, Ottawa, and Toronto, using them for triggering the campaigns to discredit those Canadian politicians, like former Canadian Prime Minister John Diefenbaker, who supported the anti-Soviet slogans of the Ukrainian diaspora in Canada. Some of those agents were infiltrated into the Ukrainian studies centers as well during the late 1970s, whose activities were commended by the KGB administration in Kyiv even during the 1980s.[84]

FIGHT WITH RUSSIAN INFLUENCES AND MISTAKES OF THE AMERICAN UKRAINIAN COMMUNITY

Since the 1970s, the Soviet KGB, and after the 1990s, Russian FSB, had targeted the American Ukrainian community, and especially Ukrainian research and teaching centers in America, using the American Ukrainians' mistakes and their gullibility, when the Ukrainian diaspora in America was fighting Russification and blindly supporting all those Soviet Ukrainians who were fluent speaking in the Ukrainian language. As former Soviet intelligence officers joked, "By the 1990s, the American Ukrainians were ready to support and applaud any Soviet Ukrainian *apparatchik*, if he spoke fluent Ukrainian and officially declared his [or her] Ukrainian patriotism; and the same time, they tried to ignore his [her] old Communist Party and KGB connections. As a result, the American Ukrainian community welcomed such KGB people, like Arnold Shlepakov, in the 1970s, and such Communist ideologists, like Leonid Kravchuk, in the 1990s."[85] The KGB administration always tried to use for communication with American Ukrainians in academic exchanges, only those representatives of Soviet Ukrainian academia who were speaking Ukrainian fluently. This became a requirement for all KGB agents who represented academic exchange programs, which involved members of the Ukrainian diaspora in both the United States and Canada, especially in the Ukrainian studies centers at Columbia and Harvard Universities, in Toronto and Edmonton.[86]

Since the 1960s until the collapse of the USSR, during the academic exchanges, the Ukrainian diaspora in America had to deal mainly with the representatives of the political and academic elites of Soviet Ukraine, who had personal connections with the communist party establishment, directly connected to various venues and organizations of Soviet intelligence. The KGB always had influence on the Ukrainian diaspora through those representatives. Even in the late 1980s and the 1990s, before and after the collapse of the USSR, the overwhelming majority of the academic guests from Soviet Ukraine in the Western colleges and research centers were *only* the representatives of the Soviet political and academic elites. As Leonid Leshchenko, who was an active participant of various exchange programs with America, explained to me later, "Look at those young Soviet Ukrainian academic visitors to the US and Canada, after 1987, who eventually settled later in America! All of them represented political and academic elites of

Soviet Ukraine! I just remind you that your dear friend Serhii Plokhy was a chair of world history and an associate dean at Dnipropetrovsk University before going to Canada; another friend of yours, Serhy Yekelchyk, before going to Australia, came from the elitist Kyiv family, related to a famous Yuri Yekelchyk, Dovzhenko's cameraman; Oxana Shevel, before going to UK and US, came from a family of the Soviet apparatchiks with her grandfather Georgiy Shevel being a minister of foreign affairs of Soviet Ukraine! And I can keep going."[87]

Eventually, Plokhy, Yekelchyk, and Shevel, whose careers in America were supported by the American Ukrainians, became the real Ukrainian patriots, distancing themselves from their Soviet past, and promoting the course of Ukrainian independence and fighting the Russian academic imperialism in America. Serhii Plokhy became Mykhailo S. Hrushevs'kyi Professor of Ukrainian History and Director of HURI at Harvard University, Serhy Yekelchyk became a Professor of Slavic Studies at the University of Victoria in Canada, and Oxana Shevel became an Associate Professor of Political Science at Tufts University. But according to officials of the Soviet/Ukrainian intelligence, who monitored the academic exchanges in the 1980s, not everybody from the post-Soviet community of Ukrainian scholars who settled in America after the collapse of the Soviet Union cut their relations with their former KGB "curators." They still have their contacts, and some of them are still used by the Russian intelligence (both by the FSB and by the GRU) to infiltrate various research and teaching institutions in the US and Canada. As one officer noted, "This will be a new problem for the Ukrainian diaspora to figure out who is who: those former Soviet Ukrainians are fluent in Ukrainian and behave like the Ukrainian patriots, but in reality, they will be used as the new sleeper agents of the Russian intelligence, targeting the Ukrainian community in America, or just as the 'useful idiots' for the Russian propaganda."[88] Many contemporaries also mentioned other important socio-cultural factors, which influenced the pro-Russian and pro-Soviet preferences among some post-Soviet Ukrainian scholars, who became active among the Ukrainian diaspora in the West, especially in the United States and Canada after the collapse of the USSR. As Leonid Leshchenko noted, "Today, historians forgot the most influential factor of pro-Russian sympathies, which was the Soviet Communist military background among those Ukrainian scholars who came from the families of Soviet military officers and whose families (moving from Russia) eventually settled in Lviv and other cities of Soviet Ukraine." He and some of his colleagues emphasized the importance of this factor, which became obvious in the writing of those Ukrainian scholars, especially after 2013, about the political developments of post-Soviet Ukraine. As one former Ukrainian KGB officer explained, such Ukrainian scholars, who live now in the West even justified Russian invasion in Donbas in 2014 as "the Donbas workers' civil war and resistance against Kyiv Ukrainian oligarchs."[89]

As Dr. Basil Dmytryshyn, a Ukrainian American, late Professor Emeritus of Russian History, told me in 2016, "There were two stages of the KGB and Russian intelligence operations to discredit the Ukrainian Diaspora in America and various centers of Ukrainian studies there: the first stage involved Soviet visiting scholars and the local (American/Canadian) leftist sympathisers, who were used by the Soviet intelligence during the 1970s and the 1980s; and the second stage involved mainly the academic refugees from post-Soviet Ukraine, who were used mostly by the FSB, after the end of the USSR." As he added later, "Unfortunately, the leaders of those Ukrainian studies centers looked some time indiscriminate and gullible by accepting and funding all (even the suspiciously connected to the Soviet political hierarchy) academic guests from post-Soviet Ukraine."[90]

If such representatives of Soviet Ukrainian elites, like Plokhy, Yekelchyk, and Shevel, demonstrated their pro-Ukrainian and anti-Russian position during their integration into American academia, other post-Soviet Ukrainian academic migrants criticized in public the post-Soviet Ukrainians as Neo-Nazis and took obviously anti-Ukrainian positions, justifying Putin's war against Ukraine in 2014. The most famous case of such an anti-Ukrainian position among the American Ukrainian diaspora is the story of the Canadian-Ukrainian political scientist Ivan Katchanovski.

Paradoxically, Katchanovski was born in 1967 in the city of Lutsk, a center of Soviet Ukrainian Volhynia, a very patriotic anti-Russian region of Western Ukraine. As a young man, he participated in the patriotic movement in Soviet Ukraine, promoting the Ukrainian language and culture during the perestroika in Kyiv, where he graduated from the Economy and Social Planning Programme at the Kyiv Institute of National Economy in 1990. In 1993, Katchanovski graduated from the Central European University in Prague as an economist. During this period of perestroika and the USSR collapse, until 1994, he was teaching economy at the Volhynian University in Lutsk. Then he moved to the United States, where he defended his PhD dissertation in political science at George Mason University in 2002. Eventually, he began teaching political science at the University of Ottawa in Canada and used the support of the local Ukrainian community there.[91] During the Maidan Revolution of 2013–2014, Katchanovski began losing this support because of his criticism of Neo-Nazi involvement in the events of this revolution. According to his research, those Ukrainian supposedly "fascist" leaders in Kyiv provoked (and organized) the deadly shooting of Maidan demonstrators, which eventually triggered the "bloody events" in Ukraine and Russian involvement in "the civil war" in Ukraine. As he noted, in 2013, "far-right groups not only provoked fighting by shooting at the police but also carried out the murder of Maidan protesters in a false-flag operation."⁹² Paradoxically, Katchanovski, who previously criticized the Russian and Soviet "imperialist" policy, in his academic activities after 2014, began supporting Putin's theory of "Neo-Nazi conspiracy" and anti-Ukrainian politics in Kyiv Maidan Revolution. As a result, his publications became widely used by the Russian pro-Putin propagandist venues during 2014–2023. Even though, recently, Katchanovski tried to distance himself from Putin's policy after the second Russian war against Ukraine in 2022, his publications about Maidan events in 2013 were actively incorporated in both the Russian anti-Western propaganda and the academic anti-Ukrainian publications by another graduate from a Canadian university, the University of Alberta, by a Swedish-American historian, Per Anders Rudling, and referred to and quoted by a retired professor from the University of Alberta, John-Paul Himka, who, during his student youth in the 1970s, had been already targeted by KGB operations.[93]

Another, most recent, mistake of the Ukrainian American community was its attempt to invite for an academic position of a Soviet historian at the Harriman Institute of Columbia University and then to support the academic career of Dr. Tarik Cyril Amar. After graduating from Oxford University in 1995, and from London School of Economics and Political Science in 1997, the young scholar of German-Turkish dissent, Tarik Amar, was accepted to Princeton University to write his PhD dissertation about the history of Soviet Ukrainian city of Lviv under supervision of Princeton historian Stephen Kotkin. In April of 2006, Amar defended his dissertation, entitled "The Making of Soviet Lviv, 1939–1963." In the fall of 2006, Amar was invited to teach as a Petro Jacyk Visiting Scholar and Adjunct Professor at the Harriman Institute and the History Department of Columbia University. In the spring of 2007, he was awarded with a Shklar Research Fellowship at the Harvard Ukrainian Research Institute. In September of the same year, Dr. Amar was invited to serve as an Academic Director at the Center for Urban History of East Central Europe in Lviv, Ukraine.[94] Eventually, in 2010, Amar's Ukrainian colleagues from Lviv, who were "impressed by his organizational talent and historical erudition," recommended his candidacy to the Ukrainian American community for an open academic position of assistant professor of Soviet History at Columbia University. As a result of this recommendation, the representatives of the Ukrainian American community not only organized their support of Amar's candidacy for a new position of Soviet historian at Columbia University in 2010, but also tried to assist him to get a US "green card."[95]

At the beginning of his teaching Soviet history in Columbia in 2010–2014, Dr. Amar just followed the traditional coverage of the historical events in American history writing about the Soviet past, concentrating his attention on the Ukrainian developments under a Soviet regime; and nobody complained about his political position and preferences. Everything changed in Amar's teaching after the Maidan Revolution of 2013–14 and the beginning of the Russian war against Ukraine in 2014. Despite the publication (in 2015) of his first book about a history of Lviv, a city, which became a symbol of the Ukrainian independence, Dr. Amar became a skeptical critic of the Maidan Revolution, blaming in public, first, the Ukrainian politicians, who supported "local Nazi nationalists," then he was trying to justify Putin's aggressive politics, regarding Ukraine in 2014–2015.[96]

Eventually, in 2016–2017, Dr. Amar took an obvious pro-Russian, pro-Putin, and anti-Ukrainian position. Paradoxically, initially using the support of the Ukrainian community in New York, Tarik Amar openly attacked the same Ukrainian community, blaming them as being fascist collaborators, racists, and anti-Semites, and provoking a political crisis in post-Soviet Ukraine. Amar's rhetoric became reminiscent of the old Soviet KGB propaganda, which was used against the Ukrainian diaspora in America during the Cold War. Even those Columbia historians, such as an Americanist Eric Foner, whose academic interests were far from the post-Soviet geopolitical space, were appalled with Tarik Amar's pro-Putin and anti-Ukrainian declarations.[97] As a result of this conflict with his colleagues, Tarik Amar left Columbia University, moved to Turkey in 2017, where he continues his criticism of Ukraine as "a Neo-Nazi state," and justifies the new war of Russia against Ukraine in 2022–2024, using such ideological platforms as television shows of RT (Russia Today) and other pro-Putin channels of influence in the West.[98] Paradoxically, Tarik Amar, working for RT, which is "a tool of Russian intelligence, used by FSB, SVR and GRU for their provocation and disinformation against the United States," became involved in Russian intelligence operations, targeting the Ukrainian diaspora in America and those very American Ukrainians who tried to assist him with getting a teaching job at Columbia University.[99] Despite his recent criticism of "the abuse of history" by Putin's propaganda, overall Amar's position still fits the same kind of propaganda, which he tried to distance from.[100]

Such mistakes of the Ukrainian community, like Tarik Amar's case, demonstrated how the Russian political propaganda and the old traditions of Soviet KGB could be used to discredit and confuse the Ukrainian diaspora and its research centers as well. At the same time, this case is also proof of how Russian academic imperialism is used not only in political propaganda and in Russian intelligence operations against Ukrainian diaspora in the West, but also in such centers of Western academia, like Columbia University in the US. Concentrating on Anglo-American material, the next chapter will discuss in detail the roots and development of such academic imperialism in Western academia.

NOTES

1. Filip Kovacevic shared his archival findings with me, demonstrating how the KGB organized their secret operations against Lithuanian diaspora in the US: Lithuanian KGB Archive, Vilnius, Lithuania: F. K-35, ap. 2, b. 844, l. 177–207 (January 1, 1965). See https://www.kgbveikla.lt/docs/show/2548/from:538.

2. Oleg D. Kalugin, *Spymaster: My Thirty-Two Years in Intelligence and Espionage Against the West* (New York: Basic Books, 2009), 221.

3. Oleg D. Kalugin, *Spymaster*, 221. See also Serhii Plokhy, *The Man with the Poison Gun: A Cold War Spy Story* (New York: Basic Books, 2016), esp. 222, 223ff.

4. I quote my interview with Leonid K., a retired KGB officer, March 3, 2019, Kyiv, Ukraine.

5. Interview with Ivan Grigorovich K., a retired KGB officer, February 3, 2019, Kyiv, Ukraine.

6. See about the role of Peter (Petro) Kravchuk and the Canadian/American Communist Ukrainians in my book: Sergei I. Zhuk, *KGB Operations against the USA and Canada in Soviet Ukraine, 1953–1991* (London and New York: Routledge, 2022), especially 50–76.

7. Arkhiv Instituta istorii Natsional'noi Akademii nauk Ukrainy (hereafter ANANU), Opys 1-L, Otdel kadrov, spr. 1277: Osobova sprava Shlepakova Arnol'da Mykolaiovycha (1978 rik, 77 arkushiv), ark. 6; Leonid Leshchenko and Ihor Chernikov, "Vsesvitnio vidomyi vitchyznianyi uchenyi: Istoryk-miznarodnyk, organizator nauky i diplomat. Do 80-litia vid dnia narodzhennia akademika NAN Ukrainy Arnol'da Mykolaivycha Shlepakova (1930–1996 rr.)," in *Mizhnarodni zv'iazky Ukrainy: naukovi poshuky i znakhidky. Vypusk 19: Mizhvidomchyi zbirnyk naukovykh prats*, Vidp. redactor S. V. Vidnians'kyi (Kyiv: Institut istorii NAN Ukrainy, 2010), 27. I also used the similar essay of memoirs about Shelpakov, published by his colleagues: V. Gulevich, B. Zabarko, L. Leshchenko, and I. Chernikov, "Cherez roky I vidstani: Do 80-richchia narodzhennia akademika NAN Ukrainy A. M. Shlepakova (1930–1996)," *Visnyk NAN Ukrainy*, no. 5 (2010): 42–46. See also Oleksii Ias,' *'Na choli respublikans'koi nauki . . . ' Instytut istorii Ukrainy (1936–1986): Narysy z instytutsional'noi ta intelektual'noi istorii (Do 80-richchia ustanovy)*, edited by V. A. Smolii (Kyiv: NAN Ukrainy: In-t istorii Ukrainy, 2016).

8. Interview with Arnold M. Shlepakov, April 4, 1991, Kyiv, Ukraine.

9. Interview with Arnold Shlepakov, August 29, 1991, Kyiv.

10. Interview with Volodymyr B. Yevtukh, December 15, 1995, Kyiv; interview with Leonid Leshchenko, June 23, 2013, Kyiv.

11. Ibid.

12. Interview with Volodymyr B. Yevtukh, December 15, 1995, Kyiv; Interview with Leonid Leshchenko, June 23, 2013, Kyiv. Leshchenko referred to the Soviet youth subculture of the late 1940s, known as "stylish boys and girls" (*styliaga* in Ukrainian).

13. ANANU, Opys 1-L, Otdel kadrov, spr. 1277, ark. 6.

14. Interview with Bolkhovitinov and Leshchenko. See especially my interview with Leonid Leshchenko, June 25, 2013, Kyiv.

15. ANANU, Opys 1-L, Otdel kadrov, spr. 1277, ark. 6.
16. Arkhiv Akademii nauk Ukrainy, Institut istorii, Opys 1-L, Otdel kadrov, spr. 1277, ark. 55. During this time Shlepakov wrote and published the typical (for Soviet historian) anti-American and anti-capitalist propaganda materials. See, e.g., A. N. Shlepakov, *Ukraina v planakh mizhnarodnoi reaktsii naperedodni drugoi svitovoi viiny* (Kyiv: Derzhavne vydav-vo politychnoi literatury URSR, 1959), idem, *V roky zrostannia voennoi nebezpeky* (Kyiv: Derzhavne vydav-vo politychnoi literatury URSR, 1963). The CIA operatives also suspected the KGB connections of the relatively young scholar such as Shlepakov. See "declassified and released the Central Intelligence Agency's material" from 1964 about Shlepakov traveling abroad with his wife. See http://www.foia.cia.gov/sites/default/files/document_conversions/1705143 /AERODYNAMIC%20%20%20VOL.%2030%20%20(OPERATIONS)_0003.pdf.
17. See his autobiography: Petro Kravchuk, *Bez nedomovok: Spogady* (Kyiv: Literaturna Ukraina, 1995). See about the Soviet financial (and other) support of the leftist Canadian Ukrainians, such as Krawchuk, in John Kolasky, *The Shattered Illusion: The History of Ukrainian Pro-Communist Organizations in Canada* (Toronto: PMA Books, 1979), especially pp. 205, 206–208. See more details about those connections of the leftist Canadians (like Krawchuk) and the Soviet administration in M. H. Marunchak, *The Ukrainian Canadians: A History* (Winnipeg/ Ottawa: Ukrainian Free Academy of Sciences, 1976), 494–495; Andrij Makuch, "Ukrainian Pro-Communists: Revolutionaries into Businessmen," *Student*, December 1979, pp. 9, 11, and other publications of Andrij Makuch about Peter Krawchuk in *The Ukrainian Weekly*, no. 15 (April 13, 1997): 4; *Journal of Ukrainian Studies*, vol. 23, no. 1 (Summer 1998): 148–150. See about the overall issues regarding the Soviet perception of Canada in Joseph Laurence Black, *Canada in the Soviet Mirror: Ideology and Perception in Soviet Foreign Affairs, 1917–1991* (Ottawa: Carleton University Press, 1998).
18. Eventually Krawchuk's book, edited and proofread by Shlepakov, was published in 1963 in Soviet Ukraine: Petro Krawchuk, *Na kanads'kii zemli* (Lviv: Knyzhkovo-zhurnal'ne vydavnytstvo, 1963). See about this in his book of memoirs: idem, *Bez nedomovok: Spogady* (Kyiv: Literaturna Ukraina, 1995), 67.
19. *Ukrains'ke tovarystvo kul'turnogo sv'iazku z zakordonom* existed during 1926–1959; from January 1959 it was renamed as *Ukrains'ke tovarystvo druzhby i kul'turnogo sv'iazku z zarubiwnymy krainamy* (1959–1985). See about a history of such Soviet organizations, created by the USSR for "cultural diplomacy" in Michael David-Fox, *Showcasing the Great Experiment: Cultural Diplomacy and Western Visitors to the Soviet Union, 1921–1941* (New York: Oxford University Press, 2012); V. M. Danylenko, *Ukraina v mizhnarodnykh, Na skryzhaliakh istorii*; and Stanislav Yu. Lazebnyk, Olha B. Havura, *Rozdumy na mostu z dvobichnym rukhom* (Kyiv: Etnos, 2004). During the late 1950s and the early 1960s, young Shlepakov was used by the "directive organs" for various contacts with the official guests from the United States and Canada. See documents in Tsentral'nyi Derzhavnyi Arkhiv Vyshchykh Organiv Derzhavnoi Vlady i Organiv Derzhavnogo Upravlinnia Ukrainy (hereafter TsDAV-OVUU), fond 5110, op. 1, tom 2, d. 1192, l. 1–3, ll. 1193, 1–5. See also in detail about the relations between Ukrainian Canadians and Soviet Ukraine in Jaroslav Petryshyn,

"The 'Ethnic Question' Personified: Ukrainian Canadians and Canadian-Soviet Relations 1917–1991," *Re-Imagining Ukrainian Canadians: History, Politics, and Identity*, edited by Rhonda L. Hinther and Jim Mochoruk (Toronto: University of Toronto Press, 2011), 223–256; Jennifer Anderson, "Polishing the Soviet Image: The Canadian-Soviet Friendship Society and the 'Progressive Ethnic Groups,' 1949–1957," *Re-Imagining Ukrainian Canadians*, 279–328.

20. I also use the Private Archive of Larissa Stavroff (Krawchuk) [hereafter Stavroff archive] in Toronto, Canada, which I visited in March 2012. Stavroff archive, file 64: Shlepakov Arnold, letter from 10 April 1957 about an invitation for submission to "the new Ukrainian periodical *Ukrains'kyi istorychnyi zhurnal.*" See also their publications after Shlepakov's joining the editorial board of *Vsesvit*: Petro Kravchuk, "Kanadtsi ukrains'kogo pokhodzhennia vchora i siogodni," *Vsesvit*, no. 9 (1981): 192–199, and Arnol'd Shlepakov, "Storinky zhyttia i borot'by," ibid., 200–201.

21. See in Petro Kravchuk, *Bez nedomovok*, 73–75, and my interview with Leonid Leshchenko, July 30, 2012, Kyiv.

22. Interview with Arnold M. Shlepakov, April 4, 1991, Kyiv. See about the similar experience in Stanislav Yu. Lazebnyk, Olha B. Havura, *Rozdumy na mostu*, chapter "Filosofiia zhyttia Petra Kravchuka," pp. 111–131.

23. A. M. Shlepakov, *Ukrains'ka trudova immigratsiia v SShA i Kanadi (kinets' XIX–poch. XX st.)* (Kyiv: Naukova dumka, 1960). See especially Stavroff archive, file 64: Shlepakov Arnold, personal letters from August 7, 1956, to December 17, 1972.

24. TsDAVOVUU, fond 4621, op. 13, spr. 217, ark. 2–37.

25. ANANU, Opys 1-L, Otdel kadrov, spr. 1277, ark. 55–64; *Visnyk NAN Ukrainy*, no. 5 (2010): 45.

26. Interview with Leonid Leshchenko, Kyiv, June 25, 2013.

27. SBU, f. 16, op. 1, spr. 1043, ark. 312–313. Shlepakov boasted about this in his conversation with me in 1991. See my interview with Arnold Shlepakov, Kyiv, August 29, 1991.

28. Interview with Arnold Shlepakov, Kyiv, August 29, 1991.

29. Interview with Leonid Leshchenko, June 25, 2013, Kyiv. Leshchenko suggested in his conversation with me that in his youth, Shlepakov had homosexual relations and was caught by the police in a kind of "illegal sexual act." The KGB used this incident for blackmailing and manipulating him. Shlepakov began drinking alcohol as a result of this situation. Other colleagues also mentioned that despite his marriage to E. N. Roslavets, deputy director of the Kyiv Museum of Western and Eastern Art, Shlepakov never demonstrated his romantic feelings to women, or expressed his interest in women in any other form, etc. See also ANANU, Opys 1-L, Otdel kadrov, spr. 1277, ark. 56.

30. Of course, occasionally, Shlepakov reproduced his old original material on Slavic immigration to the United States and US immigrational politics and published them in the prestigious collective monographs in Moscow. See, e.g., his contributions to the book, published by the Institute of Ethnography at the USSR Academy of Sciences: A. N. Shlepakov, "Slavianskie gruppy v SShA," *Natsional'nye protsessy v SShA*, edited by S. A. Gonionskiy, A. V. Efimov, and Sh. A. Bogina (Moscow: Nauka,

1973), 278–298; and idem, "Rasovo-natsional'nye osnovy immigratsionnoi politiki SShA v 20–60-kh godakh XX v.," *Natsional'nye protsessy v SShA*, 312–327.

31. I use the phrase by Sergei Burin regarding "Arbatov and Sevostianov as the officially appointed *nachal'niki sovetskoi amerikanistiki*" (the bosses and official representatives of American studies in the USSR). See A. N. Shlepakov, *Biografiia statui Svobody: Istoricheskii ocherk* (Moscow: Mysl, 1969); idem, *SShA: Sotsial'naia struktura obshchestva i ego natsional'nyi sostav* (Kiev: Naukova dumka, 1976); V. A. Gorbik and A. N. Shlepakov, *Gosudarstvennaia politika i obostrenie natsional'nykh otnoshenii v stranakh kapitala* (Kiev: Naukova dumka, 1979); I. S. Khmil, A. N. Shlepakov, *Sotsial'naia struktura i sotsial'naia politika SShA, Velikobritanii, FRG, Frantsii i Kanady* (Kiev: Naukova dumka, 1980); A. N. Shlepakov and L. A. Smirnova, *SShA: 'Pokhishchenie umov' v proshlom i nastiashchem* (Moscow: Mysl, 1983). He also edited numerous collective monographs. Altogether Shlepakov (as an author and an editor) published more than 200 books. See his various editorial projects: *Ukraina i zarubizhnyi svit*, edited by O. A. Makarenko, A. N. Shlepakov a.o. (Kyiv: Vyd-vo politychnoi literatury, 1970); *Mizhnarodna solidarnist' u borot'bi proty fashyzmu*, edited by A. N. Shlepakov, V. N. Gulevych, B. M. Zabarko a.o. (Kyiv: Naukova dumka, 1970); *Dvizhenie mezhdunarodnoi solidarnosti trudiashchikhsia, 1924–1932*, edited by A. N. Shlepakov and L. G. Babichenko (Kiev: Naukova dumka, 1980); *Sotsial'no-ekonomicheskaia i politicheskaia diskriminatsiia trudiashchikhsia v kapitalisticheskom mire, 60–70-e gg. XX v.*, edited by A. N. Shlepakov (Kiev: Naukova dumka, 1980).

32. Email correspondence with Volodymyr Yakimets, March 10–12, 2012.

33. The phrase belongs to Volodymyr Yakimets.

34. *Zarubezhnyi mir, sotsial'no-politicheskie i ekonomicheskie problemy* (Kiev: Naukova dumka, 1981–1991). See especially volume 19 for the year of 1990, pp. 103–109, 109–115. See also about how the Ukrainian Communist Party's leadership supported Shelpakov's Insitute in the memoirs of Vladymyr Shcherbytsky's personal secretary: Vitaliy K. Vrublevskiy, *Vladimir Shcherbitskiy: zapiski pomoshchnika: slukhi, legendy, dokumenty* (Kyiv: Dovira, 1993), 180–181. Note the very condescending attitude of Moscow leadership toward the Ukrainian efforts to create the first research center for American studies in Kyiv. See the documents in ANANU, Opys 1-L, Otdel kadrov, spr. 1277, ark. 77 (about Shlepakov), spr. 1198, ark. 48 (about Yevtukh joining Shlepakov).

35. *Visnyk NAN Ukrainy*, no. 5 (2010): 43.

36. Interview with Arnold Shlepakov, August 29, 1991, Kyiv, Ukraine.

37. Among the numerous publications, initiated by Shlepakov, see especially V. B. Yevtukh, *Istoriografiia natsional'nykh otnoshenii v SShA i Kanade (60–70-e gody)* (Kiev: Naukova dumka, 1982); *Rabochii klass i natsional'nyi vopros v stranakh Zapadnoi Evropy i Severnoi Ameriki, 60–80-e gg.*, edited by A. N. Shlepakov, V. B. Yevtukh a.o. (Kiev: Naukova dumka, 1985); A. M. Shlepakov, *Ukrains'ki kanadtsi v istorychnykh zv'iazkakh iz zemleiu bat'kiv* (Kyiv: Naukova dumka, 1990). However, the best study by Yevtukh in 1991 was edited by his Moscow colleague, Valery Tishkov, rather than by his mentor Shlepakov. See V. B. Yevtukh, *Kontsepsii*

etnosotsial'nogo razvitiia SShAi Kanady: tipologiia, traditsii, evoliutsiia (Kiev: Naukova dumka, 1991).

38. Interview with Arnold Shlepakov, Kiev, August 29, 1991; Petro Kravchuk, *Bez nedomovok: Spogady*, 240–241; Peter Krawchuk, *Our History: The Ukrainian Labour-Farmer Movement in Canada, 1907–1991*, translated from Ukrainian by Mary Skrypnyk, edited by John Boyd (Toronto: Lugus, 1996), 474–475.

39. Interview with Stepan Ivanovich T., a retired KGB officer, January 30, 2019, Kyiv, Ukraine.

40. Interview with Robert F. Ivanov, Moscow, September 6, 1998.

41. Interview with Arnold Shlepakov, August 29, 1991, Kiev. This conversation was in Russian, and it had more criticism of Muscovites, Arbatov, and Gorbachev than in my previous interview. He always denied his connections to the KGB, when I raised this question.

42. Robert Conquest, *The Harvest of Sorrow: Soviet Collectivization and the Terror-Famine* (New York: Oxford University Press, 1986).

43. SBU, f. 16, op. 1, spr. 1185, ark. 87.

44. Interview with Leonid Leshchenko, June 25, 2013, Kyiv.

45. Douglas Tuttle, *Fraud, Famine and Fascism: The Ukrainian Genocide Myth from Hitler to Harvard* (Toronto: Progress Books, 1987).

46. Petro Kravchuk, *Bez nedomovok: Spogady*, 244.

47. Peter Krawchuk, *Our History*, 250. See also about this story in Roman Serbyn, "Echoes of the Holocaust in Jewish-Ukrainian Relations: The Canadian Experience," *Ukrainian Quarterly*, vol. 60, no. 12 (2004): 223, and Frank Sysyn, "Thirty Years of Research on the Holodomor: A Balance Sheet," *East/West: Journal of Ukrainian Studies*, vol. II, no. 1 (2015): 7.

48. Interview with Leonid Leshchenko, June 25, 2013, Kyiv. In Ukrainian, Shlepakov's phrase about the demise of American studies sounded like this in Ukrainian "*Radians'ka amerikanistika pomerla povnistiu.*"

49. Interview with Leonid Leshchenko, June 25, 2013, Kyiv.

50. See the Private Archive of Larissa Stavroff (Krawchuk) in Toronto, Canada, which I visited in March 2012. Stavroff archive, file 64: Arnold Shlepakov.

51. Interview with Arnold Shlepakov, August 29, 1991, Kyiv.

52. The most famous case of Soviet pressure on the American left was to persuade them that Soviet suppression of Prague Spring was justifiable. As John Kolasky described this: "Sergei Molochkov, formerly in charge of relations with the CPC [Communist Party of Canada—SZh.] in the apparatus of the CC of the CPSU and the liaison between the Soviet party and the CPC and the ethnic mass organizations, had been in Canada as an employee of the Soviet embassy in Ottawa since 1967. He made a trip across Canada to persuade the Ukrainian leaders to alter their stand in the hope of finding support for the Soviet position [about an invasion of Czechoslovakia]." See in John Kolasky, *The Shattered Illusion*, 175. See about this also in Petro Kravchuk, *Bez nedomovok: Spogady*, 121–126.

53. SBU, f. 16, op. 1, spr. 970, ark. 68–73.

54. Ibid., spr. 1006, ark. 163–164.

55. Krawchuk, op. cit., 83.

56. SBU, f. 16, op. 1, spr. 1006, ark. 173–174. During the special meetings of the Ukrainian Canadian Congress and the Association of the United Ukrainian Canadians, the representatives of Ukrainian Canadians always voted for Korotich, as "the most favorable guest" from Soviet Ukraine.

57. SBU, f. 16, op. 1, spr. 974, ark. 321–322. The KGB administration ended this report to the Ukrainian communist leadership with a phrase: "We report this for your consideration."

58. SBU, f. 16, op. 1, spr. 1009, ark. 338–341; spr. 1011, ark. 102–103.

59. Interview with Leonid K., retired KGB officer, Kyiv, February 9, 2019.

60. SBU, f. 16, op. 1, spr. 1024, ark. 87.

61. Ibid., ark. 89–90. The KGB documents provided plenty of proofs of such "provocations" against the tourists from Soviet Ukraine during 1970–1971. The "Ukrainian nationalists" organized the anti-Soviet debates in New York City with representatives of SCCUA in September 1970. The similar scandal happened during the radio show with a participation of Soviet Ukrainians in Montreal, Canada. The students from Georgetown University, who specialized in the Ukrainian studies, met Soviet tourists from Ukraine with anti-Soviet demonstrations.

62. I paraphrased my interview with Igor T., a former KGB officer in Dnipropetrovsk.

63. SBU, f. 16, op. 1, spr. 1116, ark. 210–212.

64. Ibid., 176.

65. SBU, f. 16, op.1, spr. 1116, ar. 210–212. Compare with an interview with Stepan Ivanovich, a retired KGB officer in Kyiv. The result of Himka's research in Soviet Ukraine was his future book: John-Paul Himka, *Socialism in Galicia: The Emergence of Polish Social Democracy and Ukrainian Radicalism, 1860–1890* (Cambridge, MA: Harvard University Press, 1983). See also in detail this case in Sergei Zhuk, op. cit., 87–89.

66. I refer to my interview with Stepan Ivanovich T.

67. See my interview with Stepan Ivanovich T., a retired KGB officer, January 30, 2019, Kyiv, Ukraine.

68. See SBU, f. 16, op. 1, spr. 970, ark. 50, 62–63, 147ff. Among many cases of KGB disinformation in Canada, see how the KGB in Soviet Ukraine used journalist Sydney Gordon from the newspaper of the Communist Party of Canada, *The Canadian Tribune,* to promote publications of materials against Ukrainian nationalists. See SBU, f. 16, op. 1, spr. 1119, ark. 234–235.

69. See https://huri.harvard.edu/history-institute.

70. Interview with Stepan Ivanovich T., a retired KGB officer, January 30, 2019, Kyiv, Ukraine.

71. Lubomyr Hajda, "Remembering Omeljan Pritsak on His 10th Birthday" at https://huri.harvard.edu/news/remembering-omeljan-pritsak-his-100th-birthday. According to Pritsak, "The nineteen-sixties have a special place in the history of Ukraine. They witnessed the sudden explosion of Ukrainian literary talents (the shestnydesiatnyky) on the one hand, and on the other, the imperial Soviet reaction—to suppress any trace of Ukrainian cultural attractiveness. It happened that in 1964 I was invited to join the Harvard faculty. Harvard's unique scholarly potential, and the financial support of the awakened Ukrainian American diaspora under the impact of

the shestnydesiatnyky, needed to be combined and utilized. From my knowledge of Ukrainian history I realized that the Ukrainian cultural awakening of the 19th century had been regarded as a threat to the Russian imperial idea of a single high imperial culture. But in the 19th century, not all Ukrainian territories were embraced by Russia. Western Ukraine, especially Galicia with its capital of Lviv, was under Austrian constitutional rule (especially in the second half of the century), and the best talents from all the Ukrainian territories had the opportunity to participate in the development of Ukrainian high culture. In the 1960s, however, Galicia and Lviv were already under Soviet Russian domination. In such a situation, it was imperative to create Ukraine's scholarly and intellectual center at the most attractive university in the West. Since I was at that time part of such an excellent institution, namely, Harvard, I regarded it as my duty to act. First, I devoted some time to studying the challenge connected with this tremendous task. After I had obtained my answers, I discussed my project with the administration and colleagues of my university. Fortunately, they approved of my ideas, which were as follows. Ukrainian identity, which is the basis of cultural and political activity as well as a force for growth for coming generations, cannot normally exist without the help of three ethnic-national disciplines. I mean here language, the common code of national creativity, without which Ukrainianhood would lose its reason for existence; literature, as the artistic shaping of the language and spiritual nourishment for the higher levels of culture; and finally, history, the common memory of the national community, without which it would be like a robot, lacking a vision and will of its own. It was natural that a scholarly center created at Harvard would have to embrace in the first place these three disciplines. They could develop and function properly only when they were pursued simultaneously on two parallel levels: (a) instructional—the chairs of Ukrainian philology, Ukrainian literature and Ukrainian history within the respective departments of the Faculty of Arts and Sciences, and (b) research—at the Ukrainian Research Institute, an autonomous institution of the Faculty of Arts and Sciences, with library and publication facilities. ... To attain the required scholarly level, an academic body should be established: the Standing Committee on Ukrainian Studies, and also a Visiting Committee, as part of the University's Board of Overseers, which would include representatives of the broader American community, including the Ukrainian diaspora. A weekly seminar would unite the students and scholars from the three chairs as well as prominent guest scholars from the United States and abroad. An international journal of Ukrainian studies should be created, as well as a monograph series. Leading scholars from the entire world, irrespective of their nationality, should be encouraged to study Ukrainian topics and invited to work as fellows of the Institute." From "Omeljan Pritsak," published in HURI's 20th anniversary booklet (1993), https://huri.harvard.edu/history-institute.

72. Lubomyr Hajda, op. cit.
73. Ibid.
74. SBU, f. 16, op. 1, spr. 1185, ark. 272.
75. Interview with Leonid K.
76. SBU, f. 16, op. 1, spr. 1185, ark. 272–273. See similar report from the US in ibid., spr. 1192, ark. 47.

77. SBU, f. 16, op. 1, spr. 970, ark. 68–73.
78. Interview with Leonid K.
79. See https://huri.harvard.edu/history-institute#:~:text =HURI's%20Formal%20Foundation,research%20and%20share%20their%20insights.
80. Interview with Leonid K.
81. SBU, f. 16, op. 1, spr. 974, ark. 54–55.
82. Interview with Leonid K., a retired KGB officer, Kyiv.
83. SBU, f. 16, op. 1, spr. 1051, ark. 189–190. Compare with my interview with Leonid K., a retired KGB officer, Kyiv.
84. SBU, f. 16, op. 1, spr. 1077, ark. 188–195. Unfortunately, those KGB documents did not give us the names of Canadian Ukrainian scholars from Canadian universities who became the KGB agents in the 1970s and 1980s. This information is still classified.
85. Interview with Ivan Grigorovich K., a retired KGB officer, February 3, 2019, Kyiv, Ukraine.
86. SBU, f. 16, op. 1, spr. 1185, ark. 272–273.
87. Interview with Leonid Leshchenko, June 23, 2013, Kyiv. He referred to Oleksandr Dovzhenko, a famous Soviet Ukrainian film director. See also about Shevel in Olga Bertelsen, "Political Affinities and Maneuvering of Soviet Political Elites: Heorhii Shevel and Ukraine's Ministry of Strange Affairs in the 1970s," *Nationalities Papers: The Journal of Nationalism and Ethnicity*, vol. 47, no. 3 (2019): 394–411. In conversation with me, Yekelchyk denied the "elitist character" of his family. According to Professor Plokhii, Shevel did not use a support of Ukrainian diaspora at the beginning of her career.
88. Interview with Leonid K.
89. Interview with Leonid Leshchenko, June 23, 2013, Kyiv. I quote my old interview with Leonid K. of 2019, and my telephone conversation with him in June of 2023; he mentioned the names of the Ukrainian scholars, such as Georgiy Kasianov (Institute for Political Science and Administration, Maria Curie-Skłodowska University, Lublin, Poland) and Sergiy Kudelia (Associate Professor of Political Science, Baylor University, US), whose parents were Soviet military officers and settled in Lviv. See about Kudelia interpretation of the historical events in his recent essay: "Civil War Settlements and Conflict Resolution in Donbas," in *The War in Ukraine's Donbas: Origins, Context and the Future*, edited by David Marples (Budapest: CEU Press, 2022).
90. Telephone conversation with Basil Dmytryshyn in Muncie, Indiana, on October 3, 2016.
91. What follows is the information from Katchanovski's interview with Natylie Baldwin for Consortium News: https://natyliesb.medium.com/the-maidan-massacre -censorship-ukraine-my-interview-with-ivan-katchanovski-40898a2c8237 and https: //esu.com.ua/search_articles.php?id=11375.
92. See https://www.thenation.com/article/archive/the-heartbreaking-irony-of -winter-on-fire/. See also Katchanovski's article (2019): https://onlinelibrary.wiley .com/doi/abs/10.1111/wusa.12457.

93. These connections and Katchanovski's anti-Ukrainian position were criticized by many scholars such as Taras Kuzio and David R. Maples. See https://ukrainian-studies.ca/2014/12/01/taras-kuzio-study-ukrainian-nationalism-university-ottawa, and https://ukraineanalysis.wordpress.com/2014/10/23/the-snipers-massacre-in-kyiv/. Compare with: https://ici.radio-canada.ca/rci/en/news/2013351/canadian-monument-to-controversial-ukrainian-national-hero-ignites-debate.

94. See https://cdn.ku.edu.tr/resume/tcyrilamar.pdf.

95. What follows is based on my long conversations during February-April 2016, on the Columbia University campus in New York City, with Bohdan Vitvitsky and Roman Procyk, the representatives of the Ukrainian community, who assisted Tarik Amar.

96. See my review of Amar's book: Sergei I. Zhuk, "Review of Tarik Cyril Amar. The Paradox of Ukrainian Lviv: A Borderland City between Stalinists, Nazis and Nationalists. Ithaca and London: Cornell University Press, 2015," in *East/West: Journal of Ukrainian Studies*, vol. 4, no. 1 (2017): 219–221.

97. During my teaching at Columbia University in the Spring Semester of 2016, I discussed Amar's anti-Ukrainian position with Professor Eric Foner from the Department of History of Columbia University on March 30, 2016.

98. See Amar's declarations at https://www.rt.com/russia/544604-cold-war-ukraine-west; https://www.rt.com/russia/549148-ukraine-deal-anniversary-war; https://www.youtube.com/watch?v=S7jqDi8dg7g&list=WL&index=2&t=1320s. https://www.youtube.com/watch?v=5C7DE2KFJHs&t=3731s.

99. See https://www.state.gov/report-rt-and-sputniks-role-in-russias-disinformation-and-propaganda-ecosystem.

100. See Amar's interview in April of 2022: https://natyliesb.medium.com/the-abuse-of-history-in-the-russia-ukraine-war-an-interview-with-tarik-cyril-amar-cc3dbf9420dc.

Chapter 6

"Academic Imperialism"

Writing Soviet and Post-Soviet History Without Ukraine and the Role of the Russian Post-Soviet Immigration to the West

The international humanities and social sciences community experienced real epistemological shock and overall cultural division after the Euromaidan Revolution in 2013–2014. Not only experts in Slavic studies (especially former Western Sovietologists), but also the specialists in American and European studies (especially Americanists) became divided on the issue of accepting the Ukrainian war of independence against Russian aggression, especially after Russian President Vladimir Putin's Russia annexed Crimea and invaded Ukraine's Donbas. Many were undecided as to whether or not to accept that Russia was the aggressor in eastern Ukraine after Putin's government annexed Crimea in contravention of the Budapest Memorandum and other international treaties, and then sent Russian troops to Ukraine's Donbas, where Putin also had supported local pro-Russian separatists since 2005.[1]

Paradoxically, an influential part of this international community demonstrated an obvious "Russo-centrism" (or *Russophilia*) and outrageous Ukrainophobia, trying to justify Putin's politics in Ukraine and criticizing Ukraine and Ukrainians. To this day, many Western and Russian scholars, still, do not want to face the "inconvenient truth" about direct Russian military aggression and interference in the domestic politics of independent Ukraine, long before Russia's full-scale invasion of Ukraine on February 24, 2022.[2] Why did it happen? What were the reasons for the rise of such pro-Russian and anti-Ukrainian sentiments among so many Western and post-Soviet academics? Were these Russophile feelings connected to the very important epistemological and geopolitical changes affecting the humanities? This chapter is an attempt to answer these questions.

PERSONAL REACTION TO PRO-RUSSIAN POSITION OF AMERICAN ACADEMIA

As a former Soviet Ukrainian historian who moved from post-Soviet Ukraine to the United States in 1997, I had problematic relations with my cultural, professional, and ethnic identity. Despite an annual obligatory summer visit to Ukraine with my family and travels between my hometown of Dnipropetrovsk and Moscow, I felt more and more distanced from the real practical issues of everyday life in both Ukraine and Russia, identifying with my American colleagues and professional historians, sharing common professional interests and cultural practices with Americans, and gradually adjusting to American college life and values. Moreover, as a former Soviet historian-Americanist, who became a historian of imperial Russia and the Soviet Union in the US, I experienced an identity crisis, attempting to unite in my professional life, skills, and practices from both historical fields. Since the disintegration of the Soviet Union in 1991, like many of my Soviet co-citizens, I had lived through another crisis of identity, which was connected to my Soviet citizenship. As a citizen of Soviet Ukraine, who was drafted as a reservist officer for three months in May 1986 to command a platoon protecting property left in the Chernobyl zone, I experienced another cultural and identity shock, when I realized that Soviet leadership in the Kremlin and my Russian commanding officers did not care about us, "filthy Khokhols," who sacrificed our lives in Chernobyl, saving the world from a nuclear catastrophe. This exacerbated another experience of mine of an earlier cultural distancing I experienced from my Moscow colleagues, Americanists, for whom I was just "another annoying provincial Ukrainian scholar."[3]

Despite my native Russian-language skills (I spoke Russian at home), my Moscow colleagues always demonstrated a very condescending attitude to people like myself, who they viewed as (I paraphrase what Dr. Boris Shpotov from the Institute of World History said about Ukrainian scholars in 1999) "narrow-minded stupid provincials, claiming that they know something in history."[4] Therefore, I began distancing myself from my Moscow colleagues, shaping my own intellectual identity vis-à-vis Muscovites. This mental distancing from Moscow gradually increased during the 1990s when I began traveling abroad using Western research grants. I felt more Ukrainian and less Soviet than my former Moscow colleagues whom I left behind. What was shocking for me was that while I was losing ties with my Soviet past during those years, all of my Moscow colleagues, whom I was visiting almost every summer, expressed stronger and stronger feelings of "Soviet nostalgia" and blamed the West, and especially America, for the dissolution of the USSR and deterioration of their lives in post-Soviet Russia. Moreover, many of my Moscow friends also began blaming Ukrainians (including Russian speakers like me) for betraying East Slavic unity, destroying the Soviet Union, and voting in 1991 for the independence of Ukraine (which for them is still a "historical part of sacred Orthodox Christian Russia . . . with Kiev—a center of Holy Russia").[5]

Paradoxically, this kind of "Soviet nostalgia" and underlying accusations of Ukrainian "betrayal" became evident also in the writing and professional practices of my American colleagues—"Russianists" and "Sovietologists," experts in Russian, Soviet, and post-Soviet studies. When I began my new academic and teaching career as an American "Russian" historian in 2002 in the US, I encountered (surprisingly) a certain negative reaction to my Ukrainian identity and my research topics, which were related to my research work, based on material from my native Ukraine. Thus, when I finished my first American book, a cultural history of Ukrainian peasant evangelicals in the southern Ukrainian provinces of the late Russian Empire, and offered it for publication under the title *Ukraine's Lost Reformation*, all of my American reviewers immediately suggested it be replaced with a new title, *Russia's Lost Reformation*, arguing that nobody would be attracted to a book title containing a name of the new "unknown" nation of Ukraine.[6] As the late Richard Stites joked in November 2008:

> Sergei, you will be surprised to see how Russian-centered and Moscow-focused are all your American friends, historians of the Russian Empire and Soviet Union. Your new Ukrainian nation with your provincial interests just does not fit such an historical "imperial" imagination. Many of these American historians still prefer the traditional perception of all multinational history of the entire post-Soviet space from a Moscow and *Velikorusskaia* (Great Russian) point of view. They still live in their own historical nostalgic space in the Leonid Brezhnev era in Moscow or Leningrad, when they were young scholars, recalling meetings and adventures with their (mainly) Russian friends and colleagues, who are still communicating with them, strengthening their nostalgia for the Soviet past.[7]

To some extent, my second American book became another challenge to the so-called "Muscovite paradigm" in both post-Soviet Russian and Western historiography, which dominated mainstream history writing in American studies of the Soviet Union. This book was a history of Soviet cultural consumption and identity formation—not in Moscow, or in Soviet Russia, but rather in one industrial city in Soviet Ukraine, my "provincial" hometown of Dnipropetrovsk, which has now a new name—Dnipro. Portraying the cultural situation in this multinational Soviet Ukrainian city during the Brezhnev era, I traced the gradual formation of local Ukrainian identity vis-à-vis the Soviet identity imposed by Moscow, even before the collapse of the Soviet Union.[8] But despite my idealization of and fascination with Ukrainian identity in this book, I still had some ambiguous feelings about Ukraine, especially after 2010, observing rule by the most corrupt (in the entire Ukrainian history) regime of President Viktor Yanukovych and the shameful passivity and subservience to his rule of my former co-citizens. I did not like Putin's Russian militocracy, but I also disliked the high levels of corruption in Ukraine.

My ambivalence toward Ukraine changed dramatically after November 2013. By the end of February of 2014, following revolutionary events on television and via the internet, and communicating with my relatives and friends in Ukraine, I had begun feeling a tremendous respect for the Ukrainian people who challenged the corrupt regime and overthrew Yanukovych and the Donetsk criminal clan. Moreover, I felt a certain pride that my hometown of Dnipropetrovsk, led by a group of talented and patriotic Jewish-Ukrainian and Russian speaking oligarchs such as Gennadii Korban and Boris Filatov, could suppress pro-Russian separatists and transform my city into a bastion of democracy, cultural and linguistic toleration and Ukrainian patriotism in the eastern, mainly Russian speaking, region of post-Soviet Ukraine. My entire family (with our Russian, Jewish, Ukrainian, and Greek roots) in the United States became not only new patriots of a post-Maidan anti-Soviet Ukraine, but also loyal followers of our pro-Ukrainian Jewish and Russian Orthodox Dnipropetrovsk leaders, as well as of Ukrainian nationalist leader Dmytro Yarosh. The Euromaidan Revolution and subsequent political and social upheaval in our hometown of Dnipropetrovsk dealt a final blow to our Soviet identity. Moreover, watching Russian television and communicating with our Moscow relatives after November 2013 became a real cultural shock for our family as well. For us, the Euromaidan was a revolution of dignity, a revolt against the corrupt post-Soviet oligarchy, and we expected that ordinary Russians, who suffered from a similar oligarchic regime, would support such a revolution and express solidarity with it.

But alas, the Russian media and my Moscow relatives and colleagues adopted a very anti-Ukrainian position. Then the Russian leadership began open military aggression against Ukraine when it annexed Crimea in March 2014. The long campaign of demonizing the Euromaidan Revolution, which had begun in Putin's controlled Russian media in November 2013, kept portraying the brutality and violence of "fascist" Stepan Bandera followers who participated in an "American conspiracy" against Russia, claiming that they were killing and torturing innocent Russians and Jews in Ukraine. As a result of this massive and professionally organized anti-Ukrainian propaganda, not only ordinary Russian consumers of TV information, but also Russian intellectual leaders and prominent representatives of the Russian cultural establishment, such as famous film director Nikita Mikhalkov and orchestra conductor Valery Gergiev, supported Putin's aggression against Ukraine in the name of the liberation of "all Russians in Ukraine, who are threatened by [Stepan] Bandera fascists."[9]

Even the famous skeptic of Putin's politics, the last Soviet President Mikhail Gorbachev, applauded Putin's annexation of Crimea as the restoration of "historical justice" by collecting "Russian" territories.[10] Meanwhile, in response to Western sanctions, a popular presenter on Russian state television, Dmitrii Kiselev, explained to his viewers that Russia is the only country capable of turning the United States into "radioactive ashes."[11] He then went on to use animated maps to show exactly how Russia would automatically respond with nuclear missiles if its command and control were attacked or disabled by a US attack. Many Russian and Western scholars and experts, such as Stephen F. Cohen and Henry Kissinger, talked of the "justified historical role" of Russia in protecting its geopolitical interests, even if this meant the dismembering of Ukraine. Some of them justified their support for Putin through claims about Russia's "historical rights" to territories in Ukraine.[12]

Putin's imperial claims to Ukraine, his imperialist project of *Novorossiia* (the very word is derived from late imperial Russian vocabulary!) in eastern-southern Ukraine, and the sending of Russian military troops to the Donbas (Donetsk and Luhansk *oblasts*) were infused with Soviet nostalgic rhetoric and symbols in 2014. Pro-Russian proxies in the Donbas always referred to Soviet symbolism and used Soviet cultural practices. The ongoing war against Ukraine is presented as a kind of sequel to the Great Patriotic War when Soviet Donbas fought the Nazis in 1941–45. Russian instructors and volunteers, like Igor Girkin, who became leaders of pro-Russian proxies in Donbas in spring 2014, even used the discursive practices of the Great Patriotic War (including Stalin's orders in 1941 to execute criminals on occupied territories) when they controlled the city of Slovyansk in Donetsk *oblast*. For many Muscovites and residents of the Donbas, the best (and idealized) period of their life was the Leonid Brezhnev era in the 1970s and first half of the 1980s. They deny the historical existence of independent Ukraine.

Surprisingly for me, a similar rejection of Ukraine's rights to protect its territorial integrity in both Crimea and the Donbas was found among some of my American colleagues, historians of Russia and the Soviet Union. In spring 2014, this was also evident when I attempted to disseminate information about the Euromaidan, Crimea, and Putin's military aggression at the Midwest Russian History Workshop and other venues of American Slavic and East European studies. These American Slavists criticized my pro-Ukrainian position as "nationalistic," repeating Russian mass media clichés about the supposed "fascist, anti-Jewish and anti-Russian" goals of the Euromaidan, defending and justifying repression by the Yanukovych regime and security forces against protestors and activists. A year after the Euromaidan, I witnessed during academic events in Barcelona, Berlin, and Rome, some of my American and European colleagues justifying Putin's anti-Ukrainian politics as the "anti-imperialist and anti-American reaction of the Russian people."[13]

THE LEFT, REVISIONISTS, SOVIET IMMIGRANTS IN SLAVIC STUDIES, AND HISTORIOGRAPHIC SOVIET NOSTALGIA

As a historian of cultural consumption and knowledge production, I find one of the most important and interesting among the many different reasons for these pro-Russian and anti-Ukrainian feelings of American experts in Slavic studies to be what I call the methodological paradigm of "historiographic Soviet nostalgia." In my opinion, this is related to a serious paradigmatic shift in historical analysis during the late Soviet period and the rise of "revisionist" American studies of Soviet and Russian history and culture, especially during the 1990s. Earlier generations of American experts in Soviet studies concentrated on contradictions and problems in late socialist USSR, including corruption, the black market, nationalism, religiosity, and political dissent. After the disintegration of the USSR, scholars began emphasizing their research on everyday life and consumption, dismissing or avoiding serious internal problems and conflicts in late Soviet society. This approach was manifested in a lack of attention to Russian and Soviet imperialist policies against Ukraine.[14]

During the Cold War, especially before the 1980s, Soviet society was presented as a one-dimensional, monolithic, and predictable entity on both sides of the ideological divide in both Soviet studies in the West and in histories of the USSR and Communist Party in the Soviet Union. Despite the prevailing different theoretical models of interpretation—a totalitarian and modernization model in the West and Orthodox Marxism-Leninism in the USSR, Soviet studies in both the capitalist West and socialist East explained major developments in similar ways, emphasizing mostly political, economic, and ideological aspects against the backdrop of a never-changing stable Soviet civilization.

During the 1970s and the 1980s, the sudden rise of the "revisionist" school in Western historiography, especially studies by Sheila Fitzpatrick, Stephen F. Cohen, Leopold Haimson, and other Western scholars, revealed new data from the Soviet and Russian archives and introduced fresh ideas, social theories, and cultural history. A new generation of Western scholars, including Richard Stites, Vera Dunham, Laura Engelstein, Jeffrey Brooks, and

Denise Youngblood replaced the traditional one-dimensional interpretation of Soviet society with an approach that took into account different cultural practices that they had "discovered" in the everyday life of Soviet peoples. This approach changed the development of Soviet studies, and eventually contributed to the popularity of cultural studies among both Western and post-Soviet historians.[15]

The rise of the Western "revisionist" school coincided with and was further stimulated by the perestroika and then by the disintegration of the Soviet Union in 1991. During this period new archival collections were opened in the Soviet Union and post-Soviet states. Many former Soviet scholars could travel abroad and use funding and resources from Western research centers. Scholarly dialogue and collaboration between Western and former Soviet scholars were established. Many talented Soviet intellectuals with different professional backgrounds, such as Serhii Plokhy (trained as a historian of early modern Ukraine), Yuri Slezkine (originally a linguist specializing in Portuguese), Irina Paperno (trained as an expert in Russian literature and associated with the Tartu school), Dmitry Shlapentokh (a historian of France and Russia), Alexei Yurchak (a radio engineer and producer for famous Leningrad rock bands), Andrei Znamenski (a historian of American Native Peoples), Vladislav Zubok (trained as an expert in US politics), and myself (a historian of colonial British America), left their post-Soviet countries and joined Western academia where they taught Soviet, Russian, and Ukrainian studies in US universities. This experience contributed to expanding and changing the field of Soviet and post-Soviet studies. At the same time, Sovietology in the West was losing its traditional anti-Soviet critical focus and began to stress conformist (even the openly pro-Russian) features in Soviet historiography.[16]

The first serious theoretical justification for the new paradigmatic shift in the direction of the conformist, non-confrontational, non-conflict approaches for American studies of Soviet society during the Cold War was the work of a Soviet émigré from Leningrad, anthropologist Alexei Yurchak. He attempted to explore ideological aspects of everyday life, theories, and practices of late socialism, and discursive practices and identity formation in post-Stalin Soviet society. Yurchak investigated "internal shifts that were emerging within the Soviet system during late socialism at the level of discourse, ideology, and knowledge but that became apparent for what they were only much later, when the system collapsed."[17] According to Yurchak, after Khrushchev's de-Stalinization, communist ideology in Soviet society underwent a so-called *performative shift*, when Stalin's authoritative discourse lost its importance, becoming mere rituals for many Soviet people, who tried to exist outside this communist ideological discourse. He primarily used material from his hometown of Leningrad to show how different forms of cultural production and consumption in the late Soviet period, especially rock music and Western fashions, influenced Soviet youth, including *Komsomol* activists and officials. According to Alexei Yurchak, "rock and roll culture" became a part of "nonofficial discourses and practices in late socialism." In contrast to authors such as Thomas Cushman, who insisted on the countercultural character of rock music in the Soviet Union, Yurchak argued that non-official practices (such as listening and playing rock music) involved:

> Not so much countering, resisting, or opposing state power as simply *avoiding* it and carving out symbolically meaningful spaces and identities away from it. This avoidance included passive conformity to state power, the pretense of supporting it, obliviousness to its ideological messages, and simultaneous involvement in completely incongruent practices and meanings behind its back.[18]

The entire theoretical framework of Yurchak's study was directly influenced by French thinkers such as Michel Foucault and Michel de Certeau. According to de Certeau, in modern European society, "imposed knowledge and symbolisms become objects manipulated by practitioners who have not produced them." In de Certeau's interpretation, such practitioners usually subverted practices and representations that were imposed on them from within, not by rejecting them or transforming them (though that occurred as well), but in many other ways. Practitioners of knowledge production "metaphorised the dominant order: they made it function in another register. They remained within the system which they assimilated, and which assimilated them externally. They diverted it without leaving it."[19] These ideas, combined with Mikhail Bakhtin's concept of authoritative discourse, became the foundation of Yurchak's theoretical framework.[20]

As Yurchak argued, the obsession with Western cultural products became the most important feature of cultural consumption in the closed socialist society of the post-Stalin era. Yurchak focused in particular on the cultural and discursive phenomenon known among social scientists as the "Imaginary West."[21] According to Yurchak, the "Imaginary West" is a "local cultural construct and imaginary that was based on the forms of knowledge and aesthetics associated with the 'West,' but does not necessarily refer to any 'real' West, which also contributed to 'deterritorializing' the world of everyday socialism from within."[22] Yurchak rejected previous readings that emphasized the confrontational and countercultural character of the "imaginary West" in Soviet cultural consumption. Instead, he offered a consensual and conformist interpretation of this metaphor. Using the ideas of the Russian cultural critic Tatyana Cherednichenko, Yurchak attempted to show how Western music (as a part of the "Imaginary West") contributed to the "production of a whole generational identity" for the last Soviet generation.[23]

At the same time, he ignored problems of regional, national, and religious identities that were shaped by the consumption of Western cultural products in various parts of the Soviet Union. Yurchak disregarded the importance of the idea of the West for political dissent in the USSR. Yurchak's interpretation exaggerated the role of discursive practices, and in his interpretation visual elements, especially Western films, lost their role of influencing both ideological discourse and local identity among Soviet consumers.[24]

As a result, Yurchak interprets Soviet society during late socialism as a society void of any serious social problems or conflicts. Prevalent problems during this period such as the involvement of Soviet officials in the activities of the black market, Russification, street gang culture, popular religiosity, nationalism, and anti-Semitism are ignored in Yurchak's study. Yurchak also underestimated the importance of the KGB and police interference in cultural consumption, which especially affected provincial cities where the majority of the Soviet youth lived.[25]

Yurchak's study attracted many American and post-Soviet scholars who were tired of the traditional emphasis on political dissidents and who wanted the "more positive and friendly approaches toward defeated and humiliated (by the West) post-Soviet Russians, who lost their Soviet Empire at the end of the Cold War."[26] Yurchak's ideas influenced new studies about post-war Soviet history, especially the history of Soviet youth. One of the best studies of post-war Soviet youth, *Stalin's Last Generation*, drew on Yurchak's ideas and approaches. According to Juliane Fürst (who follows Yurchak verbatim), the result of the post-war socialism was the creation of a socialist "modernist" culture during late Stalinism as a "complicated conglomerate of performative practices, collective habits, individual mechanisms of survival, strategies of self-improvement, and segregated spaces for action, all of which were linked and interacted with each other in the person of the Soviet subject and citizen."[27]

In contrast to Yurchak, Fürst used not only material from the Soviet Russian cities, such as Leningrad and Moscow, she also introduced archival documents from Russian and Ukrainian regional archives and used these to create a lively picture of cultural consumption among Soviet young people during the late 1940s and early 1950s. She enriched the historiographical terrain of late Stalinism, based on classical studies by Russian historian Elena Zubkova while adding new concepts from Western cultural studies, including Yurchak's ideas.[28] Unfortunately, Fürst brought her fascination with Yurchak's theoretical framework even in her new book on the history of Soviet hippies, which was recently supported by the Russian post-Soviet reading audience, which found in a Fürst's study a Western scholar's justification of "the normalcy of the Soviet past," supporting Soviet nostalgia, which is part of Putin's propaganda in the Russian Federation today. As a result, in 2023, her study was translated into Russian and was published in Putin's Russia.[29]

Citing Yurchak's work has become practically obligatory in recent Soviet and post-Soviet studies in the West, especially in the US, UK, and Canada.[30] Even good oral history studies by Donald Raleigh, drawing on Yurchak, continued to stress the non-conflict "positive" side of Soviet history. To my knowledge, Raleigh's research about the last Soviet generation was the first Soviet oral history study by a Western scholar to be based exclusively on personal oral interviews, using only primary sources and oral history methodology in presenting and explaining these interviews.[31] For his second book, published in 2012, Raleigh interviewed sixty 1967 graduates of two Soviet magnet schools with intensive instruction in English, one in Moscow and one in the provincial city of Saratov. This project began as an extension of his previous book, which contained only interviews conducted in Saratov among former graduates from Saratov's school No. 42.[32] Some of the major characters from the first book and their interviews played an important role in his later book as well.

What is more original in the 2012 book is the addition of interviews with Muscovites, which created an important social and cultural dimension to the historical comparison of two different, but elitist cohorts of Soviet students from elite schools specializing in English—one from the "closed" Soviet provincial city of Saratov, and another from the center of Soviet civilization, a capital city of Moscow. Unfortunately, serious social and political problems, including the growth of Russian nationalism and anti-Semitism, and the exclusive position of Muscovites in the Soviet cultural hierarchy, which are the psychological foundations for Soviet Russian imperialism, completely disappeared from view in Raleigh's oral history of "Soviet baby boomers." At the same time, both Fürst and Raleigh adopted a principled anti-Putin and pro-Ukrainian position. Moreover, during the summer of 2017, Raleigh visited the city of Dnipro in Ukraine, where he presented his new research project on a biography of Brezhnev for his Ukrainian colleagues and expressed his solidarity and sympathy with Ukrainian patriots.[33]

Unfortunately, many of Fürst's and Raleigh's colleagues did not share these pro-Ukrainian sympathies. Some of their colleagues continue to prefer an image of Soviet society without social conflicts coupled with an obvious nostalgia for and idealization of the Soviet past, and rejection of Western influences on Soviet developments, even during the Brezhnev era.[34] A majority of Anglo-American studies on Soviet national politics still represent a "Moscow-centric" point of view by openly ignoring "the non-Russian republics."[35]

For many American experts in Soviet studies, the non-confrontational, conformist, and "emotionally positive" approaches to an analysis of Soviet and post-Soviet society and culture offered by Yurchak became the most popular theoretical model, leading to very dangerous epistemological and methodological consequences. This "conformist" model led to the ignoring of the "brewing" problems of Soviet Russian imperialism and Russian chauvinism. Confronted with the "unexpected" Euromaidan Revolution in Ukraine, American Sovietologists and historians of Russia and the Soviet Union were not ready to discard their old historiographical concepts. Therefore, they distanced themselves from "controversial" Ukrainian developments by denying their historical validity and focusing instead on more familiar and predictable developments in post-Soviet Russia. For the historical "nostalgic" imagination of the experts in Soviet and post-Soviet studies, the phenomenon of the Euromaidan rejected and destroyed the traditionally accepted Moscow-centered and Russian-focused approaches to political, social, cultural, and economic developments in the post-Soviet space. Eventually, this epistemological Soviet nostalgia led scholars, like Richard Sakwa and Nikolai Petro, to open support and justification of Putin's foreign and security policies in Eurasia and Eastern Europe.[36] Many American Sovietologists still dismiss problems of Russian/Soviet imperialist politics, which led to a genocide of the Ukrainian nation. One of them, Stephen Kotkin, Professor Emeritus of history at Princeton University, who published two volumes of his trilogy about Stalin's life, completely ignores the Ukrainian Holodomor, a famine artificially created by the Stalinist regime, which killed at least five million Ukrainians in 1932–33. Kotkin's students, such as Tarik Cyril Amar, not only openly support Putin's regime and its war against independent Ukraine, but also work for the Russian propagandist television station RT (Russia Today), promoting Russian imperialist and genocidal ideas.[37]

RUSSIAN ACADEMIC DIASPORA AND DISMISSING OF UKRAINE

A former Ukrainian KGB officer also mentioned another demographic and social factor, which influenced all Slavic studies centers in the West, an influx of the representatives of the Russian post-Soviet intellectual elites, who were directly connected to the Soviet government, Soviet academia, and Soviet intelligence service:

Look at the first wave of immigrants of the Russian Soviet scholars to America in the 1980s and the 1990s! All of them were either directly or indirectly connected to the KGB and the GRU. Majority of them now are teaching Soviet and Russian history at the American colleges and universities. Of course, they will promote pro-Russian and anti-Ukrainian ideas and concepts! One of the most influential Sovietologists in the US is a Russian-Jewish scholar Yuri Slezkine. He began his career as a military interpreter of Portuguese for the Soviet military mission in Mozambique. But everybody knows that such a position requires KGB and GRU clearance and connections. It means that eventually Mr. Slezkine brought those connections to America. Why did nobody ask the appropriate questions in the USA about his Russian connections and his pro-Russian position today?[38]

This officer referred to Yuri Slezkine, a professor of Russian history from the University of California, Berkeley. Yuri Slezkine was a son of the famous Soviet Russian historian-Americanist Lev Slezkine (1920–2012), who came from a family of the famous Russian writer, related to the Russian royalist nationalists, some of them were fighting the Bolshevik Soviet regime during the Russian Civil War (1918–1920). Lev Slezkine joined the Communist party and made a remarkable career as an expert of Latin America, visiting Cuba twice, and then writing about colonial British America during the late 1980s in the prestigious research institutes of the USSR Academy of Science in Moscow. Yuri Slezkine's Jewish mother, Karma Goldstein, came from the family of famous Communist Jewish activist and writer Moisei Goldstein, who migrated from Argentina to the Soviet Russia to help "build socialism there."[39] As a result of these family connections, Yuri Slezkine became a part of the Soviet Communist elite in Moscow. To some extent, he used some details of his biography for his two last books, published in the US in 2004 and 2017.[40] After finishing the philology department of Moscow State University, Yuri Slezkine was sent as a military interpreter of Portuguese with a Soviet military mission to Mozambique in Africa, where he spent 1978 and 1979. In 1982, he moved to Lisbon, Portugal, using a marriage to a Portuguese national as an official pretext to his emigration. In 1983, Yuri Slezkine moved to the US, where he joined a PhD program at the University of Texas, Austin, with Professor Sheila Fitzpatrick as his dissertation adviser.[41] After defending his dissertation about the history of "small nations" of Soviet Siberia in 1989, he began teaching at Wake Forest University in North Carolina, and then got a teaching position in 1992 at the University of California, Berkeley.[42]

Despite his publications, which criticized the Soviet Empire, Slezkine, eventually, after 2022, avoided an open criticism of Putin's Russian imperialism and the Russian imperialist war against Ukraine. In October 2022, Yuri Slezkine argued that the West maintains unity in part by characterizing Russia as "evil," noting "where would the West be without it?" He also alluded to the supposedly controversial ideas in Ukraine "which do not sit well" with the Western views: "Ukrainian nationalist ideology is in many ways the opposite of what we are taught in the United States or in the Western Europe."[43] Moreover, an FSB-created organization, the Valdai Discussion

Club, which supported pro-Russian intellectuals from the West, using them for promoting Russian geopolitical interests, awarded Slezkine with the Valdai Club award in 2020.[44] As former Ukrainian KGB officers joked, "The Russian KGB organization—Valdai Discussion Club—supported only their allies in Western academia, such as John J. Mearsheimer and Marlene Laruelle, American political scientists, who blamed the West for the war in Ukraine; and Slezkine was one of those Russian allies."[45] Moreover, Slezkine keeps traveling in Russia during the Russian war against Ukraine, delivering his public lectures about "the end of Western civilization," blaming the West (and especially the United States where he used to teach Russian history) for supporting Ukraine. He did this during his presentations on April 27, 2023, at the European University in St. Petersburg, and on May 12, 2023, at the Yeltsin Center in Yekaterinburg, and in many other locations in the Russian Federation, still introducing himself as "a professor of history from the University of California, Berkeley."[46]

Moscow intellectual immigrants, like Slezkine, represented the most prestigious centers of academic research and education in Soviet Russia, such as Moscow State University, and various research institutes of the USSR Academy of Sciences, including such infamous "spy institutes" like ISKAN in Moscow. All those Moscow academic centers were, and still are, the promoters of Russian academic imperialism. A majority of the first wave of those Russian Soviet academic emigrants to the West came from those Moscow academic centers, bringing their own personal KGB connections and influences. Many of those Moscow scholars from ISKAN eventually settled in the US, Canada, and the UK. I have already mentioned the story of Vladislav Zubok, whose first contacts with US scholars were sanctioned and permitted by ISKAN KGB supervisors during 1987. Eventually, Zubok got a teaching position as professor of history at Temple University in Philadelphia.[47] Nowadays, Professor Zubok, who has been teaching international history at the London School of Economics since 2013, took a pro-Russian position, trying to avoid any public criticism of Putin's war against Ukraine, and to stay away from the public mentioning of Russian war crimes and Russian atrocities against Ukrainians in his academic discussions of late socialism and the collapse of the Soviet Union with his Western colleagues during 2022–2023. On the eve of the Russian invasion in Ukraine, on December 28, 2021, Nick Schifrin, a PBS (American public television) journalist, interviewed Zubok as an author of the recently published book on the collapse of the Soviet Union, expecting that he would give the honest evaluation of Putin's plan for aggression against the Russian neighbor Ukraine, as an attempt of a restoration of the USSR. Zubok did not answer this question and suggested "the historians to fight over the past," avoiding any criticism of Putin, who "was massing [Russian] troops on Ukraine's border."[48] Such an attitude toward Ukraine, ignoring an obvious growing of the anti-Ukrainian hatred among Russian political elites by the beginning of 2022, and later on, avoiding any public criticism of the Russian atrocities against the Ukrainians, became the major feature of public activities of Vladislav Zubok, whose academic functions require the truthful covering of the events of the crimes against humanity committed by the Russian Federation, by the country of Zubok's origin, where his family still resides and whom he visits at least once a year.

Ironically, both MGU graduates, Slezkine and Zubok, not only shared their alma mater, which had a lot of "the KGB people" among MGU faculty, their teachers, such as Professor Nikolai Sivachev, Zubok's mentor and supervisor during his undergraduate studies, but also had the similar personal connections to the Soviet/Russian intelligence: Slezkine, via his career of the Soviet military interpreter in Africa, and Zubok, through his career at "the spy institute" of ISKAN and his connections with an ISKAN's KGB "curator" and KGB officer Radomir Bogdanov.[49] Still, Zubok, in contrast to Slezkine, tried to revise his position, and, as a decent scholar, in various roundtables about the Russian war against Ukraine, recently he began criticizing Putin and distancing himself from Slezkine, his Muscovite historian colleague.[50]

Another MGU graduate and Muscovite, Elena Osokina, Professor of Russian History at the University of South Carolina, had no such business connections to Soviet/Russian intelligence, like Slezkine and Zubok, but she still avoided any mention of Ukraine, despite the fact that her original research was about the Stalinist system of power and economy in the USSR, including the mass famine among Soviet peasants. Even her first, and the best, study of Stalinism, published in post-Soviet Russia in 1999, and based on the original archival documents, completely ignored Holodomor in Ukraine. She never mentioned the millions of Ukrainian peasants who became the victims of the Stalinist campaign of collectivization and procurement of grain for the Soviet state in 1929–1932.[51] Paradoxically, according to her MGU classmates, Osokina's first Russian husband was Sergei Semichev, a KGB officer, who helped her obtain the rare secret Soviet documents about Stalin's politics from Moscow archives.[52] Like Slezkine, Osokina, who has her family in Russia, traveled there during the bloody Russian war against Ukraine, making public presentations in June-July 2023 in Moscow, Kazan, and St. Petersburg about her recent book about Stalinist history, without even mentioning the Russian war crimes in Ukraine.[53]

This approach of "silence about Ukraine" is typical for almost all representatives of Russian academic elites, who settled in the West, and who are now teaching Russian and Soviet history/studies there. My former classmate from Johns Hopkins University graduate school, Anna Krylova, now an Associate Professor of Modern Russian History at Duke University, is another example of such a Muscovite. Originally coming from the

Communist Party/Soviet government elite from Moscow, and educated as a philologist there, she moved to Philadelphia in 1991, tried to get a degree in political science at Drexel University, and then moved to Baltimore in 1995, where she, eventually, became a graduate student of Jeffrey Brooks at the Department of History at the Johns Hopkins University. After her graduation from Johns Hopkins in 2001, she had a successful academic career, doing her original research on Soviet women in WWII, and then on human agency in history and a history of socialism.[54] Still, she had never mentioned Ukraine or Ukrainian women fighting Germans in WWII in her research, despite the significant role of Ukrainians in the socialist experiment and in the Soviet victory over fascism. Moreover, despite the anti-Russian and pro-Ukrainian position of her mentor, Jeffrey Brooks, after 2013, she always tried to avoid the discussions of the Russian atrocities committed by Putin's regime against Ukrainians. Paradoxically, Daniel Walkowitz, the husband of Judith Walkowitz, Krylova's Johns Hopkins University adviser and close friend, devoted some of his research work to a history of the working class of Ukraine and to the Ukrainian workers.[55] Krylova knew about Daniel Walkowitz's research, but she always kept silent about Ukraine, and never criticized the war crimes committed by the Russian political regime against the Ukrainian workers and the Ukrainian women, who were raped and tortured by the Russian soldiers in 2022–2023.

Unfortunately, a majority of Russian scholars who migrated from post-Soviet Russia, not just Muscovites, but also representatives of the Russian provinces, like Serguei Oushakine (originally from Altai, now at Princeton University) and Alexey Golubev (originally from Karelia, now at the University of Houston), who came with the more recent wave of post-Soviet academic emigration after Slezkine and Zubok, still keep silent about the Russian war crimes and Russian imperialism in the post-Soviet geopolitical space. Still, a few Russian scholars, like Andrei Znamenski (University of Memphis, US) and Alexander Etkind (Central European University, Vienna, Austria), who emigrated to the West and teach Russian history and culture there, openly criticize Putin's regime and its war against Ukraine and in their innovative research, and who are analyzing "the post-socialist Russia's attack on modernity."[56]

In 2005, Nikolai Bolkhovitinov, a Russian Soviet historian-Americanist and author of path-breaking studies about the beginnings of Russian-American relations, joked about Russian historians in both the US and in post-Soviet Russia:

> Nothing has changed in the Russian intellectual mindset of our specialists in American history since the times of Nicholas I. These people still dream about the restoration of the strong imperial Russian state, despising their Slavic

brothers in Ukraine and Belarus' and hating "imperialist" America, which in their imagination served the image of a Russian enemy, at least since 1917. They developed a so-called "imperial complex," which affected not only Western academia, where they found their new intellectual niche, but also the entire Russian academia, especially the humanities, including Russian *Amerikanistika* (American Studies).[57]

During the mid-1970s, as he later recalled, Ukrainian Americanist historian Arnold Shlepakov encountered manifestations of Russian nationalism among his Moscow and Leningrad colleagues:

> For many years, during my visits to Moscow, I was used to a more relaxed, liberal, and even cosmopolitan atmosphere in Moscow, especially during unofficial meetings with Russian intellectuals. I still recalled how open-minded and sympathetic toward us, the guests from Kyiv, were our colleagues, namely [Georgi] Arbatov, [Nikolai] Inozemtsev, [Nikolai] Bolkhovitinov, [Grigorii] Sevost'ianov and [Valerii] Tishkov. But at the same time, I noticed a rise in strange anti-Ukrainian and anti-Semitic Russian nationalism among a few of my colleagues who were Americanists. Certain phrases or observations made in my presence by Nikolai Sivachev from Moscow and Aleksandr Fursenko from Leningrad, regarding the "humiliation of Great Russia and Russian culture" in Soviet domestic politics and about the omnipresence of *"khokhly"* [a Russian derogatory slur for Ukrainians —SZh.]—ranging from Brezhnev to the leadership of the Soviet Academy of Sciences—put me on immediate guard. Moreover, they constantly criticized the "total domination of Soviet American Studies by the *evreiskaia shaika* [Jewish gang] from ISKAN," led by "the big Jew" Arbatov. I even complained about this to the first [KGB] department of our Institute in Kyiv. But in 1975, nobody paid attention to my complaints about the expressions of Great Russian chauvinism among my Moscow colleagues.[58]

As another Ukrainian historian-Americanist, Leonid Leshchenko, has noted, during the 1980s, Shlepakov never forgot "Sivachev's Great Russian chauvinism," and over time he became more careful in his communication with "Muscovites." He tried to distance himself from Sivachev's Moscow State University students who began playing an important role in the studies of the US political system and international relations.[59]

At the same time, Leonid Leshchenko began distancing himself from his Moscow colleagues as well. On occasion, he even felt offended by the open expression of condescension and contempt demonstrated by Americanists from MGU, ISKAN, and other Moscow centers devoted to American studies. As Leshchenko recalled in October 1991, "instead of a word of advice, which we could have used in Kyiv from our Russian colleagues in Moscow, we Ukrainian scholars often received unsubstantiated and condescending criticism of our proposals when Moscow experts simply disregarded our archival findings in Canada or the United States." During his visits to Moscow, Leshchenko witnessed overt public expression of Russian nationalism and anti-Semitism when, for example, during one such visit he overheard Sivachev complaining to his MGU colleagues that "those Jews and Ukrainians came here and overcrowded Moscow, controlling ISKAN and the Institute of World History." Eventually, he realized that Sivachev was complaining about Arbatov's leadership of ISKAN and the frequent visits to Moscow by Semion Appatov from Odesa (both Arbatov and Appatov were Jewish–Ukrainians). Paradoxically, Sivachev and his MGU colleagues, although anti-Semites, tried to be "very polite and civilized with American visiting scholars (such as Eric Foner), who were of Jewish origin," while at the same time they "openly despised the Ukrainian and Russian Jews from Soviet Ukraine." According to Leshchenko, he could still recall when he felt "unfriendly attitudes toward Ukrainian scholars from Kyiv," which were demonstrated by two Russian historians who were the organizers of American studies in the Soviet Union. One of these historians was Aleksandr Fursenko from Leningrad, while the other historian was Nikolai Sivachev from Moscow. As Leshchenko revealed in 1991,

[He] could remember only four Muscovites who were respectful towards their Ukrainian colleagues, who always tried to assist Ukrainian visitors and invited Ukrainian Americanists to participate in the compilation of Moscow publications devoted to American Studies. These were Arbatov from ISKAN, Inozemtsev from IMEMO, Bolkhovitinov from the Institute of World History and Tishkov from the Institute of Ethnography. In striking contrast to them, Fursenko (from Leningrad), Sivachev, Dementiev and Krasnov (from Moscow), who travelled to the US with Ukrainian colleagues, had always distanced themselves from Soviet Ukrainians and showed only condescension and disrespect to us. . . . Of course, I knew about Shlepakov's official complaint regarding Fursenko's and Sivachev's Great Russian chauvinism and their anti-Semitism. He filed this complaint with our KGB supervisors (from the international department) as early as 1975. But I did not follow Shlepakov's example. I did not complain officially, I simply tried to distance myself from my Moscow colleagues and concentrate on my own research in Kyiv.[60]

It is noteworthy that American colleagues in their official reports also noted expressions of "Russian nationalism," authoritarian "Stalinist" mentality, and an "exclusive" cultural mission among Soviet visitors to the US. As I mentioned before, one of Fursenko's American hosts described this manifestation of Fursenko's Russian nationalist "Stalinist" identity in the following way: "I found him [Fursenko] occasionally too Russian, almost Stalinist, sometimes too abrupt in his manners, too harsh in his judgments, too convinced of his mission and importance, too inconsiderate and inflexible, even arrogant when his work was at stake, impatient, yet trying very hard to be thoughtful."[61] Sivachev's American colleagues also noticed demonstrations of "Stalinist Russian anti-Semitic nationalism" in private conversations with Sivachev who behaved like "a stout Russian nationalist (although ethnically he is a Mordovian)."[62]

By the 1980s, some former Russian liberal scholars, such as Vladimir Lukin, who were protected by Arbatov in ISKAN from KGB persecution, also expressed Slavophile, Russian imperialist, and anti-Ukrainian views, similar to what Sivachev considered "normal Russian patriotism." Later, these Slavophile-Americanists became known as "Russian *derzhavniki* (state-builders)."[63]

But overall, during Khrushchev's thaw, through Brezhnev's détente and Gorbachev's perestroika, Westernizing concepts of American history became the prevailing trend in Soviet academia. This process was interrupted by humiliation during Boris Yeltsin's presidency and Putin's authoritarianism. The post-Soviet Russian state, with a Russian nationalist and state ideology, pushed Americanist-Westernizers to the margins of post-Soviet academia. Their place was taken by Slavophile *pochvenniki* (those who advocated a return to the "native soil") and *derzhavniki* interpretations of the American past that came to dominate historical perceptions of the US in Putin's Russia. Moreover, the traditional Soviet legacy of confrontational discourse in American studies and a tendency to view Western allies, including Americans, as unreliable replaced the discourse of cultural dialogue and mutual understanding. In his final notes, written in April 2005, Nikolai Bolkhovitinov again complained about the strong role of the post-Soviet Russian authoritarian state that had destroyed the creativity and autonomy of post-Soviet scholars and restored the "traditional Soviet state business" in the field of American studies:

> [Here in Russia] the same authoritarian regime survived without any significant changes. Our rich country remains an object of looting [by politicians]. There is no hope for progress in the social sciences and humanities. In the field of history, we have the same old leaders such as A. Fursenko and worse G. N. Sevost'ianov, who is 89 years old and still rules historical scholarship [in Russia]. . . . Now we no longer have communist party committees but the political situation in our country has not changed much [compared to Soviet times]. Putin's United Russia party is becoming more like the former monolithic CPSU [Communist Party of the Soviet Union].[64]

Since 1990s, a few talented post-Soviet Americanists became actively engaged in the development of university-level American studies programs, keeping alive Russian–American scholarly dialogue and fighting popular anti-Americanism by making frank statements to the mass media. Unfortunately, they faced manifold challenges due to the worsening Russian–American relations. On the one hand, the demand for professional knowledge about the United States in Russia is fast diminishing and American studies programs in Russia are being closed down. The post-Soviet authorities no longer need their consultations and expert opinions, unlike during the Soviet period. On the other hand, mass anti-American xenophobia is on the rise, and the Russian Putin's regime made it one of the cornerstones of the country's national identity. Now this anti-Americanism is promoted not only by political journalists without professional training who pretend to be experts in everything related to the US, but also by the Russian Americanists as well. An overwhelming majority of post-Soviet Russian scholars, including Americanists, took anti-American, Russian imperialist position.[65]

"State business" (ideologically serving the Russian state) is a prominent trend among post-Soviet scholars. Many post-Soviet Americanists in contemporary Russia, such as Andranik Migranian, have revived the "confrontational" position toward the US, blaming Americans for "creating" domestic and international problems for the Russian state. Some of them not only became official advisers to Yeltsin's and Putin's administrations, but they also play an active role as "state-builders" in Putin's nationalistic Russia. Even their children, like sons of Soviet Americanist Fursenko, not only became the personal friends of President Putin, but also actively shape politics of post-Soviet Russian imperialism.[66] As in the nineteenth century, the state (currently it is Putin's nationalist autocracy) dominates Russian interpretations of US history and politics. Meanwhile, post-Soviet Americanists, such as Viacheslav Nikonov, continue to call on Russian politicians to "resist by all available means" the "American threat" and fight "American domination and expansion in post-Soviet Ukraine."[67]

CONCLUSION

Paradoxically, Ukrainophobia in both Western and post-Soviet Russian academia was and still remains rooted in the old "imperialist epistemological complex" of Russian and Soviet history, which has influenced the humanities and social sciences in Russia and the West. Moreover, this epistemological complex was reinforced by both a significant influx of immigrant scholars from the Soviet geopolitical space into Western academia and by the rise of Soviet nostalgia among Western and post-Soviet academics who could not imagine the existence of an independent Ukraine because it would destroy their "Russian and Soviet imperialist complex" as well as challenging their nostalgic feelings for the Soviet past.

As a result, "inconvenient" facts about Ukrainian history have largely gone ignored by Western historians of the Soviet Union today, even at a time of open Russian war against independent Ukraine. Moreover, this anti-Ukrainian approach was rooted in the old KGB traditions to present the Ukrainian independence movement as "fascist," "anti-Soviet" operations run by Western (mainly American) intelligence services and funded by the Ukrainian "fascist" diaspora. Overall, through the entire Cold War, and even today, Soviet/Russian intelligence has attempted to persuade Western audiences that the Ukrainian diaspora and the entire Ukrainian movement for independence were organized by the followers of Stepan Bandera and by the "fascist" Ukrainian collaborators with the Nazis during World War II, who fled to America and who were used by the American intelligence agencies in various American "imperialist wars" against the Soviet Union, and now against the Russian Federation.[68]

Through the various KGB (and now Russian intelligence) operations in the West, Soviet/Russian intelligence agents and their "useful assets" in Western academia and media spread this disinformation about Ukraine, trying to discredit its history and culture, and justify the Russian aggression among the Western public. The peak of this blatant rejection of the independent Ukrainian history, separate from Russia, was presented in July 2021 in a historiographic essay "On the Historical Unity of Russians and Ukrainians," written by the former KGB operative Vladimir Putin, who, as President of the Russian Federation, on February 24, 2022, started a bloody war against independent Ukraine, trying to implement in practice his "historiographic imperialism."[69]

The new developments demonstrate that Russian intelligence (even after the beginning of the war against Ukraine) still continues to influence the American public (including academics) with a pro-Russian narrative of teaching, blaming Ukrainians "being racists and fascists." On April 18, 2023, the FBI announced on its website that "a federal grand jury in Tampa, Florida, returned a superseding indictment charging four U.S. citizens and three Russian nationals with working on behalf of the Russian government and in conjunction with the Russian Federal Security Service (FSB) to conduct a multi-year foreign malign influence campaign in the United States . . . to sow discord and spread pro-Russian propaganda."[70]According to the FBI investigation, "Aleksandr Viktorovich Ionov, a resident of Moscow, was the founder and president of the Anti-Globalization Movement of Russia (AGMR), an organization headquartered in Moscow, Russia, and funded by the Russian government." Ionov allegedly "utilized AGMR to carry out Russia's malign influence campaign. Ionov's influence efforts were allegedly directed and supervised by Moscow-based FSB officers, including indicted defendants Aleksey Borisovich Sukhodolov and Yegor Sergeyevich Popov."

[From] at least November 2014 until July 2022, Ionov allegedly engaged in a years-long foreign malign influence campaign targeting the United States. As a part of the campaign, Ionov allegedly recruited members of political groups within the United States, including the African People's Socialist Party and the Uhuru Movement (collectively, the APSP) in Florida, Black Hammer in Georgia, and a political group in California (referred to in the superseding indictment as U.S. Political Group 3), to participate in the influence campaign and act as agents of Russia in the United States.[71]

Moreover, these people tried to use the local American schools to promote anti-American and anti-Ukrainian propaganda, especially among Afro-American students, presenting Ukrainians as "racists and fascists":

> One focus of Ionov's alleged influence operation was to create the appearance of American popular support for Russia's annexation of territories in Ukraine. For example, in May 2020, Ionov allegedly sent a request he stated was from "Russia, the Donetsk People's Republic"—an apparent reference to a Russian-occupied region in eastern Ukraine—to Omali Yeshitela, a U.S. citizen residing in St. Petersburg, Florida, and members of other U.S. political groups to make statements in support of the independence of the so-called Donetsk People's Republic, a Russian-backed breakaway state in eastern Ukraine. Ionov later allegedly touted to the FSB that Yeshitela's video-recorded statement of support was the first time that "American nonprofit organizations congratulated citizens" of the occupied region . . . Ionov's use of the APSP to promote Russian propaganda relating to Ukraine allegedly continued after Russia's invasion of Ukraine. On the day Russia invaded Ukraine, Feb. 24, 2022, Ionov allegedly emailed Jesse Nevel, a U.S. citizen residing in St. Petersburg, Florida, an "URGENT MESSAGE" which contained pro-Russian talking points in support of the invasion. Thereafter, throughout March 2022, the APSP repeatedly hosted Ionov via video conference to discuss the war, during which Ionov falsely stated that anyone who supported Ukraine also supported Naziism and white supremacy, and Yeshitela and another APSP member allegedly made statements of solidarity with the Russian government.[72]

Another FBI case was opened in the spring of 2023 against "Russian national Natalia Burlinova, a resident of Moscow, who conspired with an FSB officer to recruit U.S. citizens from academic and research institutions to travel to Russia to participate in a public diplomacy program called Meeting Russia." This program "was operated by PICREADI, a Russian organization led by Burlinova, funded by the Russian government and devoted to promoting Russian national interests."[73] As the FBI investigation noted,

> The FSB officer provided funding and other support for Burlinova's foreign recruitment and her efforts to advance Russian interests in the United States.

In return, Burlinova provided the FSB officer with extensive information about U.S. citizens who were recruited to attend her programs, including their résumés, passport information, photographs, and analyses of their views toward Russia. Burlinova further identified for the FSB officer particular U.S. citizens who, in Burlinova's view, had expressed positive attitudes towards Russia and were prepared to continue to collaborate. During a recruitment trip to the United States in fall 2018, Burlinova met with U.S. citizens at various universities and research institutions and provided to photographs of her meetings to the FSB officer. The FSB officer used the information Burlinova provided prepare FSB intelligence reports. Burlinova never notified the Attorney General of these efforts or otherwise disclosed to the public that her recruitment efforts were supported and funded by a Russian security service.[74]

To some extent, the FSB followed the old KGB scenario from the Cold War era to discredit Ukrainian nationalism as fascism and racism, using Afro-Americans for their special operations.[75] Even today, during the bloody Russian war against Ukraine, the Russian born academics and Russian intelligence still fight for isolating and diminishing the geopolitical role of independent Ukraine, by justifying the anti-Ukrainian diplomacy and Russian aggression not only in their propaganda, but also in their history writing, which still promotes the old Russian imperialist narrative.

Finally, the Ukrainian historians began fighting with this Russian academic imperialism for restoring the correct historical portrayal of the geopolitics of Ukraine in post-Soviet history writing. At the end of November of 2023, led by Timothy Snyder, professor of history at Yale University, and by Serhii Plokhy, professor of history at Harvard University, and using the financial support of Ukrainian oligarch Victor Pinchuk, "90 international and Ukrainian historians are coming together under the umbrella of the new London-based Ukrainian History Global Initiative to wrest Ukraine's past from the shadow of Russian and Soviet narratives." This initiative will be "a major new project in the humanities, social sciences, and sciences, with the goal of establishing a scholarly and accessible presentation of the deep history of the lands of contemporary Ukraine and the peoples who have inhabited them. It aims to generate a new model of synthetic public history."[76]

NOTES

1. According to the Budapest Treaty of 1994, Russia, the UK, and the US promised to respect Ukraine's borders in accordance with the principles of the Final Act of the Conference on Security and Co-Operation in Europe, to abstain from the use or threat of force against Ukraine, to support Ukraine where an attempt is made to place

pressure on it by economic coercion, and to bring any incident of aggression by a nuclear power before the United Nations Security Council.

2. I had already tried to discuss some issues of this divide in both English and Russian languages: Sergei I. Zhuk, "Ukrainian Maidan as the Last Anti-Soviet Revolution, or the Methodological Dangers of Soviet Nostalgia (Notes of an American Ukrainian Historian from Inside the Field of Russian Studies in the USA)," in *Ab Imperio*, no. 3 (2014): 195–208; and idem, "Ukrainian Maidan and Epistemological Dangers of Soviet Nostalgia," *Historians.in.ua* website, April 6, 2015, see http://www.historians.in.ua/index.php/en/dyskusiya/1482-sergej-zhuk-ukrainskij-majdan-i-epistemologicheskie-opasnosti-sovetskoj-nostal-gii.

3. I described this personal experience of mine in Zhuk, *Soviet Americana: The Cultural History of Russian and Ukrainian Americanists* (London and New York: I.B. Tauris, 2018 [London and New York: Bloomsbury Publishing, 2019] [paperback: September 2019]), 214, 216, 229–230.

4. I quote Boris Shpotov, speaking during the International Conference in Connection with the Bicentennial of the Russian-American Company, 1799–1999: Institute of World History, Russian Academy of Sciences, Moscow, September 7, 1999.

5. I quote Dr Sviatoslav Dmitriev, Associate Professor of Ancient History at Ball State University, my Russian colleague (originally from Moscow), who took a very pro-Putin, anti-Ukrainian, Russian chauvinistic position in our discussion of the Ukrainian-Russian crisis, on January 30, 2014, in Muncie, Indiana.

6. I refer to Sergei I. Zhuk, *Russia's Lost Reformation: Peasants, Millennialism and Radical Sects in Southern Russia and Ukraine, 1830–1917* (Baltimore, MD: Johns Hopkins University Press; Washington, D.C.: Woodrow Wilson Center Press, 2004).

7. I quote my interview with Richard Stites, Philadelphia, at the 40th National Convention of the American Association for Advanced Slavic Studies, November 21, 2008. Compare with various case studies in Samuel H. Baron and Cathy A. Frierson (eds), *Adventures in Russian Historical Research: Reminiscences of American Scholars from the Cold War to the Present* (Armonk, NY: M.E. Sharpe, 2003).

8. I refer to Sergei I. Zhuk, *Rock and Roll in the Rocket City: The West, Identity, and Ideology in Soviet Dniepropetrovsk, 1960–1985* (Baltimore, MD: Johns Hopkins University Press & Washington, D.C.: Woodrow Wilson Center Press, 2010).

9. I quote Dr. Dmitriev, my Russian colleague from the Department of History, Ball State University. I explained to Dmitriev that blaming their opponents in fascism was an old KGB ideological trick. I even shared my own personal experience of my college years in the 1970s. As a DJ of the student disco, I encountered the KGB operatives who tried to criticize the American rock band Kiss for being fascists, despite our explanation that it was a nonsense because of the Jewish origin of some of those musicians, one of whom had a real Jewish "babushka" (grandmother) from Odesa, Ukraine. The KGB people did not listen to us: for them all those fascist acts like Kiss were a product of American conspiracy against the Soviet Union.

10. See "To Ukrainians, Gorbachev Remained an 'Imperialist,'" *Voice of America*, August 31, 2022. Available at https://www.voanews.com/a/to-ukrainians-gorbachev-remains-an-imperialist-/6724612.html.

11. See Robert Mackey, "Russia Could Still Turn U.S. 'Into Radioactive Dust,' News Anchor in Moscow Reminds Viewers," *New York Times*, March 16, 2014. Available at https://archive.nytimes.com/thelede.blogs.nytimes.com/2014/03/16/russia-could-still-turn-the-u-s-into-radioactive-dust-news-anchor-in-moscow-reminds-viewers.

12. Not everybody in Russia supports Putin's policy. Such Russian historians, like Andrei Zubov, and rock musicians, like Andrei Makarevich (and many other Russian intellectuals like writers Boris Akunin, Vladimir Sorokin, and Liudmila Ulitskaia) criticized publicly Putin's aggression against Ukraine.

13. Many Western historians had already described the rise and danger of Russian nationalism and Soviet (post-Soviet) imperialism. See Ben Fowkes, "The National Question in the Soviet Union under Leonid Brezhnev: Policy and Response," in Edwin Bacon and Mark Sandle (eds.), *Brezhnev Reconsidered* (New York: Palgrave Macmillan, 2002), pp. 68–89; Gerhard Simon, *Nationalism and Policy toward the Nationalities in the Soviet Union: From Totalitarian Dictatorship to Post-Stalinist Society*, translated by Karen Forster and Oswald Forster (Boulder: Westview Press, 1991); and Yitzhak M. Brudny, *Reinventing Russia: Russian Nationalism and the Soviet State, 1953–1991* (Cambridge, MA: Harvard University Press, 1998).

14. Of course, many colleagues of mine still addressed these issues. See, e.g., Yitzhak M. Brudny, *Reinventing Russia*.

15. On revisionism in American Soviet studies, see David C. Engerman, *Know Your Enemy: The Rise and Fall of America's Soviet Experts* (New York: Oxford University Press, 2009), pp. 9, 286, 294, 305–08. On the new popularity of cultural studies and on mutual influences between western and former Soviet scholars, see Laura Engelstein, "Culture, Culture Everywhere: Interpretations of Modern Russia, Across the 1991 Divide," *Kritika*, no. 2 (Spring 2001): 363–93. Soviet historians also were influenced by the charismatic medievalist Aron Gurevich who popularized the ideas of the French *Annales* among the Soviet reading audience; see Roger D. Markwick, "Cultural History under Khrushchev and Brezhnev: From Social Psychology to *Mentalités*," *The Russian Review*, vol. 65, no. 2 (April 2006): 283–301. See also Catriona Kelly, Hilary Pilkington, David Shepherd, and Vadim Volkov, "Introduction: Why Cultural Studies," in Catriona Kelly and David Shepherd (eds.), *Russian Cultural Studies: An Introduction* (New York: Oxford University Press, 1998), pp. 1–17.

16. See Engelstein, "Culture, Culture Everywhere," pp. 389ff.

17. Alexei Yurchak, *Everything Was Forever, Until It Was No More: The Last Soviet Generation* (Princeton, NJ: Princeton University Press, 2005), 32.

18. Ibid., 36–76. This thesis had already been criticized and analyzed: Sheila Fitzpatrick in *London Review of Books* vol. 28, no. 10 (May 25, 2006): 18–20; Kevin Platt and Benjamin Nathans in *Novoe literaturnoe obozrenie* no. 101 (2010): 167–84 (in Russian); and Kevin Platt and Benjamin Nathans, "Socialist in Form, Indereterminate in Content: The Ins and Outs of Late Soviet Culture," *Ab Imperio* 2 (2011), pp. 301–23 (in English). Compare with Thomas Cushman, *Notes from the Underground: Rock Music Counterculture in Russia* (New York: SUNY Press, 1995).

19. Michel de Certeau, *The Practice of Everyday Life,* trans. Steven Rendall (Berkeley: University of California Press, 1989 [1st pr.: 1984]), p. 31.

20. As he explained, "For Bakhtin, authoritative discourse coheres around a strict external idea or dogma . . . and occupies a particular position within the discursive regime of a period," while "all other types of discourse are organized around it"; Yurchak, *Everything Was Forever,* p. 14. See especially an American edition of Bakhtin's work with insightful comments: Mikhail Bakhtin, *The Dialogical Imagination: Four Essays by Mikhail Bakhtin,* edited by Michael Holquist (Austin: University of Texas Press, 1994), pp. 342–43. Compare with Slava Gerovitch, *From Newspeak to Cyberspeak: A History of Soviet Cybernetics* (Cambridge, MA: The MIT Press, 2004); Stephen Lovell, *The Russian Reading Revolution: Print Culture in the Soviet and Post-Soviet Eras* (New York: St. Martin's, 2000); and Juliane Fürst, *Stalin's Last Generation: Soviet Post-War Youth and the Emergence of Mature Socialism* (New York: Oxford University Press, 2010).

21. See how various scholars used this metaphor before Yurchak: Gordon K. Lewis, *The Growth of the Modern West Indies* (New York: Monthly Review Press, 1968), pp. 57ff.; and Robert D. English, *Russia and the Idea of the West: Gorbachev, Intellectuals, and the End of the Cold War* (New York: Columbia University Press, 2000), p. 22.

22. Yurchak, *Everything Was Forever,* pp. 34–35, 161–62.

23. See in Tatyana Cherednichenko, *Tipologiia sovetskoi massovoi kul'tury. Mezhdu Brezhnevym i Pugachevoi* (Moscow: RIK Kul'tura, 1994).

24. Most of Yurchak's material and interviews are from the Leningrad area. Moreover, the majority of his material and information came from the educated elite of this city, the loyal representatives of the Soviet middle and upper classes, and conformist Soviet intellectuals from Leningrad. He entirely ignores the working-class youth, the major consumers of heavy metal and adventure films in the Soviet society. Another problem with Yurchak's study is his uncritical attitude to interviews. Many of Yurchak's interviewees tended to idealize or exaggerate their "socialist experience" as a time without conflicts in contrast to the brutal reality of "bandit capitalism" during the Yeltsin era. In many cases, using his "speech acts" approaches, Yurchak took his interviewees' information at face value, uncritically, without checking archival sources. On his methods, see Yurchak, *Everything Was Forever,* pp. 29–33.

25. Even the list of forbidden rock bands, which Yurchak published in his book, came from the Ukrainian provincial town of Nikolaev. With only a few exceptions, all Yurchak's information derived from his hometown, Leningrad/St. Petersburg; see Yurchak, *Everything Was Forever,* pp. 214–15.

26. Author's interview with Richard Stites, Philadelphia, 21 November 2008. For an example of a defense of Yurchak against my criticism, see a review essay by a young Russian scholar: A. V. Golubev, "V poiskakh vnenakhodimosti," *Istoricheskaia ekspertiza* no. 1 (2015), esp. pp. 20–21.

27. Fürst, *Stalin's Last Generation,* p. 26.

28. Ibid., pp. 25, 100, 103, 297, 301, 362. Compare with Elena Zubkova, *Russia after the War: Hopes, Illusions, and Disappointments, 1945–1957,* translated and edited by Hugh Ragdale (Armonk, NY: M. E. Sharpe, 1998).

29. Juliane Fürst, *Flowers through Concrete: Explorations in Soviet Hippieland* (New York: Oxford University Press, 2021). I refer to this Russian edition: Iuliane

Fuerst, *Tsvety, probivshie asfal't: Puteshestvie v Sovetskuiu Xipliandiiu* (Moscow: NLO, 2023) [Цветы, пробившие асфальт: *Путешествие в Советскую Хиппляндию* / Юлиане Фюрст. – М.: Новое литературное обозрение, 2023.]

30. See the most recent and good study of the political satire in Soviet Lithuania, which still used mainly a very idealized Yurchak's theoretical framework: Neringa Klumbyte, *Authoritarian Laughter: Political Humor and Soviet Dystopia in Lithuania* (Ithaca, New York: Cornell University Press, 2022), 7, 43, 48, 80, 86, 155, 189, 216, 223ff.

31. Donald J. Raleigh, *Soviet Baby Boomers: An Oral History of Russia's Cold War Generation* (New York: Oxford University Press, 2012).

32. Donald J. Raleigh (ed.), *Russia's Sputnik Generation: Soviet Baby Boomers Talk about Their Lives* (Bloomington, IN: Indiana University Press, 2006).

33. See information about Professor Raleigh's presentation to the Dniprovsky Historical Club in the city of Dnipro, July 16, 2017. Available at http://tkuma.dp.ua/en/outreach-activities/dniprovsky-historical-club/1602-zanyattya-dniprovskogo-istorichnogo-klubu-z-prof-donaldom-rejli.

34. See especially Alexey Golubev and Olga Smolyak, "Making Selves Through Making Things: Soviet Do-It-Yourself Culture and Practices of Late Soviet Subjectivation," *Cahiers du monde russe*, vol. 54, no. 3–4 (July–December 2013): 517–41.

35. See, as a typical example, a very bad and "Moscow-centered" study by Jeremy Smith, *Red Nations: The Nationalities Experience in and after the USSR* (New York: Cambridge University Press, 2013), and its criticism for his obvious pro-Russian bias by Audrey L. Altstadt in *American Historical Review* vol. 120, no. 1 (February 2015): 358–359.

36. See especially Richard Sakwa, *Frontline Ukraine: Crisis in the Borderlands* (London: I.B. Tauris, 2016); and Nikolai Petro, "Understanding the Other Ukraine: Identity and Allegiance in Russophone Ukraine," in Agnieszka Pikulicka-Wilczewska and Richard Sakwa (eds.), *Ukraine and Russia: People, Politics, Propaganda and Perspectives* (Bristol: E-International Relations, 2015), pp. 19–35.

37. See Tarik Cyril Amar, "Politics, Starvation, and Memory: A Critique of Red Famine," *Kritika*, vol. 20, no. 1 (Winter 2019): 145 and examples such as the following: Tarik Cyril Amar, "Russia Is Right: The West Promised Not to Enlarge NATO and These Promises Were Broken," *RT*, January 15, 2022, available at https://www.rt.com/russia/546074-russia-nato-relations-lie/; and "The Origins of Ukraine's Fascists and Why It Matters, with Historian Tarik Cyril Amar," *BreakThrough News*, April 6, 2022, available at https://www.youtube.com/watch?v=5C7DE2KFJHs. See in detail about Tarik Amar in chapter 5.

38. Interview with Leonid K., a retired KGB officer, March 3, 2019, Kyiv.

39. See Yuri Slezkine, *The Jewish Century* (Princeton: Princeton University Press, 2004), 216, 226–227, 248–249, 272, 286, 310, 361; and a biography of his father in Sergei Zhuk, *Nikolai Bolkhovitinov and American Studies in the USSR: People's Diplomacy in the Cold War* (Lanham, MD and Boulder, CO: Rowman and Littlefield's Lexington Press, 2017), 89, 102, 103, 104, 157, 158, 213, 214; and in Zhuk, *Soviet Americana*, 75, 214.

40. I refer to Yuri Slezkine, *The Jewish Century* and his *The House of Government: A Saga of the Russian Revolution* (Princeton: Princeton University Press, 2017).
41. See https://www.historians.in.ua/index.php/en/intervyu/1180-yuri-slezkine-i-tend-to-do-my-own-things-and-expect-you-to-do-yours. Nikolai Bolkhovitinov, a close friend of Lev Slezkine, told me a story of his son as well. See my interview with Nikolai Bolkhovitinov, July 10, 2005, Moscow, Russia.
42. See https://ru.wikipedia.org/wiki/%D0%A1%D0%BB%D1%91%D0%B7%D0%BA%D0%B8%D0%BD,_%D0%AE%D1%80%D0%B8%D0%B9_%D0%9B%D1%8C%D0%B2%D0%BE%D0%B2%D0%B8%D1%87_(%D1%8D%D1%82%D0%BD%D0%BE%D0%B3%D1%80%D0%B0%D1%84); https://en.wikipedia.org/wiki/Yuri_Slezkine.
43. I quote his phrases from https://www.youtube.com/watch?v=uQGWpgjDiSs.
44. See https://valdaiclub.com/events/posts/articles/yuri-slezkine-author-of-the-book-the-house-of-government-is-winner-/?sphrase_id=1575974.
45. Interview with Leonid K., a retired KGB officer, July 30, 2021, Kyiv, Ukraine.
46. See https://eusp.org/events/lekciya-ocherednoy-i-na-etot-raz-okonchatelnyy-zakat-zapadnoy-civilizacii; and https://ru.wikipedia.org/wiki/%D0%A1%D0%BB%D1%91%D0%B7%D0%BA%D0%B8%D0%BD,_%D0%AE%D1%80%D0%B8%D0%B8%D0%B9_%D0%9B%D1%8C%D0%B2%D0%BE%D0%B2%D0%B8%D1%87_(%D1%8D%D1%82%D0%BD%D0%BE%D0%B3%D1%80%D0%B0%D1%84).
47. I used my conversation with Zubok, when he admitted how ISKAN officials and KGB officers assigned him to work with American academic guests in Moscow and sent him with the similar assignment to the US in 1987. See Sergei I. Zhuk, *Nikolai Bolkhovitinov and American Studies in the USSR*, 234–235, and ibid., *Soviet Americana*, 234–235.
48. See a transcript of this PBS interview in https://www.pbs.org/newshour/show/how-russia-is-trying-to-erase-its-soviet-past-in-bid-for-geo-political-strength.
49. See Sergei I. Zhuk, *Nikolai Bolkhovitinov*, 234. All former KGB officers, whom I interviewed in 2019, confirmed that a position of Soviet interpreter for the Soviet military mission abroad (like Yuri Slezkine's case) required the obligatory GRU connections.
50. See Vladislav Zubok, "The Roots of Invasion," in Roundtable "The War in Ukraine" with James Ellison, Michael Cox, Jussi M. Hanhimäki, Hope M. Harrison, N. Piers Ludlow, Angela Romano, Kristina Spohr and Vladislav Zubok, *Cold War History*, vol. 23, no. 1 (2023): 121–206, esp. 193–205.
51. I refer to her book, Elena Osokina, *Our Daily Bread: Socialist Distribution and the Art of Survival in Stalin's Russia, 1927–1941*, edited by Kate Transchel, translated by Kate Transchel and Greta Bucher (Armonk, New York: M.E. Sharpe, 2001), which was a translation of her Russian monograph: *Za fasadom "Stalinskogo izobilia": Raspredelenie i rynok v snabzhenii naseleniia v gody industrializatsii 1927–1941* (Moscow, ROSSPEN, 1999). American translation of this book was confusing, because this book was not about purely Russian, but rather Soviet distribution economic market.
52. I refer to my conversation with Dr. Mikhail Dmitriev, MGU Professor of History, July 16, 2008, Moscow, Russia.

53. See, e.g., official announcement about her public presentation in Moscow on June 29, 2023 at https://www.podpisnie.ru/events/256269/?fbclid=IwAR2CFCJ7YZFgeOJB0UPGOG5Qx8kn_fzaQkXm6qS_8DvQskR4eUfdfvZobFI.

54. Besides my numerous conversations with Anna Krylova in Baltimore during 1997–2000, I refer also to her interviews with Duke University's journalists: https://today.duke.edu/2010/11/sovietwomen.html. See also https://scholars.duke.edu/person/anna.krylova.

55. I refer to Lewis Siegelbaum and Daniel Walkowitz, *Workers of the Donbass Speak: Survival and Identity in the New Ukraine, 1989–1992* (New York: SUNY Press, 1995).

56. I refer to their recent books: Andrei Znamenski, *Socialism as a Secular Creed: A Modern Global History* (Lanham, MD: Lexington Books, 2022); Alexander Etkind, *Russia Against Modernity* (New York: Polity, 2023).

57. Interview with Nikolai Bolkhovitinov, July 10, 2005, Moscow, Russia.

58. Author's interview with Arnold M. Shlepakov, Kyiv, April 4, 1991.

59. Author's interview with Leonid Leshchenko, Kyiv, June 25, 2013.

60. I quote my interviews with Leonid Leshchenko, Berlin, Kennedy Institute, Free University Berlin, November 1–3, 1991.

61. Library of Congress. IREX Papers (Hereafter—LC. IREX), RC 21, F 109, letter by Theodore Von Laue, May 15, 1973, pp. 1–2. And he finished his letter with the phrase, "Poor man: his visit in the U.S. was so hectic, too much to be observed and digested! I wonder how he feels now, back in Leningrad, with all his presents and his memories . . . "

62. LC. IREX. RC 21, F 17, Vladimir Petrov's letter of 3 February 1975, p. 2.

63. Russian historian Robert Ivanov mentioned this in 1991. See also Robert English, *Russia and the Idea of the West*, pp. 236–237.

64. Nikolai N. Bolkhovitinov, *Vospominaniia* (Moscow, 2005), unpublished, typewritten manuscript of 62 pages, which begins with the crossed-out title "Schastlivaia pora detstva," pp. 60, 61, 62.

65. See ibid., p. 62.

66. Among numerous publications of former Soviet Americanists in Russia, see E. Ia. Batalov, M. G. Noskov, *Amerika, Evropa, Rossiia v transatelnticheskom prostranstve* (Moscow: In-t Evropy: Rus. souvenir, 2009); and Andranik Migranian, "Putin Triumphs in Ukraine," *The National Interest*, March 6, 2014. On the role of Andranik Migranian as an adviser to both Presidents Yeltsin and Putin, see Eugeniusz Górski, *Civil Society, Pluralism and Universalism (Polish Philosophical Studies, VIII)* (Washington, DC: The Council for Research in Values and Philosophy, 2007), pp. 57, 58, 61.

67. V. A. Nikonov, *Sovremennyi mir i ego istoki* (Moscow: Izd-vo universitea, 2015), pp. 371–80, 427–46.

68. See about this in detail in Sergei I. Zhuk, *KGB Operations against the USA and Canada in Soviet Ukraine, 1953–1991* (London and New York: Routledge, 2022). Compare with the best description of Russia's war against Ukraine in Luke Harding, *Invasion: The Inside Story of Russia's Bloody War and Ukraine's Fight for Survival*

(New York: Vintage Books, 2022) and Serhii Plokhy, *The Russo-Ukrainian War: The Return of History* (New York: W.W. Norton, 2023). Compare with the best geopolitical analysis in Jim Sciutto, *The Return of Great Powers: Russia, China, and The Next World War* (New York: Dutton, 2024).

69. Vladimir Putin's essay is "On the Historical Unity of Russians and Ukrainians," published on the official Kremlin site on July 12, 2021. Available at http://en.kremlin.ru/events/president/news/66181. See also about this in Harding, *Invasion*, pp. 23–26. Compare with Serhii Plokhy, *The Russo-Ukrainian War*, 214–216.

70. See the detailed information on the FBI site: https://www.justice.gov/opa/pr/us-citizens-and-russian-intelligence-officers-charged-conspiring-use-us-citizens-illegal. See also an article by Mike Eckel: https://www.rferl.org/a/russia-fsb-fbi-burlinova-arrest-warrant-spying/32373997.html. Compare with article by Julian Barnes "Russia Pushes Long-Term Influences Operations Aimed at the U.S. and Europe," https://www.nytimes.com/2023/08/25/us/politics/russia-intelligence-propaganda.html.

71. See https://www.justice.gov/opa/pr/us-citizens-and-russian-intelligence-officers-charged-conspiring-use-us-citizens-illegal.

72. See https://www.justice.gov/opa/pr/us-citizens-and-russian-intelligence-officers-charged-conspiring-use-us-citizens-illegal.

73. See the website of this organization: https://www.picreadi.com.

74. See https://www.justice.gov/opa/pr/us-citizens-and-russian-intelligence-officers-charged-conspiring-use-us-citizens-illegal.

75. See chapter 4 about the KGB using Afro-American students against American Ukrainians in 1982.

76. See https://uhgi.org. See also https://www.theguardian.com/world/2023/nov/29/historians-come-together-to-wrest-ukraines-past-out-of-russias-shadow#:~:text=Now%2C%2090%20international%20and%20Ukrainian,of%20Russian%20and%20Soviet%20narratives.

Chapter 7

"The Agents of Influence"

Post-Soviet Oligarchs, Russian Intelligence Service, and Slavic Studies Centers in the West

"What many historians forgot nowadays is the role of the so-called agents of influence of the Putin's intelligence service in western academia," one retired Ukrainian KGB officer noted. And he continued,

> Since the beginning of their history, all the most prestigious academic centers of research in the West, like the Wilson Center in the USA, became the target for the KGB operations as early as 1968. Now the Russian intelligence is using the new money of post-Soviet oligarchs, following the same tradition of influencing this organization in pro-Russian direction. Another old KGB tradition was influencing various international organizations for Slavic Studies, especially in the United States. After the collapse of the Soviet Union, Russian intelligence continues the same politics with only one difference—with more financial capital, money, which the Russian agents use for influencing the "useful" pro-Russian representatives in western academia. At the same time, Putin and his comrades use the Russian public organizations, such as Russkii mir [Foundation] and Valdai discussion club, created by the Russian intelligence for spreading the Russian ideas and influences among the western academics. The historians, who study the Russian intelligence's influences in western academia, need to start with a story of those think tanks, like the Wilson Center, and concentrate on such Putin's organizations like Russkii mir [Foundation] and Valdai club.[1]

So, this chapter follows this former KGB officer's suggestion and explores how Putin's regime uses the Western think tanks, like the Wilson Center, and the Russian cultural diplomacy, which includes various Russian "front organizations," like the Russkii Mir Foundation and Valdai discussion club, to influence Western academia nowadays.

THE WILSON CENTER, THE KENNAN INSTITUTE, AND THE RUSSIANS

As early as late October of 1968, the KGB officers reported to their administration in Moscow and Kyiv that the US Congress established a special think tank, the Woodrow Wilson International Center for Scholars, as

> (1) a living institution expressing the ideals and concerns of [the US President] Woodrow Wilson, which would be an appropriate memorial to his accomplishments as the twenty-eighth President of the United States, a distinguished scholar, an outstanding university president, and a brilliant advocate of international understanding; (2) that the Woodrow Wilson Memorial Commission, created by joint resolution of Congress, recommended that an International Center for Scholars be constructed in the District of Columbia in the area north of the proposed Market Square as part of the Nation's memorial to Woodrow Wilson; (3) that such a center, symbolizing and strengthening the fruitful relation between the world of learning and the world of public affairs, would be a suitable memorial to the spirit of Woodrow Wilson; and (4) that the establishment of such a center would be consonant with the purposes of the Smithsonian Institution . . . [created by Congress in 1846] for the increase and diffusion of knowledge among men.[2]

Immediately, the KGB noted this organization as a new target for its operations against American think tanks and academia as well. Since 1968, the KGB analysts followed closely the expansion and various structural changes in the Wilson Center.[3]

When, among many research groups and institutes of the Wilson Center, the Kennan Institute for advanced studies of Russia and the Soviet Union was created in 1974, it became the new goal of the KGB operations against American academia. Soviet intelligence followed closely the creation of this institute and the career of its first (founding) director, Professor S. Frederick Starr (1975–1980). It was a part of the KGB operation against the US diplomacy and the American centers for Soviet studies during the détente period, especially after both Soviet and American intelligence services cooperated in preparation of the official visits by US President Richard Nixon, to Moscow and Kyiv in 1972. Soviet intelligence decided to use the American think tanks, such as the Kennan Institute, not only to influence US politics in pro-Soviet directions, but also to collect information about the reaction of American experts and politicians to the improvement of the US-Soviet relations after 1972.[4]

The KGB had already known that the Kennan Institute was established by "a joint initiative" of George F. Kennan, a former US Ambassador to the Soviet Union in 1952, James Billington, a director of the Wilson Center

"The Agents of Influence" 157

(1973–1987), and historian S. Frederick Starr from Oberlin College. This new think tank was named after Ambassador Kennan's relative, George Kennan "the Elder" (1845–1924), a nineteenth-century explorer of Russia and Siberia. Soviet intelligence officers provided their supervisors with the published official information about this organization as well:

> George Kennan has always been fascinated by the Soviet Union, which Winston Churchill characterized as "a riddle wrapped in a mystery inside an enigma." A former U.S. Ambassador to Moscow and fellow at Princeton's Institute for Advanced Study, Kennan, 72, is now engaged in his most ambitious effort to solve that riddle. With Princeton Colleagues James Billington and Frederick Starr, he has set up the first major center for Russian studies to open in the U.S. in more than a decade. Located in the Smithsonian Institution's Victorian-Gothic headquarters building and affiliated with the Woodrow Wilson Center for Scholars, the new Kennan Institute will bring experts from round the world to Washington for all-expense-paid weekend seminars, short-term research projects and yearlong fellowships. Its goal: to deepen U.S. understanding of the Soviet Union. Says Kennan: "This is the only truly national institution devoted to Soviet studies. It can serve as an anchor in bad times and a channel for improved communications in good times."[5]

At the same time, providing this kind of published information, the KGB analysts, emphasized a role of private "capitalist" funding for this think tank:

> Applications have been pouring in for the first full fellowship program, slated to begin this fall. Among the proposals: studies of Soviet society under Stalin, Russian nationalism, Soviet biological research, and 19th century Russian ideology. The institute is already sponsoring a full schedule of conferences on Soviet history, politics, and culture. Last week, for example, experts gathered to assess the work of the Soviets' recently concluded 25th Congress of the Communist Party. This spring the center will sponsor a festival of silent Soviet films rarely seen in the West. Kennan began planning the institute five years ago when he realized that "Russian studies were in for a bad time. Money was drying up; resources and facilities were scattered. Many leaders in the field were dead. It was felt that if I didn't do something, nobody else would." So as not to drain foundation money from existing university centers for Soviet studies, Kennan approached companies that do business with the Russians, including PepsiCo, Chase Manhattan, Bank of America and General Electric. They responded with enthusiasm—and generous grants.[6]

These kinds of publications were filed almost every month after 1975 by the KGB analysts for their administration. They noted that the founding director of the Kennan Institute and a president of Oberlin College, Professor Starr "expressed in public his friendly feelings towards the Soviet Union and Russian culture." At the same time, the KGB analysts recommended to the KGB administration to look for availability of "the inside analysis of this American Anti-Soviet center [and think tank—SZh.]."[7] They were looking for any Soviet scholar who could get an official American invitation to visit the Kennan Institute. The KGB analysts were especially interested in sending a Soviet Americanist there. As the KGB officials from the Institute of World History of the USSR Academy of Sciences (IVI) explained in December of 1974, "We need a Soviet specialist, who understands the realities of both American politics and a development of the American studies of the Soviet Union."[8]

That is why those KGB officials invited Nikolai Bolkhovitinov, a Soviet Americanist, and a famous Soviet historian of Russia-US relations, for a special personal interview to discuss his possible visit to the Kennan Institute in the United States. They knew that in the fall of 1974, Bolkhovitinov's American colleague, Dr. Richard Morris, a professor of US history from Columbia University, sent Bolkhovitinov an official invitation to take part in the celebration of the American Revolution Bicentennial in the US in 1975. For this visit, Professor Morris suggested a few options for funding Bolkhovitinov's visit, including the Guest Fellowship from the recently established Kennan Institute in Washington, D.C. The KGB officials from the first (international) department, which was responsible for the foreign connections of IVI, became "very interested in this Professor Morris' proposal," and they decided to use Bolkhovitinov for their intelligence purposes. They had a series of long conversations with Bolkhovitinov, explaining to him what he was supposed to do during his visit to the Kennan Institute. As they instructed him, "we need to know the goals, structure, and financial sources of this organization, how the Kennan Institute was connected with the CIA and other US intelligence organizations, and how it was involved in the special anti-Soviet intelligence operations."[9]

Bolkhovitinov flew to the United States in April of 1975. On May 1, 1975, Bolkhovitinov presented his research paper about the establishment and development of Russian-American relations during the eighteenth and nineteenth centuries at the Woodrow Wilson International Center for Scholars in Washington, D.C. The Kennan Institute in this center financially supported his visit, granting him affiliation as a guest scholar, with his subsequent participation in the US government–sponsored project "The Impact of American Revolution Abroad." On May 8–9, 1975, Bolkhovitinov took part in the fourth symposium on the American Revolution Bicentennial, organized and funded by the Library of Congress. In the Library's Coolidge Auditorium, he presented his paper "The American Revolution and the Russian Empire." In Washington, D.C., Bolkhovitinov met and established friendly personal connections with James Billington, a director of the Wilson Center, and S. Frederick Starr, Kennan Institute's director.[10]

After his return to Moscow, Bolkhovitinov submitted the obligatory travel report to the institute's international (KGB) department with his positive analysis of "the Kennan Institute's goals and structure," demonstrating "the establishing the productive connections" with Billington and Starr. During the next year, in 1976, the KGB continued its collection of information about the Kennan Institute's activities, using not only Bolkhovitinov's reports, but also the communications of Bolkhovitinov's colleagues from the Institute of the USA and Canada (ISKAN).[11] Until 1991, almost every year, the KGB used the recommendations of Soviet Americanists, like Bolkhovitinov, to monitor the policy and academic research discussed in such American think tanks, like the Kennan Institute.[12]

During 1976–1978, Nikolai Bolkhovitinov and other Soviet Americanists, received additional instructions from their KGB supervisors in Moscow, Leningrad, and Kyiv: "Soviet academic guests in the United States need to promote and support pro-Soviet positions and ideas of the members of such anti-Soviet centers, like the Kennan Institute, and do all the best to influence those centers in the pro-Soviet and pro-Russian directions." Other venues for the pro-Soviet and pro-Russian ideas were "various professional associations for Slavic studies, Russian historical and political science research in America, which could be used as the important platforms for promoting the pro-Soviet and pro-Russian approaches in academic research, regarding the Soviet geopolitical space."[13] At the same time, the KGB analysts especially noted and praised those leaders of the American think tanks, like Kennan Institute's directors, who "distanced themselves from the confrontational attitudes towards the Soviet Union and supported the Soviet cultural diplomacy in the USA and promoted Russian culture in the American society during the Cold War." According to the KGB officers, the Kennan Institute's directors included Frederick Starr (1975–1980), Abbott Gleason (1980–1983), Herbert Ellison (1983–1985), and Peter Reddaway (1985–1989). Still, the KGB administration suspected the existing "strong personal and direct connections" of all those Kennan Institute's leaders to the CIA.[14]

Such traditional orientation of the KGB anti-American operations and the strong interest of the Soviet and Russian intelligence in a development of various centers of Slavic and Soviet studies (like the Kennan Institute) and in various professional organizations for scholars of the Slavic and Soviet studies has survived the period of perestroika and the changes in Soviet foreign policy during the 1980s and the 1990s. Even after the collapse of the USSR, the new generation of post-Soviet scholars with their connections to post-Soviet Russian intelligence, continued the similar contacts with the same Western venues for Slavic and Soviet studies (like the Kennan Institute) to promote the same, but now purely pro-Russian, interests. As Nikolai Bolkhovitinov noted,

> We have the new generation of young post-Soviet scholars with the strong connections to Russian intelligence: 1) who, like Vladislav Zubok, a talented and open-minded grandson of the founding father of Soviet American Studies, Lev Zubok, began traveling to the United States since 1987 on a regular basis, or 2) like the sons of the professional KGB officers, Vyacheslav Nikonov and Alexei Miller [son of one of the founders of the Institute of Slavic Studies, Ilia S. Miller.—SZh.], or 3) the sons of scholars, who worked for the KGB, like Alexei Arbatov [son of ISKAN director Georgy Arbatov—SZh.], who brought their old family KGB connections not only to their academic fields of the American and Slavic studies in Moscow, but also to the infrastructure of their foreign professional organizations in the US and Europe, and who used those connections for the pro-Russian anti-Western activities inside those organizations as well.[15]

Paradoxically, during the perestroika and immediately after the dissolution of the Soviet Union, those KGB and GRU connected scholars, especially post-Soviet Americanists, became the major consultants regarding the post-Soviet geopolitical space not only for the American think tanks, like the Kennan Institute, but also for various American grant-awarding organizations. During Gorbachev's perestroika, their American colleagues idealized the role of Soviet Americanists, forgetting about (or trying not to notice) their KGB connections. As they explained Soviet Americanists' role in the opening of diplomatic and academic dialogue with the Americans in the 1980s, "They [Soviet Americanists] ended up absorbing a good deal about Western political institutions and values which they . . . put to use once perestroika was under way."[16] Eventually, all major centers of Soviet American studies, which played a role of the Soviet foreign policy advisers, in Moscow (IMEMO and ISKAN), and in Kyiv (the Institute of Social and Economic Problems of Foreign Countries), contributed to shaping Gorbachev's "new thinking" policy. According to the US political scientists,

> [The researchers from those centers] helped change the intellectual and political climate in which policy decisions were made. This change in climate only became dramatic once the specialists gained some access, whether direct or indirect, to members of the [Soviet] leadership favoring reform; the ideas espoused by specialists in the 1970s and early 1980s were used by [this] leadership to legitimize and guide controversial policy decisions of the mid and late 1980s.[17]

In 1989 and 1990, IREX and other US funding agencies organized a series of official meetings and conferences, involving the US scholars and the leaders from various research centers of the Soviet Academy of Sciences in both Moscow and Kyiv, such as Valery Tishkov from the Institute of Ethnography, Yuri Levada from the All-Union Center for Public Opinion on Social and Economic Problems, and Andrey Kokoshin from ISKAN. It is noteworthy that Soviet Americanists from ISKAN (a place known in the West as a Soviet "spy institute"), KGB-connected scholars such as Viktor Sergeyev, Vladimir Averchev, and Pavel Parshin, became the active "advisers" for American granting agencies and US scholars, recommending and justifying the inclusion of the talented Soviet scholars, like Levada, in the list of the participants of the Soviet-US conferences during perestroika. Such a role was played also by other Moscow scholars, specializing in Ukrainian and East European History, such as Alexei Miller, who became active in the Soros Foundation and in establishing the Central European University in Budapest in 1991.[18]

Paradoxically, an intensification of those academic contacts between Soviet scholars and their American colleagues did not dramatically change the "discursive landscape" of American studies in Russia and Ukraine during perestroika. But at the same time, the new openness and travels abroad led to a change of the research topics and fields—instead of US history, American political science, and anthropology, Soviet Americanists from Moscow and Kyiv began studying Russian/Soviet history, Soviet diplomacy, and anthropology. Eventually, the personal academic adjustment to the new requirements of the international job market by Soviet Americanists led to the gradual changes in their academic identity: former Soviet Americanists became the new Western Sovietologists and experts in Russian/Ukrainian history, Soviet political science, and Soviet anthropology.[19]

In late 1992, former Soviet Americanist Vladislav Zubok was awarded with a Kennan Institute research fellowship, which allowed him to move from Moscow, Russia, to Washington, D.C., in February of 1993, to begin his new academic career in the United States.[20] In 1994, Zubok became a research fellow at the National Security Archive, affiliated with the Institute for European, Russian and Eurasian Studies, George Washington University. In 1995, he was appointed a director of the Russian and East European Document Database Project of the National Security Archive, and at the same time he joined the Cold War International History Project at the Wilson International Center for Scholars, which was funded by the Smith Richardson Foundation, where he created an English language catalogue of newly available documentation from 1996 to 2001.[21] Eventually, after many years looking for a teaching tenured job in the US, Zubok found a teaching position at Temple University in Philadelphia, where he earned tenure, as a professor of history in 2004. Meanwhile, he became an active consultant of different media projects in the US, including Sir Jeremy Isaac's twenty-four-episode series *Cold War* on CNN television. At the same time, Zubok was awarded various prestigious research grants from the MacArthur Foundation and Carnegie Corporation. Since 2013, he has been teaching at the London School of Economics in the United Kingdom. Zubok's brilliant academic career in the West was a typical example of how the talented scholars from the Soviet "spy institutes" such as the Moscow Institute of the USA and Canada, became easily integrated into Western academia, using various American think tanks, such as the Wilson Center and the Kennan Institute.[22]

SOVIET AND RUSSIAN FINANCIAL SOURCES OF "COVERT" OPERATIONS

After the collapse of communism, many Russian experts with open or hidden connections to the Soviet/Russian intelligence became incorporated into various Western think tanks. The most scandalous case of such "incorporation" was the story of Dmitri Trenin. In 1994, Trenin, a retired colonel of GRU (Russian military intelligence), joined a Carnegie Moscow Center, a regional affiliate of the Carnegie Endowment for International Peace. In December of 2008, Trenin was appointed a new Director of Carnegie Moscow Center.[23] After 2012, Trenin took openly the pro-Putin and anti-Western position, criticizing the US foreign policy and so-called "colored" anti-Russian revolutions in post-Soviet geopolitical space. As a result of his anti-American position, a few Putin critics, such as Maria Lipman and Lilia Shevtsova, left the Carnegie Moscow Center. In early 2022, Trenin openly supported Putin's war against Ukraine, and, finally, "the Carnegie Endowment for International Peace ended its affiliation with Dmitri Trenin."[24]

Unfortunately, the Russian, GRU, and KGB/FSB connected experts, like Trenin, were actively promoting pro-Putin and pro-Russian ideas in other American think tanks, such as the Kennan Institute and Middlebury Institute of International Studies at Monterey, as early as 2005, and until the beginning of the Russian war against Ukraine in 2022.[25]

After the collapse of the USSR and the sudden rise of post-Soviet oligarchs, the Russian intelligence services (FSB, SVR, and GRU) began using various financial tools of those oligarchs to influence the Western think tanks. The "new" Russian money became the active player, especially in those Western organizations, which were involved in various Russian studies and East-European studies programs. To some extent, post-Soviet intelligence used the old KGB traditions to bribe the Western politicians, journalists, and academics to influence them and use them as the "agents of influence" for various KGB operations. The most scandalous cases of such KGB financial operations of bribing included the special state-sponsored programs of providing money in the 1950s–1970s to the left "pro-Communist" representatives of the Ukrainian diaspora in America, like Peter Krawchuk,[26] or "compensating financially, Iosif Zatirka, a US citizen of the Ukrainian origin, for offering classified information about the American military forces" in 1960,[27] or "secretly offering" financial aid to Hubert Humphrey, the US Vice-President to Lyndon Johnson, in the spring of 1968 during the presidential elections in the US.[28] The KGB used various financial sources for those "bribing" operations. Initially, the main sources for such operations came not only through the official Soviet state-sponsored financial venues, but also as a result of blackmailing the Soviet Jewish immigrants in America, requesting from them "special payments" to the KGB agents. According to Oleg Kalugin, a former KGB officer, during the 1970s, many Jews were allowed to immigrate to the US and Israel after their agreement to collaborate with the KGB during their emigration. As a result, "huge numbers of Russian criminals and KGB spies . . . did inundate the United States."[29]

At the same time, during the emigration process, the KGB officers recruited Soviet Jews as their active agents and used this Jewish immigration in the US for their own financial operations. All of those KGB intelligence practices from the 1950s became "normalized" in the forms of the KGB active measures during the 1960s and the 1970s.[30] Since the 1970s, the KGB operatives began using their "assets" among the Soviet Jewish immigrants in "capitalist America" for their various secret operations against the US, which survived the collapse of the Soviet Union and now are under control of the FSB, a Russian successor of the KGB. Some of those old Jewish immigrants, like Semyon Kislin in New York City, co-owner of Joy-Lud Electronics, which was allegedly owned by the KGB, became instrumental in keeping control over Jewish immigrants' business by Russian intelligence nowadays as well.[31]

During the same time, beginning with the 1960s, the KGB infiltrated various banking and financial organizations in the West, which were used by Soviet intelligence for their "financial operations" as well. Eventually, by the 1980s, at the beginning of perestroika, the KGB operatives collected and implemented new financial and technological experiences of their American opponents, which became useful for opening the new banking system (and other financial and technological practices) in late Soviet and post-Soviet geopolitical space (all KGB reports in 1989–1991 discuss such information and practices on a regular basis).[32] Using its previous American experience and connections with the "useful" Americans, the KGB administration, including its Ukrainian office, founded a series of financial organizations in the West, especially in the United States and Canada, which became important venues for various banking and other financial operations of the KGB.[33] By the end of the 1990s, the post-Soviet successors of the KGB began using the "new money" of the new capitalist class of post-Soviet Russia, which became known as post-Soviet oligarchs, or as just "Putin's kleptocracy."

This "new money" became an active element of the new Russian "cultural and academic diplomacy," which affected various think tanks in the West, including the Woodrow Wilson International Center for Scholars and the Kennan Institute in Washington, D.C. According to the retired KGB officers,

> By the end of perestroika, the KGB, first, and after 1991, its successor—FSB, later, engaged the Soviet and post-Soviet "new riches," the people, we call now oligarchs, in the Soviet and later Russian intelligence operations, which targeted the Wilson Center and other American think tanks, investing money and using various financial donations as the tools, influencing those think tanks in the direction, which could be favorable for the Russian politics. The best example of this scenario is a rise of Renova financial group in 1990, founded by Russian-Ukrainian Jews Viktor Vekselberg, Leonard Blavatnik and their former Jewish classmates from Moscow colleges, a financial syndicate, which expanded later in the oil and aluminum business. Approximately the same time, Alfa Financial Group (with its Alfa Bank) was founded by another Jewish graduate from Moscow college, Mikhail Fridman. Seven years later, in 1997, both Renova and Alfa groups united their efforts in establishing their financial control over a variety of businesses in Russia, and after emigration of Blavatnik to the United States, in America as well. Of course, these developments were monitored and controlled by the Russian intelligence. After the rise of Putin to power in the 2000s, these businesses became an important part of Putin's political tools. Putin began using them for his own political interests, influencing the ruling elites and academia in the West.[34]

Such an involvement of Putin's kleptocracy became important in the financial life of many American think tanks, like the Wilson Center. On May 26, 2005, for the first time in its history, the Wilson Center awarded a Russian post-Soviet oligarch, one of Putin's most important kleptocrats, Vagit Alekperov, president of the Russian oil company LUKOIL. Alekperov received "the Woodrow Wilson Award for Corporate Citizenship at a dinner to benefit the Wilson Center's Kennan Institute."[35] According to American scholars, like Karen Dawisha, who were Kennan Institute research fellows, Alekperov had old connections to Yevgeniy Primakov and Russian intelligence.[36] Co-chair of this ceremony was an old late Soviet connection to Renova and Alfa Financial Groups, a "Ukrainian-born" and now "a British-American businessman" Len (Leonard) Blavatnik, who had links to Pyotr Aven, "the first oligarch to make friends with Vladimir Putin."[37]

On October 18, 2007, "the Woodrow Wilson Center's Kennan Institute held its inaugural Kathryn and Shelby Cullom Davis Awards Dinner, an annual event intended to raise public awareness of individuals demonstrating outstanding corporate citizenship and public service in connection with the U.S.-Russian relationship." One of those "individuals" was Viktor Vekselberg, who received "the Woodrow Wilson Award for Public Service for his outstanding contributions to the rebirth of Russian philanthropy."[38] In October of 2010, the Kennan Institute sponsored the US-Russian Business Council's eighteenth meeting with the participation of Viktor Vekselberg as well, who was only one representative of Russian business during this ceremony.[39] As we see, this financier of Putin, who eventually became sanctioned by the US government for supporting the Russian wars against Ukraine in 2018, also had his old connections to the Wilson Center.[40]

Another scandalous case, which connected both the Kennan Institute and the Wilson Center to Putin's kleptocracy, was the story of another Russian (Latvian-born) billionaire, Petr Aven, who had provided funding for various Western think tanks since 2001, including the Wilson Center.[41] On November 3, 2015, in Washington, D.C., during the special Kathryn and Shelby Cullom Davis Awards Dinner, Petr Aven was awarded with "the Woodrow Wilson Award for Corporate Citizenship for his role in expanding understanding between Russians and Americans during his career as a Russian government official in the early 1990s, his tenure at Russia's largest private bank (Alfa Bank), and for his role as co-founder of the Alfa Fellowship Program." According to the Wilson Center's explanation, "The Alfa Fellowship Program brings early career Americans to work in Russia, and the alumni of this program represent a rising generation of American experts on Russia working in the private sector, government, and non-profit community."[42] On November 21, 2014, during the ongoing war of Russia against Ukraine, Melissa Graves, Program Director at Alfa Fellowship Program, made a public presentation at the Wilson Center about "American engagement with Russia" without even mentioning the Russian-Ukrainian conflict of 2013–2014.[43]

Moreover, on November 30 and December 1, 2017, the Wilson Center's Kennan Institute organized a special meeting for "over fifty Alfa Fellowship Program alumni and current fellows to celebrate fifteen classes of fellows and reconnect over discussions about Russia and the region." As the official Wilson Center website informed, "The alumni event kicked off with a dinner and reception at the W Hotel [in Washington, D.C.] on November 30, featuring a keynote address by Mr. Mikhail Fridman, Chairman of the Supervisory Board, Alfa Group Consortium, who emphasized the importance of the Alfa Fellowship Program as a key international exchange initiative for young professionals to learn first-hand about business and culture in Russia."[44] The Wilson Center's site, which I quote, never mentioned the direct and very personal connections of Mikhail Fridman and his friend Petr Aven and their Alfa Bank to Russian President Putin. As Kateryna Smagliy noted in 2018, "The Wilson Center turned a blind eye to various reports that implicated Petr

Aven of corruption and his ties to the Kremlin. Information about the Alfa Group's involvement in organized crime, narcotics trafficking, money laundering and rigged auctions of state assets through government connections became publicly available in 2000, when the Center for Public Integrity—one of America's oldest investigative news organizations—published its report on the Alfa Group."[45]

Only much later, on May 26, 2022, during the new bloody Russian war against Ukraine, the Wilson Center administration publicly announced that, "due to the recent sanctions by the U.S. Government related to Russia's war on Ukraine, it is rescinding and no longer recognizes previous awards [by the Wilson Center] given to . . . Viktor Vekselberg and Petr Aven."[46] At the same time, in a response to this decision, during the peak of the Russian invasion in Ukraine, the Russian Federation openly cut off its relations with the Wilson Center and the Kennan Institute, officially announcing the Wilson Center as a "foreign agent" and banning its activities on the territory of Russia.[47]

Unfortunately, the serious damage to the studies of the post-Soviet geopolitical space in the West, including the United States and Canada, had been done already. The pro-Russian bias was maintained not only by the Russian billionaires' donations, but also by the financial support of various studies of the post-Soviet countries by the Western (mostly American) academics, who traveled to the Russian Federation, using various Russian fundings (including Alfa Fellowship since 2004). Officially, the Alfa Fellowship Program denied that it supports the "purely academic research" in Russia, insisting on its financing only the young Western "professionals," who "demonstrated interest in Russian, European, and Eurasian affairs."[48] In fact, 200 Western young academics (from the US, the UK, and Germany), like Associate Professor of International History Christopher Miller from Tufts University, were awarded an Alfa Fellowship at the beginning of their academic career in the United States, which allowed them to finish their academic research, using the money of pro-Putin's oligarchs, such as Petr Aven and Mikhail Fridman, who created the notorious Alfa Financial Group in post-Soviet Russia. Paradoxically, many of those Western young academics used the Russian Alfa Bank stipends, living in the Russian Federation, when Putin had already begun the first war against Ukraine in 2013–2014. Many of them did not even pay attention to this war in their official appreciation of the Russian funding of their research during this time, noting that they used their time "in Moscow to help launch [their] career as [analysts] of Russian politics and economics, deepening [their] experience with the country and taking advantage of the Alfa Fellowship's network to build professional relationships that have been crucial to [their] career development."[49]

THE VALDAI DISCUSSION CLUB AND THE RUSSKII MIR FOUNDATION AS FRONT ORGANIZATIONS OF RUSSIAN POST-SOVIET INTELLIGENCE

Other venues of influence on the Western academia, especially in the United States and Canada, were the special organizations, created and sponsored by the Russian post-Soviet intelligence agencies (especially by FSB, GRU, and SVR), the venues called by some scholars "front organizations" of the Russian intelligence service.[50] Such "front organizations" were used by the KGB during the entire Cold War period, and those intelligence practices survived the collapse of the Soviet Union and still are functioning in post-Soviet Russia. The archival KGB documents and interviews with the retired KGB officers demonstrate how the Soviet intelligence used various international pacifist anti-war organizations, including the Soviet Peace Fund, created in April of 1961, as the "KGB front organizations," and had promoted Soviet political and cultural interests among the Western public.[51]

According to some scholars, the predecessors of the recent Russian front organizations, connected to the Russian intelligence, like *Rossutrudnichestvo*, the Gorchakov fund, the Valdai Discussion Club, and the Russkii Mir Foundation, included the Soviet and post-Soviet venues such as the All-Union Society for Cultural Relations with Foreign Countries (VOKS) in 1925–1958, the Union of Soviet Societies of Friendship and Cultural Relations with Foreign Countries (SRTD), and the Russian Agency for International Cooperation and Development (1992–1994).[52] As a former KGB officer emphasized, this was "the old KGB tradition to create such organizations and attract the foreigners, who could be used as supporters of Soviet politics and diplomacy." According to him, the post-Soviet Russian intelligence service, a successor of the Soviet KGB, "continued the same strategy and kept creating the similar organizations in post-Soviet Russia, the most effective and influential among them are the Valdai Discussion Club and the Russkii Mir Foundation." And he joked,

> If you want to know who is used by the Russian intelligence as their "agents of influence," look for the Western names of so-called experts, or participants, or the awards' receivers of those two venues: the Valdai Discussion Club and the *Russkii Mir* Foundation. Those organizations were founded by the former KGB people, and they still work for those former KGB people, who now, like Putin and Patrushev, rule post-Soviet Russia.[53]

The Valdai Discussion Club was created in 2004 as a Russian think tank and discussion forum, "with the goal to engage the Western academics and political experts in a dialogue with their Russian colleagues." The name of this venue was derived from the location of its first meeting at Velikii Novgorod near Lake Valdai in the Russian Federation. In 2011, the Russian oligarchs and political advisers, like Petr Aven, who were close to Putin, established the Valdai Club Foundation. Since 2014, this foundation became the official manager of the Valdai Club. According to the club's official website, the same year it "moved away from the format of 'telling the world about Russia' to practical work aimed at forming the global agenda and delivering a qualified and objective assessment of global political and economic issues. One of its main objectives is to promote dialogue among the global intellectual elite in order to find solutions to overcome the crises of the international system."[54] Officially, the leadership of the Valdai Foundation was represented by the Board of the Foundation for Development and Support,

> Which is chaired by Andrey Bystritskiy, renowned Russian media manager, author of articles and publications, and media and communications researcher. Fyodor Lukyanov, well-known Russian international relations and foreign affairs expert and editor-in-chief of the Russia in Global Affairs journal is Research Director of the Foundation. The Foundation's day-to-day activities are run by Executive Director Nadezhda Lavrentieva, Honoured Economist of the Russian Federation, and former top manager at major Russian media outlets (NTV Plus, RIA Novosti, TASS Russian News Agency).[55]

According to the former KGB analysts, all those names were connected to the KGB from the 1980s and 1990s. Moreover, the official founders of Valdai Discussion Club were organizations, which incorporated the officers from the Russian intelligence service (FSB, SVR, and GRU): the Russian International Affairs Council (RIAC) and Council of Foreign and Defense Policy (CFDP).[56]

As Western observers noted, from the early beginning, Valdai Club became the tool of official propaganda for Putin's regime, the "propagandist" venue to promote the Russian political ideas among Western academics.[57] Some scholars, like Lilia Shevtsova and Marcel H. Van Herpen, described the Western participants in Valdai Club's discussions as "Putin's useful fools"; some of the intelligence experts connected those participants directly to Putin's "agents of influence."[58] They define such "institutional agents of influence" (like Valdai Club) as "Russia's major state federal agencies, large state-affiliated grant-making foundations, and private charities linked to Russian oligarchs."[59]

An analysis of the so-called "experts list" of the Valdai Club reveals the names of prominent experts in Slavic/Russian/Soviet studies, who became engaged in a dangerous academic dialogue, sponsored by the Russian intelligence service. Some of these experts were characterized by the Russian intelligence researchers like the "useful fools/idiots," or the "agents of influence" of the Russian successors of the Soviet KGB. The most typical example of such experts from the Valdai Discussion Club is the story of Matthew Rojansky, who served as Kennan Institute's director from 2013 to 2022.[60] He has had a brilliant career as a Russian expert in various American think tanks, as a Deputy Director of the Russia and Eurasia Program at the Carnegie Endowment for International Peace and as a President and CEO of the U.S. Russia Foundation. The only problem for many observers was that "Rojansky was too soft on Russia."[61] When Jane Harman, a Wilson Center president, recommended in 2021 to US President Biden to hire Rojansky for the position of Russia director of the National Security Council, "several current and former senior officials [including such activists as Bill Browder and Garry Kasparov] warned the White House against hiring Rojansky, arguing that appointing him would signal a conciliatory U.S. policy toward Moscow."[62] Moreover, much earlier, when Rojansky "dismissed Dr. Kateryna Smagliy, Director of the Kennan Institute Kyiv Office, and simultaneously appointed Dr. Mikhail Minakov as Principle Investigator on Ukraine," closing the Kyiv office, as a reaction to this decision, in February 2018, the Ukrainian alumni of the Kennan Institute wrote an open letter to the administration of the Wilson Center criticizing the Kennan Institute and its director Rojansky as an "unwitting tool of Russia's political interference."[63] Eventually, on April 12, 2021, the Ukrainian Congress Committee of America (UCCA) sent a letter to President Biden,

> [E]xpressing great concern "with the reported potential appointment of Matthew Rojansky as Russia Director at the National Security Council. This appointment is fraught with many problems—not least of which is his belief that Ukraine is expendable to secure closer U.S.-Russia relations. Mr. Rojansky's work is a source of much anxiety and has drawn criticism not only from Ukrainians, but from Central and Eastern European countries and those domestically who are concerned about Russia's influence in the United States. As exemplified by his support of a 'Pro Unity' Russian concert tour in 2017—led by a Russian conductor known to support and defend Putin—Mr. Rojansky's actions and incendiary comments over the years would send the wrong message not only to our strategic partner Ukraine but also to reformers in Russia and the entire world."[64]

As a result, Rojansky's candidacy was not approved by Biden's administration in 2021, and in 2022, Rojansky was replaced by William Pomerantz as a new director of the Kennan Institute. Unfortunately, until now (March of 2024) Matthew Rojansky still keeps his position of "an expert" of the Valdai Discussion Club.[65]

According to the former KGB analysts, Soviet and Russian intelligence always wanted to attract "political and academic stars" in their "front organizations," to use those "big shots" from politics and academy as their "agents of influence" to attract more "useful fools" from the West. So, the list of Valdai Club's "experts" includes the scholars from the most prestigious universities and think tanks from the West.[66] This list contains such names as Jon Alterman, Zbigniew Brzezinski Chair in Global Security and Geostrategy, Director of Middle East Program at the Center of Strategic and International Studies (CSIS), Georgetown University; Samuel Charap, the Rand Corporation; Professor Julian M. Cooper, Centre for Russian and East European Studies (CREES), University of Birmingham; Timothy Colton, Professor of Government and Russian Studies, Harvard University; Clifford Gaddy, Senior Fellow at the Brookings Institution in Washington, D.C., Professor of Economy, Johns Hopkins University; John Mearsheimer, Professor of Political Science, University of Chicago; Charles Kupchan, Professor of International Affairs, Georgetown University; Angela Stent, Director of the Center for Eurasian, Russian & East European Studies, Georgetown University; Marlene Laruelle, Director, Institute for European, Russian and Eurasian Studies (IERES), Co-Director, PONARS-Eurasia, Director, Central Asia Program, George Washington University; and Thomas Remington, Goodrich C. White Professor of Political Science, Emory University. Even famous American journalists, like Jill Dougherty from CNN, who was a Global Fellow at the Wilson Center and Kennan Institute in 2016–2022, were included in the list of Valdai Club's "experts."[67] The Western experts, who took openly pro-Putin and anti-Ukrainian positions, blaming the West in the new Cold War and anti-Russian politics, play an important role in this Valdai Club's list. I had already mentioned such names, as Professor Mearsheimer and Dr. Laruelle, who always criticized the West, especially the United States for "the unjust mistreatment of Russia." The special group of pro-Putin Western scholars in the Valdai Club "experts list," even more anti-Western and anti-Ukrainian, than Mearsheimer, is represented by such Slavic studies specialists like Richard Sakwa, Emeritus Professor of Russian and European Politics at the University of Kent at Canterbury, who was also a Senior Research Fellow at the National Research University-Higher School of Economics in Moscow and an Honorary Professor in the Faculty of Political Science at Moscow State University;[68] and Nicolai N. Petro, Professor of Political Science, University of Rhode Island.[69] It is noteworthy that those Valdai Club Western experts are still very active, using prestigious Western academic venues, such as George Washington University in 2024, to discuss how "the West failed to prevent a second Cold War" with Russia and openly criticize the US support of Ukraine, fighting for its independence.[70]

Many of the active participants in Valdai Club events are the recent emigrants from Russia, such as Yuri Slezkine, Professor of History, the University of California, Berkeley (a recipient of 2020 Valdai Discussion Club Award), and Andrey Tsygankov, Professor at the Departments of Political Science and International Relations, San Francisco State University. The most influential Russian experts of Valdai Club came from the famous families of Soviet experts in foreign relations, who were either KGB/GRU officers, or worked as KGB agents. Those children and grandchildren of those famous families, and now the Valdai Club's experts, are such important figures in Russian diplomacy (in both political and academic spheres), like Viacheslav Nikonov, Chairman of the Executive Board at Russkii Mir Foundation, Dean at the School of Public Administration, Lomonosov Moscow State University (grandson of Stalin's minister of foreign affairs, son of a professional KGB officer); Yevgeniy Primakov, Jr., a head of *Rossutrudnichestvo* (grandson of a Soviet politician and spy, connected to both KGB and GRU); Alexei Miller, Professor of History, the European University in St. Petersburg (son of SMERSH and KGB officer); Nadezhda Arbatova, Head of Department of European Political Studies at the Institute of World Economy and International Relations (IMEMO) (a wife of the son of Georgy Arbatov, a director of the Institute of USA and Canada, and a famous "KGB man" among Soviet Americanists).[71]

Another "front organization" of the Russian intelligence, openly funded by the Russian government is the Russkii Mir Foundation.[72] According to the official site of this organization,

> In June 2007 President Putin signed a decree establishing the Russkiy Mir Foundation, for the purpose of "promoting the Russian language, as Russia's national heritage and a significant aspect of Russian and world culture and supporting Russian language teaching programs abroad." The Foundation is a joint project of the Ministry of Foreign Affairs and the Ministry of Education and Science and supported by both public and private funds. The Russkiy Mir Foundation is headed by Vyacheslav Nikonov, Dean of History and Political Science at the International University in Moscow and founder of the Polity Foundation. The Foundation's Board of Trustees consists of prominent Russian academics, cultural figures, and distinguished civil servants, and is chaired by Dmitry Kozak, Deputy Chief of Staff of the Presidential Executive Office.[73]

Its mission statement emphasized that "the three meanings of this small but eloquent word inspire and define Russkii Mir's mission—to promote understanding and peace in the world by supporting, enhancing and encouraging the appreciation of Russian language, heritage and culture."[74] According to President Putin's decree on June 21, 2007, the Russian state established this Foundation: "The founders of the Foundation, on behalf of the Russian Federation, are the Ministry of Foreign Affairs of the Russian Federation and the Ministry of Education and Science of the Russian Federation; The

Foundation's assets may be composed of federal budget funds and voluntary contributions and other sources in accordance with the legislation of the Russian Federation."[75]

Almost all the leadership of the Russkii Mir Foundation was connected to Soviet and Russian intelligence. A chair of the Foundation Board of Trustees was a professional GRU officer, Dmitry Kozak, who was born in Soviet Ukraine and began his career in the late 1970s in the GRU Speznaz (military special forces). Kozak, who moved to Leningrad in the 1980s, where he graduated from the Law School (faculty of law) of Leningrad State University, maintained his personal connections with Soviet Russian intelligence, which were strengthened by his old friendship with Vladimir Putin, who graduated from the same school.[76] Another connection to the old "KGB people" in the Soviet ruling elites was represented by Alexei Gromyko, the Director of the Russkii Mir Foundation's European programs, who was a grandson of Andrei Gromyko, the USSR Foreign Minister from 1957 to 1985 and Chairman of the Presidium of the Supreme Soviet from 1985 to 1988.[77]

But the true ideological leader of Russkii Mir Foundation was another "KGB man," Vyacheslav Nikonov, who symbolized a symbiosis of the Soviet traditional political establishment with the Russian intelligence, also rooted in the Soviet KGB/GRU past. Nikonov was born in 1956 in Moscow into the privileged family of the ruling Soviet elite. His mother, Svetlana Molotova (1929–1989), was a daughter of Vyacheslav Molotov, Stalin's Minister of Foreign Affairs. Eventually, she got a PhD degree in history.[78] During her studies she met her future husband, father of Vyacheslav Nikonov, Alexei Nikonov. Alexei (1917–1992) began his career as an undergraduate student at the department of history of Moscow State University (MGU) before WWII. During the war he joined the Soviet army and began working in the Soviet intelligence, as a NKVD/KGB officer. After WWII he returned to Moscow as a graduate student of history at MGU, where he defended his PhD in history. In the 1950s, Alexei Nikonov became an associate professor of history at MGIMO. Some contemporaries noted how Alexei Nikonov divorced his first wife, left his first family, and then he got married to Svetlana Molotova, "who was not very attractive, but very useful [for his career promotion]."[79] This marriage to Molotov's daughter contributed to the promotion of Alexei's academic and communist party career, the pinnacle of which was his position of one of the editors of the most influential ideological journals in the USSR, *Communist*. Eventually, Alexei Nikonov easily defended his doctoral dissertation as well. His son, Vyacheslav Nikonov, used to joke that he was "a son of two professional historians, mother and father, both *doktora istoricheskikh nauk*."[80]

Despite the firing of his father from the prestigious journal's editorial board because of his opposition to Khrushchev reforms in 1957, and constant criticism of Molotov as "Stalinist," Alexei Nikonov survived as a "professional Soviet historian," working for various research institutes of the USSR Academy of Sciences and maintaining the "useful connections" in Moscow, which allowed his son, Vyacheslav, to receive a good education at the MGU department of history in the 1970s and successfully build not only his academic, but also political career in the Soviet Union and post-Soviet Russia as well.[81]

Vyacheslav Nikonov chose the research field of US History, and his adviser was a famous MGU Americanist historian Professor Evgenii Yaz'kov.[82] Eventually, in 1981, he defended his kandidatskaia dissertation (Soviet version of Western PhD degree), and in 1989 his dosktorskaia dissertation on political history of the Republican Party of the United States after WWII. During this period of time, using his parents' KGB connections, Nikonov traveled to the United States as a part of MGU's student exchange with American universities. As some contemporaries noted, during his travels he became a "KGB person" in the group of those Soviet exchange students.[83] After 1989, being a leader of the Communist organization at the MGU department of history, Nikonov also started his political career, becoming a political adviser of Soviet Russian politicians, such as Gorbachev and Yeltsin. At some point, Nikonov worked, during 1991–1992, as a deputy of the chair of the KGB. Paradoxically, at the same time, Nikonov was invited to teach the Fall Semester of 1992 at California Institute of Technology in the US. Using his American connections after his travels to the United States, he even tried to create the first "Americanized" political science think tank, called "Polity" in post-Soviet Russia.[84]

After 2000, Nikonov stopped his liberal experiments with political science at MGU and became the "new Russian conservative." Eventually, he established his political reputation as an anti-American, Russian patriotic, pro-Putin politician, working in the Russian parliament, Russian government, and actively participating in various Russian television shows, supporting all Putin's political decisions. From June 2007 to September 2023, following Putin's orders and recommendations, Nikonov served as a leader of the Russkii Mir Foundation.[85] As some scholars noted, during his leadership of this foundation, Nikonov always expressed publicly his "anti-Ukrainian and anti-Western rhetoric," with its main "leitmotif" of "an unprecedented confrontation between Russia and the entire Western world, combined with the pressing need to expand the 'Russian world' in any way possible."[86]

Throughout his entire political and academic career under Putin, Nikonov took publicly anti-American positions, criticizing the Orange Revolution and Maidan Revolution in Ukraine as an "American conspiracy against Russia." In his textbook, whose publication was funded by his organization, the Russkii Mir Foundation, Nikonov presented the United States as the major geopolitical enemy of Russia. He interpreted all events in Georgia, Moldova, and Ukraine since the collapse of the Soviet Union as a result of "US expansionism." According to Nikonov, the major goal of the United States is to "weaken" and to "punish" Russia, using the recent developments in Ukraine and Russia. Moreover, Nikonov supports the Russian expansionism, Russian annexation of Crimea, and Russian military presence in eastern Ukraine. He justifies the Russian war in Ukraine by the "historical mission" of the Russian state to "defend" its state national interests against "American imperialism" in Eastern Europe, in post-Soviet geopolitical space.[87] Other Russian ideologists also follow Nikonov in their criticism of US "public diplomacy" criticizing Americans in "masterminding" "Ukrainian revolutions." They accuse US politicians in attempts to "take out" Ukraine from the Russian sphere of influence in Eastern Europe as early as 2003. According to them, US "public diplomacy" focused its efforts on pro-Western Ukrainian youth, trying organized so-called "Orange" and other anti-Russian revolutions in Ukraine. These Russian ideologists repeat Nikonov's old concepts about "American anti-Russian conspiracy." Nikonov's Russian colleagues emphasized that since 2003 "the USA were able to create [in Ukraine] a solid human potential, oriented to the West."[88] Although Nikonov stepped down from the leadership of the Russkii Mir Foundation at the end of 2023, his ideas, projects, and, especially, his connections to Russian intelligence still shape and orient major developments of this organization.[89]

The most important influence of the Russkii Mir Foundation was implemented through its grant awarding strategy (*grantovaia programma fonda* in Russian). From the early beginning of this foundation, its major goal was to provide financial assistance for research, especially to the former Russian emigrants in the Western academia, who were "promoting, popularizing, and expanding" Russian culture and Russian cultural and political interests. One of the first Western recipients of Russkii Mir Foundation grants was Vladislav Zubok, Professor of the International History at the London School of Economics (LSE), a former Professor of History at Temple University in the US. As Zubok put on his official LSE website: "Professor Zubok received numerous grants from the McArthur Foundation and Carnegie Corporation of New York, and from the Yeltsin foundation and the Russkii Mir foundation."[90] According to his own vita, Zubok received those grants at least twice in 2008: for the "International Summer School Grant," Foundation "Russkii Mir"; and for "Research and Writing Grant," Foundation "Russkii Mir."[91]

Such practice of granting financial awards was targeting mostly former Russian citizens who lived in the West and worked in Western academia. The major goal of such practice was "integrating Russian academia by incorporating Russian diaspora in the West." Almost every Russian emigrant, who became a famous scientist or scholar in the West, was approached by the

Russkii Mir Foundation's representatives, and was invited to participate in various venues—roundtables, international summer schools, conferences— organized by this organization, which covered all of those Russian emigrants' travel expenses and provided them with generous stipends. One of the active participants (at least since 2009) of all those meetings was Yuri Slezkine, Professor of History from the University of California, who praised the Russkii Mir Foundation during the special roundtable on "Russia in Global Social Sciences and Global Social Sciences in Russia: The Role of National Academic Diaspora," which was held in October of 2009 at the Marriott Grand Hotel in Moscow. As Slezkine explained to his Moscow hosts, "I don't know what has changed at all in Russia or whether anything has, in fact, changed. But I do know that the Russkii Mir Foundation has appeared. This event, in my opinion, has pretty much changed the picture of our cooperation with Russia. In any case, I have personally participated in several academic forums sponsored by Russkii Mir."[92]

As some scholars noted, "In contrast to Western institutions of cultural diplomacy, which attract more and more adherents of their cultures through academic opportunities, language learning, and creating an appealing image, Russian cultural diplomacy is more focused on uniting the base of supporters, relying on the dispersed diaspora of ethnic Russians and 'Russian-speakers' (often Russified members of other ethnic groups)."[93] At the same time, some recent researchers emphasized how this organization expanded internationally, "The Foundation is one of the primary nodes of the state-controlled ecosystem of organizations devoted to expanding Russia's influence abroad, including Rossotrudnichestvo, the Gorchakov Fund, universities and their departments, research centers and think tanks, smaller oligarchic foundations, state-supported NGOs, state-focused media, etc."[94]

As a result, the geographical expansion of the Russkii Mir Foundation was a real success of this organization: by March 2022, the "Foundation had 104 active Centers in 52 countries, 128 Cabinets in 57 countries, and over 5,700 friendly organizations in nearly 160 countries (including 2700 such friendly organizations in Russia)."[95] Russian intelligence also played the most important role in the foundation's centers located in foreign countries. The most active were those centers, which were associated with the universities in Western Europe, the UK, and the US. Despite the fact, that as a reaction to Russia's war against Ukraine, by April 2023, 23 centers were closed in the West, some of those centers' local participants are still active at the University of Durham, the American University, and other academic locations in both the UK and the US.[96]

Two other Russian organizations—*Rossutrudnichestvo* in 2008, Alexander Gorchakov Public Diplomacy Fund in 2010—were created on the model of the Russkii Mir Foundation with the strong influences of Russian intelligence.

176   Chapter 7

The Russkii Mir Foundation, *Rossutrudnichestvo*, Alexander Gorchakov Public Diplomacy Fund, and many other Russian public diplomacy groups, which are the "front organizations" for Russian intelligence, still target the Western academics, their "agents of influence," trying to persuade them that only the West, and especially the Americans are guilty of the new wave of wars and the West's confrontations with Russia.[97] The KGB/FSB ideologists in Russia, who represent those organizations, like Andranik Migranian, a former director of the New York office of the Kremlin's Institute for Democracy and Cooperation, a think tank, which was founded both in Paris, France, and in the United States by FSB connected Russian oligarchs, blame only the Americans in "creating" all domestic and international problems for the Russian state.[98]

CONCLUSION: RUSSIAN ACADEMIC DIASPORA AND ITS INCORPORATION INTO THE WESTERN ACADEMIA

After the collapse of the Soviet Union in 1991, the West, and, especially, the Western academia, and, particularly, the American academic institutions, have witnessed the massive exodus of the former Soviet scholars to the West, especially to the United States and Canada. According to my research, the demographic model of this exodus was completely the same as a demography of the academic exchanges between the Soviet Union and the West during the détente and afterward. In both cases—the 1970s through the 1980s' Soviet visiting academic programs and the post-Soviet academic emigration after 1991—we observe the same patterns: more than 70 percent of both Soviet visitors and post-Soviet migrants came from the ruling Soviet political elites, and more than 80 percent of them represented only one city of the Soviet geopolitical space—Moscow.[99]

Between 1991 and 2005, the overwhelming majority (85 percent) of post-Soviet academic migration to the United States, at least, was Russian by origin. If we add the number of those Soviet Russian academics who settled in the US before 1991, we will have a growing Russian academic diaspora in the West, especially in the United States and Canada. More than 80 percent of that diaspora in the West consists of Muscovites, the residents of Moscow![100]

As some contemporaries described this demographic situation in the Russian diaspora in America, "After 1991, the Russians dominated the entire post-Soviet academic emigration to America, and the Russian residents from the city of Moscow, those Russian *CHMO*, prevailed. In Canada and the United States, two from three post-Soviet immigrants were *CHMO* from

Moscow, plus, we need to include a role of female *CHMO*-immigrants, who imposed their pro-Russian view on their American husbands."[101]

Another colleague of mine, whom I criticized for his collaboration with the KGB during his "American travels" before 1991, explained to me that:

> [He] had to do this [collaboration with Soviet intelligence] to get the official support for his trips to America, but all [his] Moscow colleagues, who immigrated to the USA and Canada, were either KGB agents, or KGB officers [they had *pogony KGB*, according to his words]. But now those Muscovites have their American jobs, teaching at various Canadian or American universities, and they distance themselves from Putin. At the same time, they are afraid to criticize Russian political regime, having their families and close friends, still living in Moscow. How could they be against the Russian politics, if they are linked to those Russian ruling elites by their origin, by their families, by their education! And do not forget about the strong pro-Moscow influences of those Russian women, who successfully married American specialists in the Slavic studies and encourage their husbands to support pro-Russian pro-Putin politics, not only to do their research. Frankly speaking, now, those Muscovites [he used a word *Moskvichi*—SZh.] in the Western academia, especially in the field of the Slavic Studies, play role of the "fifth column" of Putin's regime in the West, especially in the United States and Canada![102]

Many years after these interviews, the recent developments in Western academia prove the truth of those observations. Numerous Russian scholars, like Yuri Slezkine from the University of California, openly support Putin's political regime in its confrontation with the West.[103] On January 3, 2024, another Russian national working in Western academia, Dr. Viacheslav Morozov, "a professor of international political theory at the University of Tartu was detained by Estonia's internal security service (ISS)" "on espionage charges in a case that his university said shows Russia's intent to 'orchestrate anti-democratic action' in the Baltic country."[104] As the Russian-language sources, such as *Meduza* blog, described, "The head of the ISS said that Russia maintains a high-level of interest in spying in Estonia. According to him, Morozov's case 'illustrates the Russian special services' desire to penetrate different spheres of life in Estonia, including academia."[105] It is noteworthy that a majority of Russian academic diaspora criticized Estonia's decision to arrest Morozov as a Russian spy and supported Morozov as "an innocent victim of anti-Russian hysteria" in the West.[106]

The most typical reaction to Morozov's arrest in Estonia was demonstrated by Ivan Kurilla, another Russian scholar-Americanist, who avoids public criticism of Putin's regime's aggression and the Russian war crimes in Ukraine, and who is a frequent participant of numerous American venues for Slavic studies, such as the annual meetings of ASEEES (the Association for Slavic, East European, and Eurasian Studies) and who is a recipient of the Kennan Institute awards.[107] Dr. Kurilla, who is now a professor of history and international relations at the European University in St. Petersburg, Russia (a former professor of history at Volgograd State University), criticized Morozov's arrest as a "criminal prosecution on the basis of [his Russian] citizenship." Paradoxically, Kurilla blamed the Estonian authorities not in their protection of Estonian statehood against the Russian interference, but rather in their imitation of the old Soviet legal practices: "The University of Tartu fired Morozov based on an arrest, before the trial and proof of guilt. Well, we know what country does that. The university proved that, in practice, its Soviet heritage is stronger than its European one."[108] Unfortunately, according to Kurilla's biography, his Soviet Americanist's past influenced his pro-Russian, anti-American, and anti-Western criticism. Despite his liberal academic approaches, which he demonstrated during the meetings with his American colleagues, his reaction to Morozov's arrest reminds us that Dr. Kurilla worked in 2002–2003 as a Vice Rector for International Programs at Volgograd State University.[109] This position, which in Russian is known as *a prorector po rabote s inostrantsami*, was officially part of Russian intelligence "nomenklatura," a position, which was historically "directly connected to a KGB/FSB approval and required KGB/FSB security clearance."[110] Before getting this KGB/FSB position in Volgograd University, which was from 1998 to 2001, Kurilla worked as a regional coordinator for Lower Volga at the Open Society Institute, which was sponsored by the George Soros Open Society Foundation in post-Soviet countries.[111] According to the former KGB analysts, "Only KGB/FSB approved Russian scholars with old KGB Soviet connections were allowed to work with the foreign financial organizations, such as Soros Open Society Foundation."[112]

Unfortunately, this case with all of those reactions to Morozov's arrest by the Estonian authorities and by the Russian academics, such as Kurilla, also illustrated another reality: the deep integration of the Russian academic diaspora into the Western academia, not only in the US and Canada, where Russian emigrants and Russian visitors built their new post-Soviet academic career, but also in the former Soviet republics, like Estonia, where the Russians tried to dominate the academic and political discourse.

NOTES

1. Interview with Ivan Grigorovich K., a retired KGB officer, March 3, 2019, Kyiv, Ukraine.

2. I quote my interview with Leonid K., a retired KGB officer, March 3, 2019, Kyiv, Ukraine, who suggested to me this quotation from the original official

American documents about the founding of the Wilson Center: https://www.govinfo.gov/content/pkg/STATUTE-82/pdf/STATUTE-82-Pg1356.pdf.
3. See my interview with Leonid K., and SBU, f. 16, spr. 1077, ark. 343 ff., and spr. 116, ark. 210–212.
4. See about how the KGB monitored the Soviet-US relations in the 1970s: SBU, f. 16, op. 1, spr. 1045, ark. 19–247, and spr. 1046, ark. 51–228.
5. In all KGB operatives' reports, they always quoted the *Time* magazine article "Education: Studying the Soviets," from April 25, 1976. All KGB officers, whom I interviewed in 2019, gave me their own old Xerox copies of this American publication with their own notes on it, which was quoted by the KGB administration in both Moscow and Kyiv during the 1970s in their reference for KGB operations against the Kennan Institute. See this link, the most quoted by the KGB publication: https://content.time.com/time/subscriber/article/0,33009,913990,00.html.
6. See https://content.time.com/time/subscriber/article/0,33009,913990,00.html.
Some KGB analysts also emphasized how the American periodical described the reaction of the Soviet officials, who were "also impressed. Says one: 'We do not have entirely fond memories of Ambassador Kennan himself [the Kremlin declared him persona non grata after he denounced Stalinism in 1953], but we regard the formation of his institute as a positive development.' Indeed, the Russians feel that in *the Institut Imyeni Kennana* the U.S. finally has a worthy counterpart to Moscow's U.S.A. Institute—a think tank for Americanologists in the Soviet Union." I refer to my interview with Leonid K.
7. Interview with Leonid K.
8. I quote my interview with Leonid K. and my interview with Nikolai Bolkhovitinov, June 12, 1991, Moscow.
9. I quote my interview with Nikolai Bolkhovitinov, June 12, 1991, Moscow. See in detail this story of Bolkhovitinov's travels to the US in 1975 in Sergei I. Zhuk, *Nikolai Bolkhovitinov and American Studies in the USSR: People's Diplomacy in the Cold War* (Lanham, MD: Lexington Books, 2017), 161–163.
10. See a story of these symposia in Lawrence S. Kaplan, "The American Revolution in an International Perspective: Views from Bicentennial Symposia," *The International History Review*, vol. 1, no. 3 (July 1979): 408–426, esp. pp. 423, 424, and N. N. Bolkhovitinov, "Simpoziumy Biblioteki Kongressa v sviazi s 200-letiem Amerikanskoi revoliutsii," *Novaia i Noveishaia Istoria*, no. 6 (1975): 227–229. His paper was published the next year in English as Nikolai N. Bolkhovitinov, "American Revolution and the Russian Empire," *The Impact of the American Revolution Abroad*: Papers presented at IV Symposium, May 8 and 9, 1975 (Washington, D.C.: Library of Congress, 1976), 80–97. See also Philip Ranlet, *Richard B. Morris and American History in the Twentieth Century* (Lanham, MD: University Press of America, 2004), 141–149, especially p. 145. There were four annual symposia—each year from 1972 to 1975.
11. Interview with Nikolai Bolkhovitinov, June 12, 1991, Moscow.
12. Even in May–June of 1991, on the eve of the collapse of the USSR, Alexei Arbatov, a young Soviet Americanist, the son of the ISKAN director, Georgy Arbatov,

was a guest scholar of the Kennan Institute: https://www.wilsoncenter.org/person/alexei-georgievitch-arbatov.

13. Both Bolkhovitinov from Moscow and Arnold Shlepakov from Kyiv described in the same words these KGB instructions. I quote my interview with Nikolai Bolkhovitinov, June 12, 1991.

14. I quote my interview with Leonid K. Compare with the documents about the KGB analysis of American academic diplomacy and its CIA connections in SBU, f. 16, op. 1, spr. 1141, ark. 380–381 ff.

15. Interview with Nikolai Bolkhovitinov, July 18, 2008, Moscow, Russia.

16. Strobe Talbott in Arbatov, *The System: An Insider's Life in Soviet Politics* (New York: Random House, 1992), xv.

17. Sarah E. Mendelson, *Changing Course: Ideas, Politics, and the Soviet Withdrawal from Afghanistan* (Princeton: Princeton University Press, 1998), 89.

18. See about this in the documents of IREX and ACLS. Some of them are available online. See especially http://digitalcollections.library.cmu.edu/awweb/awarchive?type=file&item=54988. See also numerous publications about these academic connections, e.g., *Milestones in Glasnost and Perestroyka*, edited by A. Hewett and Victor H. Winston (Washington, D.C.: The Brookings Institution, 1991), 412, 429. Compare with a more critical evaluation of Soviet Americanists from ISKAN in Ted Hopf, *Peripheral Visions: Deterrence Theory and American Foreign Policy in the Third World, 1965–1990* (Ann Arbor: University of Michigan Press, 1994), 130ff. See also https://people.ceu.edu/alexei_miller.

19. See about this in detail in Sergei I. Zhuk, *Soviet Americana: The Cultural History of Russian and Ukrainian Americanists* (London and New York: I.B. Tauris, 2018), 237ff.

20. See https://www.wilsoncenter.org/person/vladislav-zubok.

21. See https://nsarchive.gwu.edu/search?s=zubok&op=Search.

22. See https://www.lse.ac.uk/international-history/people/academicstaff/zubok/zubok.

23. See https://carnegieendowment.org/2009/02/03/dmitri-trenin-appointed-director-carnegie-moscow-center/4ndc.

24. See https://english.gordonua.com/news/exclusiveenglish/who-is-dimitri-simes-and-why-is-he-trying-to-sink-mayflower-investigation-by-yuri-felshtinsky-316154.html, and in: https://carnegiemoscow.org/experts/287.

25. See the links about their activities at https://www.wilsoncenter.org/publication/why-russia-and-america-need-each-other and about other Trenin's colleagues, like Alexey Arbatov, Alexei Miller, Yuri Slezkine, and Vladislav Zubok in https://www.middlebury.edu/institute/academics/centers-initiatives/monterey-initiative-russian-studies/mssr-2018/experts; https://www.middlebury.edu/institute/academics/centers-initiatives/monterey-initiative-russian-studies/mssr-2022/experts; https://www.middlebury.edu/institute/academics/centers-initiatives/monterey-initiative-russian-studies/geopolitics-move/experts; and https://www.middlebury.edu/institute/academics/centers-initiatives/monterey-initiative-russian-studies/visiting-experts/bios.

26. See Sergei I. Zhuk, *KGB Operations against the USA and Canada in Soviet Ukraine, 1953–1991* (London and New York: Routledge [Taylor & Francis] Publishing Company, 2022), Chapter 3, pp. 50–76.

27. SBU, f, 16, op. 1, spr. 944, ark. 98–101.

28. Sergei I. Zhuk, *KGB Operations*, 171–173.

29. Quoted from Craig Unger, *American Kompromat: How the KGB Cultivated Donald Trump, and Related Tales of Sex, Greed, Power, and Treachery* (New York: Dutton, 2021), 31.

30. In the early 1960s, the KGB continued to monitor the families of the Ukrainian Jews, who used to live in the US before WWII and later returned to the USSR as Soviet citizens. After their experience with Soviet realities, some of those families tried to re-immigrate back to the US and contacted American officials from the US Embassy. The KGB arrested them and used "their Zionist-American" connections, as a pretext for their persecution. See the Rosenberg family (father, son, and daughter) case in the Kyiv KGB office in SBU, f. 16, op. 1, spr. 944, ark. 70–77.

31. Craig Unger, *American Kompromat*, 30–32. See about Kislin's connections with Russian intelligence on pp. 17, 26, 28, 35–36, 45, 46.

32. See, e.g., in SBU, f. 16, op.1, spr. 1271, ark. 21–25; spr. 1295, ark. 52–54, 83–85 ff.

33. SBU, f. 16, op.1, ark. 83–91. See about a creation of hundreds of front companies by the KGB in the 1980s in Craig Unger, *House of Trump, House of Putin: The Untold Story of Donald Trump and Russian Mafia* (New York: Penguin, 2019), 70–71, 144–145; see about KGB recruiting useful Americans, so-called American assets on pp. 28–29, 46–47.

34. I quoted my interviews with Leonid K. and with Ivan Grigorovich K. (Both interviews were done in 2019 in Kyiv.)

35. See this link on the Wilson Center's official site: https://www.wilsoncenter.org/article/wilson-center-to-honor-pickering-and-alekperov-for-contributions-to-us-russian-relations. Compare with Kateryna Smagliy (with Ilya Zaslavskiy), "Hybrid Analytica: Pro-Kremlin Expert Propaganda in Moscow, Europe and the U.S. A Case Study on Think Tanks and Universities," p. 38: https://www.underminers.info/publications/hybridanalytica.

36. Yevgeniy Primakov was a head of KGB of its First Directorate (foreign intelligence) in 1991, and afterward he was a head of SVR (Russian foreign intelligence). See https://www.britannica.com/biography/Yevgeny-Primakov. Karen Dawisha was a Public Policy Scholar at the Wilson Center in 2012. See https://www.wilsoncenter.org/person/karen-dawisha.

37. Kateryna Smagliy, "Hybrid Analytica," p. 38. See about those connections in Karen Dawisha, *Putin's Kleptocracy: Who Owns Russia?* (New York: Simon & Schuster, 2014), 277, 19–20, and Mikhail Zygar, *All the Kremlin's Men: Inside the Court of Vladimir Putin* (New York: Public Affairs, 2016), vii, 26. Compare with Craig Unger, *House of Trump, House of Putin*, 216–217.

38. See https://www.wilsoncenter.org/article/wilson-center-honors-vekselberg-and-cloherty-first-kathryn-and-shelby-cullom-davis-awards.

39. See https://www.wilsoncenter.org/article/kennan-institute-pleased-to-support-the-us-russian-business-council-18th-annual-meeting.
40. Craig Unger, *House of Trump, House of Putin*, 293. Compare with: https://apnews.com/article/russia-ukraine-putin-new-york-manhattan-viktor-vekselberg-a30 82f5072ad5a8ce5784038ccbfbfb1.
41. See various studies of Putin's regime, including Karen Dawisha, *Putin's Kleptocracy*, 19–20, 101, 118, 119, 196; Mikhail Zygar, op. cit., 57; Steven Lee Myers, *The New Tsar: The Rise and Reign of Vladimir Putin* (New York: Simon & Schuster, 2015), 251.
42. See https://www.wilsoncenter.org/article/wilson-center-honors-petr-aven-and-susan-carmel-lehrman.
43. See https://www.wilsoncenter.org/event/preparing-for-the-future-assessing-the-conditions-and-capacity-for-american-engagement-russia.
44. I quote the Wilson Center's website: https://www.wilsoncenter.org/article/alfa-fellowship-program-celebrates-15-classes-fellows-collaboration-the-kennan-institute.
45. Kateryna Smagliy, op. cit., 38.
46. See https://www.wilsoncenter.org/article/statement-rescinded-awards-viktor-f-vekselberg-and-petr-aven.
47. See https://data-scripts.ovd.info/agents/?lang=en.
48. See the official site of this program: https://alfafellowship.org/participant-profile.
49. I quote from Christopher Miller's page on Alfa Fellowship Program's site: https://alfapro.wpengine.com/?p=660. Christopher Miller did this in Moscow, in 2013–2014, during the period of this first Russian war, before defending his dissertation at Yale University. Compare with other Alfa Fellows: https://alfafellowship.org/alumni.
50. I refer to Olga Bertelsen, "Russian Front Organizations and Western Academia," *International Journal of Intelligence and Counterintelligence*, vol. 36, no. 4 (2023): 1184–1209.
51. See Yuri Goriachev's publication in 1991: https://www.taylorfrancis.com/chapters/edit/10.4324/9781003062493-36/soviet-peace-fund-united-nations-yuri-goriachev?context=ubx. Compare with KGB documents about the international organizations, including the United Nations Organization, which were used by the KGB during the 1960s and the 1970s: SBU, f. 16, op. 1, spr. 938, ark. 92–109.
52. See in detail in *Russian Cultural Diplomacy Under Putin: Rossutrudnichestvo, the "Russkii Mir" Foundation, and the Gorchakov Fund in 2007–2022*, edited by Nadiia Koval and Denys Tereshchenko (Stuttgart: ibidem-Verlag, 2023), 29–31. See also Michael David-Fox, *Showcasing the Great Experiment: Cultural Diplomacy and Western Visitors to the Soviet Union, 1921–1941* (New York: Oxford University Press, 2012).
53. I quote Leonid K. He referred to Nikolai Patrushev, who served as a FSB director in 1999–2008, and since 2008 he is a Secretary of the Security Council of Russia.
54. See https://valdaiclub.com/about/valdai.
55. See https://valdaiclub.com/about/valdai.

56. Interview with Ivan Grigorovich K., a retired KGB officer, March 3, 2019, Kyiv, Ukraine, and interview with Leonid K. See Valdai Club site about those names: https://valdaiclub.com/about/founders.

57. See https://www.washingtonpost.com/posteverything/wp/2016/10/26/is-there-value-in-valdai.

58. Marcel H. Van Herpen, *Putin's Propaganda Machine: Soft Power and Russian Foreign Policy* (Lanham, MD, and Boulder, CO: Rowman and Littlefield's Lexington Books, 2017), 62, 68. See especially the official US government documents: https://www.govinfo.gov/content/pkg/CPRT-115SPRT28110/html/CPRT-115SPRT28110.htm; https://www.foreign.senate.gov/imo/media/doc/FinalRR.pdf, p. 48; and Orysia Lutsevych, *Agents of the Russian World: Proxy Groups in the Contested Neighbourhood*, Chatham House, at 11 and 12 (Apr. 2016).

59. Orysia Lutsevych, *Agents of the Russian World.*

60. See https://www.wilsoncenter.org/person/matthew-rojansky.

61. I quote from https://www.axios.com/2021/04/10/biden-national-security-council-russia-director.

62. See https://www.politico.com/news/2021/04/19/biden-russia-expert-483000.

63. See https://archive.kyivpost.com/article/opinion/op-ed/alumni-deeply-concerned-kennan-institutes-growing-pro-kremlin-policies.html.

64. See https://ucca.org/wp-content/uploads/2020/03/Biden-Rojansky-Letter-Apr-2021.pdf.

65. See https://valdaiclub.com/about/experts/425/?sphrase_id=1606195.

66. I quote Leonid K.

67. See https://valdaiclub.com/about/experts/10200/. See also Wilson Center's site: https://www.wilsoncenter.org/person/jill-dougherty.

68. See https://valdaiclub.com/about/experts/434/?sphrase_id=1604180.

69. See https://valdaiclub.com/about/experts/403/?sphrase_id=1604183.

70. I refer to a Richard Sakwa's book discussion, organized by Marlene Laruelle at the Institute of European, Russian and Eurasian Studies, George Washington University, in Washington, D.C., on January 24, 2024: https://myemail.constantcontact.com/The-Lost-Peace--How-the-West-Failed-to-Prevent-a-Second-Cold-War.html?soid=1110347635144&aid=d2147F6Uevw.

71. See https://valdaiclub.com/about/experts/370/?sphrase_id=1603575; https://valdaiclub.com/about/experts/4127/?sphrase_id=1603822.

72. See in detail about this organization in: *Russian Cultural Diplomacy Under Putin*, 99–159.

73. See https://russkiymir.ru/en/fund.

74. Ibid.

75. See https://russkiymir.ru/en/fund/decree.php.

76. See Kozak's biography and his Ukrainian roots at https://web.archive.org/web/20160411023734/http://perebezhchik.ru/person/kozak-dmitriy-nikolaevich.

77. *Russian Cultural Diplomacy*, 159.

78. I use my interview with Nikolai Bolkhovitinov, who knew Nikonov as his colleague-Americanist from Moscow. Bolkhovitinov used the words "KGB men" to characterize Nikonov and his father. See also Vyacheslav Nikonov's story about his

father at https://www.vremyan.ru/news/prazdnik_pobedy_dlja_menja_ochen_lichnyj_nikonov.html.

79. I quote from Mikhail Voslensky, *Nomenklatura: The Ruling Class in the Soviet Union* (*Nomenklatura: Gospodstvuiushchii klass Sovetskogo Soiuza*), Second Edition (London: Overseas Publications Interchange, 1990), p. 126: «Так попал в номенклатуру доцент Никонов, бросивший семью и презревший угрозы парторганизации, для того лишь, чтобы жениться на дочери Молотова, отнюдь не блещущей красотой».

80. I follow my interview with Nikolai Bolkhovitinov, July 15, 1995. See also how Nikonov's connections to Molotov helped him to get an editor's position in *Communist*: https://www.imemo.ru/inozemtsev-ocherkcherkasov#_ftnref20.

81. See https://russianlife.com/magazine/jan-feb-2002/100-young-russians-to-watch/vyacheslav-nikonov-historian.

82. See about MGU Americanists, such as Yaz'kov in Sergei I. Zhuk, *Soviet Americana*, 28, 130, 189.

83. I refer to my conversations in 1991 in Moscow with both Yaz'kov and Nikolai Bolkhovitinov.

84. See Caltech publications: https://campuspubs.library.caltech.edu/2449/1/1993_02_27_01.pdf; and https://calteches.library.caltech.edu/3739/1/Constitution.pdf.

85. *Russian Cultural Diplomacy Under Putin*, 116–117.

86. Ibid., 117.

87. V. A. Nikonov, *Sovremennyi mir i ego istoki* (Moscow: Izd-vo Moskovskogo universiteta, 2015), esp. 302–304.

88. N. A. Tsvetkova, "Publichania diplomatiia SSHA: ot kholodnoi voiny k novoi kholodnoi voine," in *Rossiia i SShA: poznavaia drug druga. Sbornik pamiati akademika Aleksandra Aleksandrovicha Fursenko*, edited by Vladimir V. Noskov (Saint-Petersburg: Nestor-Istoriia, 2015), 82–97, citations are from pp. 92 and 93.

89. See https://www.vedomosti.ru/politics/articles/2023/09/18/995847-vyacheslav-nikonov-pokinet-russkii-mir.

90. See https://www.lse.ac.uk/international-history/people/academicstaff/zubok/zubok.

91. See https://www.lse.ac.uk/International-History/Images/People/Academic-Staff/zubok/ZubokCV2016.pdf, p. 8.

92. I quote an article "Integrating Russian Academia" from https://russkiymir.ru/en/magazines/article/144532.

93. *Russian Cultural Diplomacy Under Putin*, 158.

94. Ibid.

95. Ibid., 139.

96. Ibid., 147–148.

97. See in detail about *Rossutrudnichestvo* and Gorchakov Fund in *Russian Cultural Diplomacy Under Putin*, 23–97 and 161–198. Compare with Olga Bertelsen, "Russian Front Organizations and Western Academia."

98. Andranik Migranian, "Putin Triumphs in Ukraine," *The National Interest*, March 6, 2014. See about the role of Andranik Migranian as an adviser of both Presidents Yeltsin and Putin in Eugeniusz Górski, *Civil Society, Pluralism and*

Universalism (Polish Philosophical Studies, VIII) (Washington, DC: The Council for Research in Values and Philosophy, 2007), 57, 58, 61.

99. See my calculations from Sergei I. Zhuk, *Soviet Americana*, 96, and idem, *KGB Operations*, 88, 93, 171–187. Compare with the documents of IREX and other US organizations from Manuscript Collection at the Library of Congress and SBU archival documents from fond 16, Kyiv, Ukraine.

100. I checked numerous specialists in Russian studies (history, anthropology, political science) among faculty of the major big schools—universities and colleges—in the US and Canada. The typical schools in my search included the University of South Carolina, where in its department of history I found a Muscovite, Professor Elena Osokina; and York University, where in its department of politics I found another Muscovite, Associate Professor Sergei Plekhanov.

101. Interview with Leonid K. He referred to the old anti-Moscow Soviet folklore. As early as the 1950s, provincials began calling Muscovites *chmo* (acronym from combination of the Russian words *chelovek Moskvy i Moskovskoi oblasti*—a resident of Moscow and the Moscow region). According to the retired Soviet military officers, in the 1950s a sudden influx of the physically weak and effeminate young conscripts from the Moscow region into the Soviet Army resulted in their senior officers complaining about unpreparedness of these young soldiers from Moscow for the requirements of military service. Eventually, Soviet military officers used *chmo* in their documents to mark the names of the conscripts from Moscow and the Moscow region. In the 1960s and 1970s this acronym left Soviet army circles, penetrated Soviet civilian population, and became a popular word used to characterize any weak and effeminate male character. As a result, people forgot about the Soviet army origin of this term. Traditionally, provincial population in the USSR distanced themselves from Muscovites, using various bad words, including *chmo*. See in Sergei Zhuk, *Nikolai Bolkhovitinov*, 244. Usually, American scholars-Slavists married to Russians (especially to Muscovites) try to avoid any public criticism of Putin's Russia and Russian atrocities in Ukraine.

102. I quote my interviews with Leonid Leshchenko, June 23, 2012, and June 25, 2013, Kyiv, Ukraine.

103. See in detail about this in chapter 6.

104. See https://www.theguardian.com/world/2024/jan/16/russian-professor-arrested-in-estonia-on-espionage-charges.

105. See https://meduza.io/en/feature/2024/01/19/well-known-in-his-field.

106. See, among many Russian emigrants' reactions, a position of Dmitry Dubrovsky, a former associate professor at Russia's Higher School of Economics and Morozov's colleague, who works now in various East European academic venues, at https://meduza.io/en/feature/2024/01/19/well-known-in-his-field.

107. See https://www.wilsoncenter.org/person/ivan-kurilla.

108. Quotation is from https://meduza.io/en/feature/2024/01/19/well-known-in-his-field.

109. See his c.v. at https://eu-spb.academia.edu/IvanKurilla/CurriculumVitae.

110. See Mikhail Voslensky, *Nomenklatura,* 128. See also in detail about this university's position in Sergei I. Zhuk, *Soviet Americana*, 11. Compare with my old

interview of Nikolai Bolkhovitinov, who criticized the conservative Soviet political position of the "young Americanist from Volgograd." See his criticism of Kurilla in my interview with Nikolai N. Bolkhovitinov, January 4, 2004, Moscow, Russian Federation. Compare with the recent analysis of FSB functions in Russian universities: https://www.opendemocracy.net/en/odr/what-fsb-is-doing-in-russian-universities.

111. See https://eu-spb.academia.edu/IvanKurilla/CurriculumVitae.

112. Interview with Leonid K. In early 2024, Dr. Kurilla was fired by his Russian employer for *proguly* (absenteeism), and now he is looking for asylum in the US.

Epilogue
KGB Legacy and Failed "Westernization" of Russia

After the collapse of the Soviet Union in 1991, many Western (especially American) observers and historians shared a euphoria of the downfall of communism and the end of the Cold War. This euphoria was reinforced by the rise of the new revisionist school in the Soviet studies in the US, and by a massive emigration of post-Soviet Russian scholars to the West, who brought the nostalgic, idealistic vision of their Soviet past, which fit the revisionist version of Sovietology in various Western centers of Slavic studies as well. As a result, the Western Slavists, and especially Sovietologists, ignored the very serious legacy of the Soviet past in post-Soviet geopolitical space: the KGB influences in all spheres of life, from politics to culture. This KGB legacy, which became obvious today in the confrontational character of Russian foreign policy, Russian special aggressiveness in its relations with the West, was (and still is) a dangerous element of both domestic and international politics of the Russian Federation. For many years, the former Soviet dissidents, like Vladimir Bukovsky, tried to explain this "KGB threat" to the Western public, which began forgetting about an existence of this KGB legacy after 1991.[1]

For me, personally, it was a real shock, after my emigration to the United States in 1997, to see how my American colleagues, especially historians and political scientists, idealized post-Soviet Russian politics, completely ignoring KGB legacy there. I tried to explain this KGB danger to all my American friends, but they did not listen to me, idealizing their post-Soviet Russian connections. But I had a very different personal experience with this KGB legacy. Coming from the Ukrainian patriotic region of "*Shevchenkiv krai*" (Zvenigorodka district, Cherkasy Region of Ukraine, where poet Taras Shevchenko, a symbol of Ukrainian independence, lived in the 19th century), I entered the university in 1976 in a big industrial Soviet Ukrainian city, which experienced a massive and very aggressive Russification campaign. This "rocket" city, famous for its production of the Soviet military missiles, was closed by the KGB to any foreign influences, and the KGB used it for its various anti-Western ideological operations all the time. Moreover, at the department of history of Dnipropetrovsk University, where I spent five years as an undergraduate student, I experienced not only processes of forceful Russification, but also a constant presence of the KGB people there. The assistant chair of our department was Professor Anatolii O. Gusak, a retired KGB officer; some faculty members were infamously known for denouncing to the KGB office my classmates for their criticism of Soviet realities and for reading the "forbidden dissident" literature. Eventually, later on, I described my frustration with this situation in my books about Dnipropetrovsk and the strong KGB connections of this city.[2] Moreover, when Taras Kuzio proposed me in 2020 to co-edit a project about a prominent post-Soviet, patriotic Ukrainian role of this city, I was reluctant to collaborate with him, because I did not like the city, which was associated in my historical imagination ONLY with Brezhnev/KGB Mafia there.[3] So, by publishing my research on the KGB and post-Soviet Russian intelligence influences in post-Soviet space, I tried to attract my Western colleagues' attention to this KGB legacy. But all was in vain. The Western (especially American) think tanks kept hiring the Soviet Russian intelligence officers, like Dmitri Trenin, as their Russian post-Soviet administrators (like Carnegie Foundation did); various Slavic associations and schools in the West kept inviting and financing Russian scholars, like Alexei Miller, who were connected to Russian intelligence and to its "front organizations" such as the Valdai discussion club.

AMERICANIZATION AS PART OF WESTERNIZATION OF RUSSIA

Only the open Russian war against Ukraine in 2022, officially announced by Putin as a "special military operation" against the Western/American influences in post-Soviet geopolitical space, revealed not only the KGB nature of Putin's regime, but also the failure of the Western politicians and academics to bring Russia "back into the Western civilization." Now the same observers, who wanted "Russian integration into the West," suddenly noted how Putin's "Americanized" Russia imitated the American political practices, such as "the US intrusion under Hilary Clinton into Russian domestic politics" or using the US military contractors for foreign military operations in Iraq and Afghanistan. As a result of this copycatting of American actions, Russia interfered in US politics in 2016, supporting Donald Trump, and used a private military mercenary organization, Wagner group, in the Russian war against

Ukraine in 2022–23.⁴ Paradoxically, Putin's Russia, which became openly anti-Western and anti-American, still incorporates and utilizes the typical forms of cultural production/consumption and political practices, traditionally known as "American/Western" ones. The events of the Russian wars against independent Ukraine in 2014, and especially in 2022–24, revealed the ambivalent ("love-hate") attitudes toward this concept of "Westernization/ Americanization" among not only the Russian political elites, especially among the Russian/former Soviet intelligence officers, who play an important role in shaping such attitudes in Putin's Russia, but also among the ordinary Russians at least since 2001, since the rise of "the KGB oligarchy," or the "Chekist regime" in the post-Soviet geopolitical space.

Historically, the prevailing form of Russian Westernization was "Americanization" of Russian politics, economy, and culture. This beginning of the fascination with American civilization among the people, who lived in the geopolitical space of the former Russian Empire/Soviet Union, was directly connected to their reading of the adventure novels of American writers such as James Fenimore Cooper (1789–1851) and British writer Thomas Mayne Reid (1818–1883), who portrayed brave Indigenous Americans fighting the European colonizers in North America. Eventually, more American literature and the films and music from the United States, especially after 1917, strengthened this "cult of America" among the citizens of Soviet Russia. According to many scholars, this massive consumption of cultural products from "capitalist America" became the major tool of Russian "Americanization."⁵

Another source of interest in American civilization was directly connected to a notion of modernity, which, since the nineteenth century, became associated in the Russian imagination and scholarship with "American modernity."⁶ This fascination with America especially influenced the Marxists in the Russian/Soviet imperial space. All major leaders of the Bolshevik regime in the Soviet Union idealized the American experience as a model for Soviet socialism since the early days of the Bolshevik Revolution in 1917. Even the socialist industrialization, "a peculiar version of the industrial revolution in the USSR," used the American industrial towns, like Gary, Indiana, as a model for creating the Soviet "Magnetic Mountain" towns for initiating the industrial modernization of Soviet socialist landscape.⁷ Both Lenin and Stalin emphasized a significance of the American models of modernity for Soviet socialism. As Stalin noted in 1924, "The combination of Russian revolutionary sweep with American efficiency is the essence of Leninism in party and state activity."⁸ Eventually, all major industrial and technological projects of the Stalinist Soviet Union used the American innovations and financial investments.⁹

During WWII, despite all ideological and political differences, the USSR and the US became political allies, justifying to some extent the role of American civilization as a model for Soviet socialist modernity. Even during the Cold War confrontation, since 1945, this trend of idealization of American civilization continued in the USSR. The Cold War was also a process of a paradoxical imitation of capitalist America, the major geopolitical opponent of the Soviet Union, especially in the spheres of cultural production and consumption. This process led to the peculiar forms of Americanization, which reflected both domestic and international issues of the special chronological conditions. The first stage of this "Soviet Americanization" took place during late Stalinism (1945–1953); the second stage of Americanization was triggered by Nikita Khrushchev's anti-Stalin reforms and opening the Soviet society to the Western influences (1953–1964); the next, third, stage was a result of Leonid Brezhnev's détente, a relaxation of international tensions and collaboration with the West (1968–1984). Finally, the last, fourth, stage of such Americanization became as a Soviet reaction to Mikhail Gorbachev's perestroika and the opening of politics of dialogue with the United States (1985–1991).

The beginning of détente in US-Soviet relations in the 1970s not only resulted in some important changes in the distribution and consumption of American cultural products such as films among Soviet consumers, but also in the direct appropriation (even copycatting) of certain American cultural practices related to cinema and television, such US film genres as the western, musical comedy, and even sitcoms for Soviet television. A very important role in this process belonged to various Soviet Americanists, the experts in US history, politics, and culture. During the 1970s, 600 of them became active participants in the various political, cultural, and academic exchanges between the US and the USSR, directly contributing to the Americanization of cultural politics of the Soviet administration.[10]

To some extent, during the peak of Soviet Americanization, in the détente of the 1970s and perestroika of the 1980s and the 1990s, this process followed the same paradigm of two previous ones (during late Stalinism and Khrushchev): an imitation of US cultural and political forms and practices, on the one hand, and fighting the same practices as "dangerous capitalist propaganda," on the other hand. The most important controller of this Americanization was the KGB and other institutions of Soviet intelligence.

Since the beginning of the Cold War, Soviet political police had tried to push and promote the pro-Soviet, pro-Russian narrative in Western, especially in the American, interpretations of history, politics, and culture. At the same time, various Soviet ideologists and the KGB blamed the Americans in their rejection of the pro-Soviet and pro-Russian explanations of the geopolitics and betrayal of the Soviet-American political dialogue. Even the reasons for the Cold War confrontation with the former allies, like the United States, were interpreted and presented by the KGB, and after the collapse of communism, by the FSB, as a fault and betrayal of the Americans. The KGB used not only the official textbooks and scholarly monographs, but also popular culture such as adventure novels, films, and television shows to promote its narrative among the general audience in both the Soviet Union and post-Soviet Russia, blaming the Americans in the anti-Russian politics and preferences.

"SEDUCTIVE ADVERSARY," OR "AMERICANIZATION" AND THE RISE OF THE KGB OLIGARCHY

After the Second World War, during the Cold War, Soviet political police and major intelligence agency, the KGB, targeted the United States as the "main enemy in the world" for the Soviet Union. According to Christopher Andrew, "Throughout the Cold War, Soviet intelligence regarded the United States as its 'main adversary.'"[11] In their everyday counterintelligence activities inside the Soviet Union, through the entire period of post-Stalin socialism, the KGB operatives still dealt mainly with the intelligence from the "main adversary," the United States. According to the official counterintelligence research of KGB in Kyiv, a number of the spies from the US always dominated regarding the number of spies from other capitalist countries. Thus, in January–August of 1969, there were 133 cases of espionage in Soviet Ukraine, committed by foreigners. Of them, 74 were committed by Americans, 12 by Englishmen, 19 by French, and 11 by West Germans.[12] This was the typical ratio for the KGB operations in Ukraine. During the 1970s and the 1980s, more than 60 percent of all recorded and reported KGB counterintelligence operations in Soviet Ukraine targeted the US and Canada only.

"Capitalist America" became not only the "main" but also the "seductive" adversary of the KGB, creating the attractive cultural products and practices for Soviet consumers. Paradoxically, the KGB operatives were also attracted to various "material and cultural items" they associated with the "seductive America." As one retired KGB officer recalled, "despite all our ideological communist upbringing, we, young KGB officers, still dreamed about the products 'made in the USA,' about a possibility to get a special assignment involving a 'business trip' to America, which would allow us to bring the desired items from America to Ukraine."[13] Former KGB officers, like Oleg Kalugin, recalled how the KGB agents, living in the US on intelligence assignments, enjoyed consumption of American products and services, "falling in love with America" and the American way of life. As Kalugin (who was sent officially to the US as an exchange student of journalism) described his own fascination with America in his memoirs, "I was twenty-four and had been turned loose in New York City with the princely sum of $250 a month in Fulbright spending money. I was living for free in Columbia's John Jay Hall," he continued, "taking journalism courses, and being encouraged by the school newspaper—and the KGB—to sniff around New York and get acquainted with American life . . . I visited scores of neighborhoods and all the major museums. I saw ball games and went to the Metropolitan Opera. I rode buses and subways for hours and saw more than one hundred films. I went to a strip club in Greenwich Village, shelling out $40 for a drink with one of the dancers."[14] But the most important effect of the exchange program on Soviet Americanists was the developing, even among the "KGB people," of a psychological phenomenon, which some contemporaries called "a fondness of America and its people."[15] As Allen H. Kassof from IREX explained this phenomenon:

> We know in retrospect that many of the Soviet Americanists who came to do research on the United States as adversaries developed a very complex symbiotic relationship with their subjects. Beginning as analysts of American life, they gradually became supporters: the internal messengers of new conceptions of Soviet-American relations and, ultimately, spokesmen for alternatives. On the personal level, they developed significant friendships not only with their counterparts in the American sovietological community, who were their most readily accessible colleagues, but with a representative spectrum of American elites.[16]

This hidden curiosity, and fascination, about "capitalist America" was obviously present in all individual KGB reports (including the counterintelligence ones), which were submitted to their administration by the KGB operatives, who worked with the American visitors in Soviet Ukraine. Those KGB officers, who "worked" with the American tourists in Kyiv, recalled that "after a long communication with an American visitor, besides the classified intelligence information, a KGB agent usually reported the numerous details of everyday life in America of his visitor: about American cars, education, food, fashions, even films and television shows."[17] As KGB operatives joked, by participating in those anti-American operations, the KGB officers "discovered the various details of everyday life in American civilization: it was a peculiar process of the 'discovery of America/the American Other' by struggling not only with the alleged American intelligence agents, but also with American propaganda during consumption of the 'seductive American products.'"[18]

During the Cold War détente period, institutionalization of various academic centers for American studies in Moscow and Leningrad/St. Petersburg was used by the officers of the KGB and GRU (military intelligence), the two Soviet intelligence agencies, to create cover positions for themselves, to invite American policymakers and academics to the Soviet Union and to undertake intelligence-related missions to the United States. Even the first group of four Soviet students of American studies, who participated in the initial academic exchange with Americans at Columbia University in 1958, included three professional Soviet intelligence officers. American hosts were aware of this mission from Soviet research centers, which sent their representatives to the US "to spy and to interfere with American politics." According to the available documents, the most influential "KGB man" among the Soviet experts in US politics, history, and culture was Georgi Arbatov, who had been a director of the Institute of the USA and Canada since 1967. Arbatov, who had the KGB code name of "Vasilii," built up an influential circle of high-level contacts in America, and he was regularly required to cultivate these connections.[19] Three other leaders of the Soviet Americanist centers were either KGB officers or KGB agents. I refer to Grigorii Sevostianov, Soviet intelligence officer, who was a head of a center at the Institute of World History in Moscow between 1968 and 1988; to Nikolai Sivachev, a KGB agent, a former Sevostianov's student, leader of the similar center at Moscow State University between 1974 and 1982; and to Aleksandr A. Fursenko (1927–2008), a KGB person, and a founder of St. Petersburg school of Russian Americanists. Another prominent "KGB/FSB person" among Soviet and Russian Americanists was Vladimir Sogrin, a Sivachev student, who became a director of the Center for North American Studies at the Institute of World History in Moscow after 2008. Many of those centers included the professional intelligence officers, who were officially retired from their KGB service. Sevostianov's center in Moscow had at least two of those officers: Vadim A. Koleneko (1943–2011), a specialist in Canadian studies, and Vladimir V. Poznyakov (1946–2021), an expert in Soviet American intelligence before and during the early Cold War.[20]

As we had already seen, from the early beginning, the academic exchanges between the United States, and the USSR were used for infiltration with the "KGB people." These "people" included a wide variety of the experts, from the ranked KGB officers to various scholars and scientists (including Soviet Americanists), who collaborated with the KGB and provided those "directing organs" not only with intelligence information and necessary "informal" contacts in academic and diplomatic circles, but also with the very important expertise in such different fields of knowledge as the functions of the US Department of State, computer science, or the banking system. Many Soviet participants recalled how their KGB supervisors requested them to provide information about different functions of US banks "to use this experience for organization of the Soviet foreign banks, working abroad."[21] According to former Soviet KGB officers, who participated in these exchange programs, this information about banking and financial services in the West would be used for future financial operations in post-Soviet Russia.[22]

The main result of the KGB's operations in "capitalist America" was a typical industrial and technological espionage. The KGB provided with precious technological and industrial information the Soviet military factories and research centers. As the KGB officers, who supervised these operations in Kyiv, revealed,

> [Between] 1965 and 1987, almost 90 percent of all technological innovations in all research institutes and the factories of the "military-industrial complex" of Soviet Ukraine were based on the stolen information from the capitalist countries by the specially trained KGB agents. And at least 80 percent of all those "secret samples" of important technological "inventions" came directly from the United States of America. Paradoxically, a majority of these technological secrets were stolen from the American laboratories and colleges by the Soviet engineers and scientists, who participated in the international academic exchanges programs and who executed the KGB orders, performing the functions of the Soviet spies on the American soil.[23]

Soviet Americanists and their KGB supervisors began their own participation in the creation of an international community of scholars, becoming partners in academic exchange with their American colleagues. They established good relations not only with American experts in US history, politics, and culture, but also with American specialists in Russian/Soviet studies. To some extent, participation of Soviet Americanists in this international community would not only shape the development of American studies in the USSR, but also influence Russian studies in America. After visiting America, Soviet Americanists became hosts for American guests, experts in Russian studies, building strong personal connections with them. Eventually, through these personal connections Soviet Americanists, including the KGB agents, and their American colleagues created the important academic international network, controlled now by the Russian intelligence and the network, which involved their students as well, and which survived the collapse of the Soviet Union in 1991.[24]

CRISIS OF THE RUSSIAN AMERICANIZATION UNDER THE KGB REGIME OF PUTIN, THE PARADOXICAL RISE OF UKRAINIAN IDENTITY, AND THE DANGEROUS ROLE OF THE RUSSIAN DIASPORA

The process of "Americanization" for Russian politics and culture was gradually changed after 2000, when a new Russian President, Vladimir Putin, a former KGB officer, began transforming the political system of the Russian Federation into the so-called "KGB kleptocratic regime."[25] This process of "Americanization" never influenced the deep social, economic, political, and ideological foundations of the Soviet, and after 1991, of the Russian political regimes. Both the political elites, including Putin's KGB kleptocracy, and ordinary Russians, enjoyed only the material comfort and various forms of entertainment they associated with this Americanization, mostly through various venues and forms of consumption, starting with reading James Fenimore Cooper's novels and watching the American western films, or listening to Anglo-American rock and roll music. They never understood and never accepted the rules of the democratic system of politics and the rule of law in Russia. Moreover, after a 2007 Munich speech of Putin, where he blamed the West and especially the US in anti-Russian politics, the Russian ruling elites, supervised by Putin's kleptocracy, gradually began distancing themselves from the old perceptions of Americanization. This distancing from the "dangerous American influences" reached a peak in July of 2021, when Putin published a historical essay, in which he blamed the USA for using Ukraine against Russia. This publication became his theoretical justification for the open war against Ukraine in 2022, which was publicly presented as a "Russian war" ("a special military operation" in the official Russian documents) against the American/NATO threat to the Russian security.

Paradoxically, a Russian indigenization of the American influences in a process of its "Americanization" led to the complete rejection of those influences. And the very people who used to provide and justify those influences into Russian society, the Russian experts in the American studies (many of them were, and still are, KGB/FSB officers and agents), like Vyacheslav Nikonov, are now justifying Putin's expansionism and his anti-Americanism.

Instead of following the American influences, Russian intelligence is trying to influence America and US domestic politics as well. Russia's meddling in the US presidential elections in 2016 became the most important news in media, provoking various political debates and affecting the new administration of President Donald Trump for many years to come. This chapter of cyber warfare between the Russian Federation and the US is rooted in the old legacy of the Cold War, when both the United States and the Soviet Union tried to influence and interfere in the domestic policies of their adversaries. Since Stalin's rule, the Soviet Communist leadership tried to influence American politics on behalf of the Soviet political interests. As Georgi Arbatov, a director of the Institute of the USA and Canada in Moscow and political adviser to Leonid Brezhnev, noted in 2002, "Soviet leaders were always looking for various ways how to influence US domestic politics, beginning with funding American communists, then supporting the Afro-American and American Indian movements, and finally, assisting American politicians with the obvious pro-Soviet interests. And this strategy of interference in US politics became more efficient with the beginning of cultural and academic exchanges between the US and the USSR in 1958 when the first Soviet guests had begun visiting America on a regular basis."[26]

Another Soviet political adviser and director of the Ukrainian center for American studies in Kyiv, Arnold Shlepakov, emphasized that the beginning of such exchanges under Khrushchev and Brezhnev intensified the different strategies of Soviet meddling in American politics,

> During détente, Soviet leadership began an intensive interference in the life of various ethnic communities in Northern America, especially Ukrainian community in Canada and the US. Using various representations of Ukrainian national identity, Soviet official guests tried to project to their American hosts (especially to American/Canadian Ukrainians) only positive images of Ukrainian economy, culture and scholarship, which had flourished in the Ukrainian SSR since the October Revolution of 1917. Paradoxically, this cultural diplomacy, as a result of the active personal contacts of Soviet Ukrainians with American Ukrainians, led to the unexpected growth of awareness of Ukrainian national identity among the Soviet participants of these contacts.[27]

The beginning of relaxation of international tensions between the Soviet Union and the Western capitalist countries during the Khrushchev Thaw, and especially Brezhnev's détente, created the new conditions for a cultural dialogue between Soviet Ukraine and Ukrainian diaspora in "capitalist America," which in Soviet geopolitical imagination included both the United States and Canada. Soviet leadership tried to use this dialogue and established political, cultural, and economic connections between Soviet and American Ukrainians to influence a political life in both the US and Canada in a favor of the Soviet Union, by promoting the attractive images and positive notions of Soviet life, and simultaneously suppressing any negative and critical impressions and reactions about Soviet realities, and vigorously fighting "Ukrainian bourgeois nationalism," which in Soviet ideological discourse was always related to the Ukrainian diaspora in America. At the same time, Soviet administration tried to engage the leftist, pro-Communist elements in the Ukrainian diaspora, like Peter Krawchuk in Canada, for a support of Soviet interests in America. The re-establishing of Soviet-Canadian diplomatic relations in 1954 and a signing of the first US-USSR exchange agreement on October 29, 1958, laid a foundation for an active Soviet cultural diplomacy in "capitalist America." Soviet Ukraine became an important participant in this cultural diplomacy, especially after February of 1958, when the Central Committee of Communist Party of the Soviet Union officially decided to create a separate Soviet Ukraine's Permanent Mission to the United Nations Organization in New York City. Since 1958 Soviet diplomacy had begun using national culture of Soviet Ukraine and various manifestations of Ukrainian national identity as an important tool in cultural Cold War. The KGB and, after 1991, the Russian FSB, tried to stop and destroy this Ukrainian identity as "a dangerous Ukrainian bourgeois nationalism" and "Ukrainian Neo-Nazism" misinterpreting this phenomenon as a result of the "American intelligence anti-Soviet and anti-Russian operation." At the same time, both Soviet and Russian intelligence ignored the rise of Russian nationalism and imperialism inside Soviet and post-Soviet Russia. Moreover, since the Cold War, Soviet and Russian intelligence had supported and encouraged the similar feelings among the Russian diaspora abroad, especially in the United States and Canada, using the Russian emigrants against the Ukrainians and "Ukrainian nationalism," as a "dangerous product of the American anti-Russian campaign."[28]

As this book demonstrated, Russian academic diaspora in the West joined enthusiastically Putin's anti-American campaign as well, promoting Russian academic imperialism, which affected the Western (especially American) academia, including its think tanks and college system of education, especially in the United States and Canada. Instead of its integration into the West, Putin's Russia tried to influence Western politics and academia, using the old KGB legacy of interference and "active measures" against the academic centers of the Western world, and especially the American civilization, which used to be the object of fascination of the Soviet predecessors of Putin. Paradoxically, now, the most important "agents of influence" for pro-Putin anti-American politics in the West, especially in the United States, are the very Americanized Russian representatives of a former Soviet civilization, who became an influential part of the Russian diaspora, promoting the same KGB legacy with its pro-Russian nationalistic imperial concepts in Western academia, which they tried to avoid by their emigration to the West, especially to "capitalist America." Tragically, today, this Russian diaspora in Western academia is engaged by Putin's genocidal regime and its intelligence in Russian war against "imperialist America" and "Americanized Ukraine," in the war, which looks like the military campaign of 1938 by Hitler's Nazi regime that used the German diaspora, engaging it in promoting the pro-Nazi politics in Europe.[29] This historical comparison is a reminder about an existing political danger of Russian academic imperialism, which still influences the Western, especially American, academia.

NOTES

1. See especially Vladimir Bukovsky, *Judgment in Moscow: Soviet Crimes and Western Complicity*, translated by Alyona Kojevnikov (Westlake Village, CA: Ninth of November Press, 2019). Compare how this legacy contributed to the wave of so-called "new Cold Wars" in David E. Sanger with Mary K. Brooks, *New Cold Wars: China's Rise, Russia's Invasion, and America's Struggle to Defend the West* (New York: Crown, 2024), especially pp. 35–36.

2. I refer to Sergei I. Zhuk, *Rock and Roll in the Rocket City: The West, Identity, and Ideology in Soviet Dniepropetrovsk, 1960–1985* (Baltimore, MD: Johns Hopkins University Press & Washington, D.C.: Woodrow Wilson Center Press, 2010 [paperback: March 2017]), idem, *Popular Culture, Identity and Soviet Youth in Dniepropetrovsk, 1959–1984* in The Carl Beck Papers in Russian and East European Studies, no. 1906 (Pittsburgh, PA: University of Pittsburgh Press, 2008), and idem, *KGB Operations against the USA and Canada in Soviet Ukraine, 1953–1991* (London and New York: Routledge [Taylor & Francis] Publishing Company, 2022).

3. I refer to this publication: *Ukraine's Outpost: Dnipropetrovsk and the Russian-Ukrainian War*, edited by Taras Kuzio, Sergei I. Zhuk, and Paul D'Anieri (Bristol, England: E-International Relations Publishing, 2022).

4. See various publications of British journalist Shaun Walker about this war, the role of the Wagner group, etc., in *The Guardian*: https://www.theguardian.com/world/2023/jan/24/yevgeny-prigozhin-the-hotdog-seller-who-rose-to-the-top-of-putin-war-machine-wagner-group.

5. Sergei I. Zhuk, "Reading James Fenimore Cooper in the USSR: The American Western Frontier and Native Americans in Soviet Imagination and Cultural Practices," in *The Western in the Global Literary Imagination*, edited by Christopher Conway, Marek Paryż, and David Rio (Leiden-Boston: Brill, 2022), 149–163.

6. Maxim Kovalevsky, "American Impressions," *Russian Review*, vol. 10, no. 3 (July 1951): 176–184, esp. 178–179; idem, *Istoriia amerikanskikh uchrezhdenii*: Litograf lektsii (Saint Petersburg, 1908); A. S. Sokolov, "Amerikanskaia tema v nauchno-literaturnom nasledii M.M. Kovalevskogo," *Amerikanskii ezhegodnik* [hereafter—*AE*] *1989* (Moscow: Nauka, 1990), 155–173.

7. Stephen Kotkin, *Magnetic Mountain: Stalinism as a Civilization* (Berkeley: University of California Press, 1995), 42, 47, 52, 362–363, and Paul Josephson, "Industrial Deserts: Industry, Science and the Destruction of Nature in the Soviet Union," *The Slavonic and East European Review*, vol. 85, no. 2 (April 2007): 294–321.

8. This quotation is from Joseph Stalin, *The Foundations of Leninism*, section ix. See https://www.marxists.org/reference/archive/stalin/works/1924/foundations-leninism/ch09.htm.

9. See how the Soviets used American assistance in building Dniproges in Zaporizhzhia: Serhii Plokhy, *The Gates of Europe: A History of Ukraine* (New York: Basic Books, 2015), 247–248.

10. Robert D. English, *Russia and the Idea of the West: Gorbachev, Intellectuals, and the End of the Cold War* (New York: Columbia University Press, 2000).

11. Christopher Andrew and Vasili Mitrokhin, *The Sword and the Shield: The Mitrokhin Archive and the Secret History of the KGB* (New York: Basic Books, 1999), 150. See also John Earl Haynes, Harvey Klehr, and Alexander Vassiliev, *Spies: The Rise and Fall of the KGB in America* (New Haven: Yale University Press, 2009), esp. 293–481; Oleg D. Kalugin, *Spymaster: My Thirty-Two Years in Intelligence and Espionage Against the West* (New York: Basic Books, 2009), 221.

12. Galuzevyi Derzhavnyi Arkhiv Sluzhby Bezpeky Ukrainy (hereafter SBU), f. 16, op. 1, spr. 988, ark. 138.

13. Interview with Leonid K., a retired KGB officer, March 3, 2019, Kyiv, Ukraine. Leonid was a personal friend of the Soviet Ukrainian Americanists, such as Arnold Shlepakov and Leonid Leshchenko, who introduced me to this officer in 1992.

14. Oleg D. Kalugin, *Spymaster*, 27, 29.

15. Pavel Palazchenko, *My Years with Gorbachev and Shevardnadze: The Memoir of a Soviet Interpreter* (University Park: Penn State University Press, 1997), p. 95. Palazchenko, Mikhail Gorbachev's interpreter, wrote in his book of memoirs: "Most [Soviet] experts on the United States, regardless of differences of view on particular issues, seemed genuinely to like America and the Americans." Ibid. See also Yale Richmond, *Cultural Exchange and the Cold War: Raising the Iron Curtain* (University Park: Penn State University Press, 2003) 91.

16. Allen H. Kassof, "Scholarly Exchanges and the Collapse of Communism," *The Soviet and Post-Soviet Review*, vol. 22, no. 3 (1995): 263–274, citation is from p. 270.

17. Interview with Leonid K.

18. Interview with Igor T., a retired KGB officer, May 18, 1991, Dnipropetrovsk, Soviet Ukraine.

19. Christopher Andrew and Vasili Mitrokhin, op. cit., 211–212, 213.

20. Interview with Nikolai N. Bolkhovitinov, Moscow, May 21, 2001.

21. Interview with Nikolai Bolkhovitinov, March 23, 1991, Moscow.

22. See Kalugin, op. cit., 424.

23. Interview with Stepan Ivanovich K. in Kyiv, and Igor T., former KGB officers from Kyiv and Dnipropetrovsk, Ukraine. See about the KGB espionage in America in: Sergei I. Zhuk, *KGB Operations against the USA and Canada in Soviet Ukraine, 1953–1991* (London and New York: Routledge [Taylor & Francis] Publishing Company, 2022).

24. See about this in detail in my book: Sergei I. Zhuk, *Soviet Americana: The Cultural History of Russian and Ukrainian Americanists* (London and New York: I.B. Tauris, 2018 [London and New York: Bloomsbury Publishing, 2019]).

25. See about this in Karen Dawisha, *Putin's Kleptocracy: Who Owns Russia?* (New York: Simon & Schuster, 2014), and Mikhail Zygar, *All the Kremlin's Men: Inside the Court of Vladimir Putin* (New York: Public Affairs, 2016).

26. Interview with Georgi A. Arbatov, Moscow, July 12, 2002.

27. Interview with Arnold Shlepakov, Kyiv, April 28, 1990.

28. See in V. A. Nikonov, *Sovremennyi mir i ego istoki* (Moscow: Izd-vo Moskovskogo universiteta, 2015), 302–304.

29. See such an analogy in Jim Sciutto, *The Return of Great Powers: Russia, China, and The Next World War* (New York: Dutton, 2024), especially about the role of Russian intelligence on pp. 134–137.

Appendix
List of Interviews

Interview with Bohdan Josypovych K., a retired KGB/SBU officer, February 9, 2019, Kyiv, Ukraine.
Interview with Nikolai N. Bolkhovitinov, January 4, 2004, Moscow, Russian Federation.
Interview with Igor T., a retired KGB officer, May 15, 1991, Dnipropetrovsk, Ukraine.
Interview with Ivan Grigorovich K., a retired KGB officer, February 3, 2019, Kyiv, Ukraine.
Interview with Leonid K., a retired KGB officer, March 3, 2019, Kyiv, Ukraine.
Interviews with Leonid Leshchenko, June 23, 2012, and June 25, 2013, Kyiv, Ukraine.
Interview with Stepan Ivanovich T., a retired KGB officer, January 30, 2019, Kyiv, Ukraine.
Interview with Vitalii Pidgaetskii at the Department of History, Dnipropetrovsk University, February 10, 1996, Dnipro, Ukraine.
Interview with Arnold Shlepakov, August 29, 1991, Kyiv, Ukraine.

Selected Bibliography

Andrew, Christopher, and Vasili Mitrokhin, *The Sword and the Shield: The Mitrokhin Archive and the Secret History of the KGB* (New York: Basic Books, 1999).
Antons, Jan-Hinnerk, "Displaced Persons in Postwar Germany: Parallel Societies in a Hostile Environment," *Journal of Contemporary History*, January 2014, vol. 49, no. 1, 92–114.
Arkhiv Nathional'noi Akademii Nauk Ukrainy [Kyiv, Ukraine], Opys 1-L, Otdel kadrov, Files of Shlepakov, Arnol'd; Leshchenko, Leonid, etc.
Bertelsen, Olga, "Political Affinities and Maneuvering of Soviet Political Elites: Heorhii Shevel and Ukraine's Ministry of Strange Affairs in the 1970s," *Nationalities Papers: The Journal of Nationalism and Ethnicity*, 2019, vol. 47, no. 3, 394–411.
Bertelsen, Olga, "Russian Front Organizations and Western Academia," *International Journal of Intelligence and Counterintelligence*, 2023, vol. 36, no. 4, 1184–1209.
Black, Joseph Laurence, *Canada in the Soviet Mirror: Ideology and Perception in Soviet Foreign Affairs, 1917–1991* (Ottawa: Carleton University Press, 1998).
Bukovsky, Vladimir, *Judgment in Moscow: Soviet Crimes and Western Complicity*, translated by Alyona Kojevnikov (Westlake Village, CA: Ninth of November Press, 2019).
Cacciatore, Francesco Alexander, *"Their Need Was Great": Émigrés and Anglo-American Intelligence Operations in the Early Cold War.* PhD dissertation, University of Westminster, March 2018.
Corera, Gordon, *Russians Among Us: Sleeper Cells, Ghost Stories, and the Hunt for Putin's Spies* (New York: William Morrow Paperbacks, 2021).
Darczewska, Jolanta, and Piotr Żochowski, "Active Measures: Russia's Key Export," *Point of View*, June 2017, Number 64 (Warsaw: Center for Eastern Studies), pp. 5–71.
Danylenko, V. M., *Ukraina v mizhnarodnykh naukovo-tekhnichnykh zv'iazkakh (70-80-i rr.)* (Kyiv: Instytut istorii Ukrainy. Instytut ukrais'koi arkheografii, 1993).
Dawisha, Karen, *Putin's Kleptocracy: Who Owns Russia?* (New York: Simon & Schuster, 2014).
Derzhavnyi arkhiv Dnipropetrovs'koi oblasti, Dnipropetrovs'k, Ukraine: Fond 19, Dnepropetrovskii Obkom KPU (Kommunisticheskoi partii Ukrainy); Fond 9870,

Dnepropetrovskii Obkom KPU (Kommunisticheskoi partii Ukrainy). Otdel: Osobyi sector. Sektor: Sekretnaiu chast.'

Dobrynin, Anatoly, *In Confidence: Moscow's Ambassador to America's Six Cold War Presidents (1962–1986)* (New York: Times Books, 1995).

Dubov, D., A. Barovska, T. Isakova, I. Koval, and V Horbulin; general editorship by D. Dubov. *"Active Measures" of USSR against USA: Preface to Hybrid War. Analytical Report* (Kyiv: The National Institute for Strategic Studies, 2017).

Engerman, David C., *Know Your Enemy: The Rise and Fall of America's Soviet Experts* (New York: Oxford University Press, 2009).

English, Robert D., *Russia and the Idea of the West: Gorbachev, Intellectuals, and the End of the Cold War* (New York: Columbia University Press, 2000).

Galeotti, Mark, *Putin's Wars: From Chechnya to Ukraine* (London: Osprey Publishing, 2022).

Galuzevyi Derzhavnyi Arkhiv Sluzhby Bezpeky Ukrainy (The Branch State Archive of the Security Service of Ukraine [SBU]), Kyiv, Ukraine: Fond 1, The Second Main (Counterintelligence) Directorate of the KGB; Fond 16, The Secretariat of GPU-KGB of Ukraine.

Garthoff, Raymond L., *A Journey through the Cold War: A Memoir of Containment and Coexistence* (Washington, DC: Brookings Institution Press, 2001).

Geelhoed, E. Bruce, *Diplomacy Shot Down: The U-2 Crisis and Eisenhower's Aborted Mission to Moscow, 1959–1960* (Norman: University of Oklahoma Press, 2020).

Hanusiak, Michael, and Sam Pevzner, *Lest We Forget* (New York: The Ukrainian American League, 1973).

Harding, Luke, *Invasion: The Inside Story of Russia's Bloody War and Ukraine's Fight for Survival* (New York: Vintage Books, 2022).

Haynes, John Earl, Harvey Klehr, and Alexander Vassiliev, *Spies: The Rise and Fall of the KGB in America* (New Haven: Yale University Press, 2009).

Hollingworth, Mark, *Agents of Influence: How the KGB Subverted Western Democracies* (London: Oneworld Publications, 2023).

Jones, Seth G., *A Covert Action: Reagan, the CIA, and the Cold War Struggle in Poland* (New York: W.W. Norton, 2018).

Kalugin, Oleg D., *Spymaster: My Thirty-Two Years in Intelligence and Espionage Against the West* (New York, NY: Basic Books, 2009).

Kassof, Allen H., "Scholarly Exchanges and the Collapse of Communism," *The Soviet and Post-Soviet Review*, 1995, vol. 22, no. 3, 263–274.

Kovacevic, Filip, "The Chekist Monitor" website: https://thechekistmonitor.blogspot.com.

Khrushchev, Sergei N., *Nikita Khrushchev and the Creation of a Superpower* (University Park, PA: The Pennsylvania State University Press, 2000).

Kramer, Mark, ed., "Ukraine and the Soviet-Czechoslovak Crisis of 1968 (Part I): New Evidence from the Diary of Petro Shelest," *Cold War International History Project Bulletin*, 1998, no. 10, 234–247.

Kravchuk, Petro, *Bez nedomovok: Spogady* (Kyiv: Literaturna Ukraina, 1995).

The Kremlin's Malign Influence inside the US, edited by Michael Weiss (Washington, D.C.: Free Russia, 2021).
Kuzio, Taras, *Crisis in Russian Studies? Nationalism (Imperialism), Racism and War* (Bristol, England: E-International Relations, 2020).
Kuzio, Taras, *Russian Nationalism and the Russian-Ukrainian War: Autocracy-Orthodoxy-Nationality* (London and New York: Routledge [Taylor & Francis] Publishing Company, 2022).
LaFeber, Walter, *America, Russia, and the Cold War 1945–2006*, 10th Edition (Boston: McGraw-Hill, 2008).
Lazebnyk, Stanislav, *Zakordonne ukrainstvo: vytoky ta siogodennia* (Kyiv: Istyna, 2007).
Lazebnyk, Stanislav, and Olha B. Havura, *Rozdumy na mostu z dvobichnym rukhom* (Kyiv: Etnos, 2004).
Library of Congress, Manuscript Collection, (1) International Research and Exchanges Board (IREX), Files of Soviet Visiting Scholars: Sivachev, Fursenko, etc.; (2) American Council of Learned Societies (ACLS), Files about Soviet-US academic exchanges (1958–1990s).
Lutsevych, Orysia, "Agents of the Russian World. Proxy Groups in the Contested Neighborhood," Chatham House, April 2016: https://www.chathamhouse.org/publication/agents-russian-world-proxy-groups-contested-neighbourhood.
Marunchak, M. H., *The Ukrainian Canadians: A History* (Winnipeg/Ottawa: Ukrainian Free Academy of Sciences, 1976).
McCauley, Kevin N., *Russian Influence Campaigns Against the West: From the Cold War to Putin* (North Charleston, SC: CreateSpace Independent Publishing Platform, 2016).
McGlynn, Jade, *Memory Makers: The Politics of the Past in Putin's Russia* (London: Bloomsbury, 2023).
McGlynn, Jade, *Russia's War* (New York: Polity, 2023).
Mickolus, Edward, *The Counterintelligence Chronology: Spying By and Against the United States From the 1700s Through 2014* (Jefferson, NC: McFarland & Company, Inc., 2015).
Mikkonen, Simo, "Soviet-American Art Exchanges during the Thaw: From Bold Openings to Hasty Retreats," in *Art and Political Reality*, edited by M. Kurisoo. Proceedings in the Art Museum of Estonia, vol. 8 (Tallinn: Art Museum of Estonia—Kumu Art Museum, 2013), 57–76.
Motyl, Alexander J., "The Foreign Relations of the Ukrainian SSR," *Harvard Ukrainian Studies*, March 1982, vol. 6, no. 1, 62–78.
Muszyński, Wojciech Jerzy, "The Polish Guards Companies of the U.S. Army After World War II," The Polish Review, 2012, vol. 57, no. 4, 75–86.
Na skryzhaliakh istorii: Z istorii vzaiemozv'iazkiv uriadovykh struktur i hromads'kykh kil Ukrainy z ukrains'ko-kanads'koiu hromadoiu v drugii polovyni 1940–1980-ti roky, edited by P. Tron'ko a. o. (Kyiv: Instytut istorii Ukrainy NANU, Fundatsiia ukrains'koi spadshchyny Al'berty, 2003).
Nikonov, Vyacheslav A., *Sovremennyi mir i ego istoki* (Moscow: Izd-vo Moskovskogo universiteta, 2015).

Palazchenko, Pavel, *My Years with Gorbachev and Shevardnadze: The Memoir of a Soviet Interpreter* (University Park, PA: The Pennsylvania State University Press, 1997).

Parrish, Michael, *The Lesser Terror: Soviet State Security, 1939–1953* (Westport, CT: Praeger Publishers, 1996).

Peebles, Curtis, *Twilight Warriors: Covert Air Operations against the USSR* (Naval Institute Press, 2005).

Plokhy, Serhii, *The Man with the Poison Gun: A Cold War Spy Story* (New York: Basic Books, 2016).

Plokhy, Serhii, *Chernobyl: History of a Tragedy* (New York: Penguin, 2019).

Plokhy, Serhii, *Nuclear Folly: A History of the Cuban Missile Crisis* (New York: W.W. Norton, 2021).

Plokhy, Serhii, *The Russo-Ukrainian War: The Return of History* (New York: W.W. Norton, 2023).

Re-Imagining Ukrainian Canadians: History, Politics, and Identity, edited by Rhonda L. Hinther and Jim Mochoruk (Toronto: University of Toronto Press, 2011).

Russian Active Measures: Yesterday, Today and Tomorrow, edited by Olga Bertelsen (New York: Ibidem Press and Columbia University Press, 2021).

Russian Cultural Diplomacy Under Putin: Rossutrudnichestvo, the "Russkii Mir" Foundation, and the Gorchakov Fund in 2007–2022, edited by Nadiia Koval and Denys Tereshchenko (Stuttgart: ibidem-Verlag, 2023).

Russian Misinformation and Western Scholarship: Bias and Prejudice in Journalistic, Expert, and Academic Analyses of East European and Eurasian Affairs, edited by Taras Kuzio (Stuttgart, Germany: ibidem-Verlag / ibidem Press, 2023).

Sanger, David E., with Mary K. Brooks, *New Cold Wars: China's Rise, Russia's Invasion, and America's Struggle to Defend the West* (New York: Crown, 2024).

Sciutto, Jim, *The Return of Great Powers: Russia, China, and The Next World War* (New York: Dutton, 2024).

Shlepakov, Arnold M., *Ukrains'ka trudova immigratsiia v SShA i Kanadi (kinets' XIX – poch. XX st.)* (Kyiv: Naukova dumka, 1960).

Shultz, Richard H., and Roy Godson, *Dezinformatsia: Active Measures in Soviet Strategy* (New York, NY: Pergamon-Brassey's International Defense Publishers, 1984).

Smagliy, Kateryna (with Ilya Zaslavskiy), "Hybrid Analytica: Pro-Kremlin Expert Propaganda in Moscow, Europe and the U.S. A Case Study on Think Tanks and Universities": https://www.underminers.info/publications/hybridanalytica.

The Soviet Invasion of Czechoslovakia in 1968: The Russian Perspective (The Harvard Cold War Studies Book Series), edited by Jozef Pazderka (Lanham, MD, and Boulder, CO: Rowman and Littlefield's Lexington Books, 2019).

Stengel, Richard, *Information Wars: How We Lost the Global Battle against Disinformation & What We Can Do About It* (New York: Atlantic Monthly Press, 2019).

Taubman, William, *Khrushchev: The Man and His Era* (New York: W. W. Norton, 2003).

Tromly, Benjamin, *Cold War Exiles and the CIA: Plotting to Free Russia* (New York: Oxford University Press, 2019).
Tsentral'nyi derzhavnyi arkhiv vyshchykh organiv vlady ta upravlinnia, Kyiv, Ukraine, Fond 5116, Ministerstvo kul'tury URSR.
Tsentral'nyi Derzhavnyi Arkhiv Gromads'kykh Ob'ednan' Ukrainy, Kyiv, Ukraine, Fond 7, Viddil kul'tury, Viddil Propagandy i agitatsii.
Tuttle, Douglas, *Fraud, Famine and Fascism: The Ukrainian Genocide Myth from Hitler to Harvard* (Toronto: Progress Books, 1987).
Unger, Craig, *House of Trump, House of Putin: The Untold Story of Donald Trump and Russian Mafia* (New York: Penguin, 2019).
Unger, Craig, *American Kompromat: How the KGB Cultivated Donald Trump, and Related Tales of Sex, Greed, Power, and Treachery* (New York: Dutton, 2021).
Vrublevskiy, Vitaliy K., *Vladimir Shcherbitskiy: zapiski pomoshchnika: slukhi, legendy, dokumenty* (Kyiv: Dovira, 1993).
Yekelchyk, Serhy, *Ukraine: Birth of a Modern Nation* (New York: Oxford University Press, 2007).
Zhuk, Sergei I., *KGB Operations against the USA and Canada in Soviet Ukraine, 1953–1991* (London and New York: Routledge [Taylor & Francis] Publishing Company, 2022).
Zhuk, Sergei I., *Nikolai Bolkhovitinov and American Studies in the USSR: People's Diplomacy in the Cold War* (Lanham, MD: Lexington Books, 2017).
Sergei I. Zhuk, *Rock and Roll in the Rocket City: The West, Identity, and Ideology in Soviet Dniepropetrovsk, 1960–1985* (Baltimore, MD: Johns Hopkins University Press; Washington, D.C.: Woodrow Wilson Center Press, 2010).
Zhuk, Sergei I., *Soviet Americana: The Cultural History of Russian and Ukrainian Americanists* (London and New York: I.B. Tauris, 2018).
Zhuk, Sergei I., "The 'KGB People,' Soviet Americanists and Soviet-American Academic Exchanges, 1958–1985," *The Soviet and Post-Soviet Review*, 2017, vol. 44, no. 2, 133–167.
Zhuk, Sergei I., "'Academic Détente': IREX Files, Academic Reports, and 'American' Adventures of Soviet Americanists during the Brezhnev Era," *Cahiers du monde russe*, janvier–juin 2013, vol. 54, no. 1–2, 297–328.
Zhuk, Sergei I., "'Academic Imperialism:' Writing Soviet and Post-Soviet History without Ukraine," *Russian Misinformation and Western Scholarship: Bias and Prejudice in Journalistic, Expert, and Academic Analyses of East European and Eurasian Affairs*, edited by Taras Kuzio (Stuttgart, Germany: ibidem-Verlag / ibidem Press, 2023), 61–85.
Zubok, Vladislav M., *Collapse: The Fall of the Soviet Union* (New Haven: Yale University Press, 2021).
Zyarnyuk, Andriy, "Historians As Enablers? Historiography, Imperialism, and the Legitimization of Russian Aggression," *East/West: Journal of Ukrainian Studies*, 2022, vol. ix, no. 2, 191–212.

Index

Abel, Rudolf, 72, 73, 84, 87, 89
Academic exchanges, v, xix, 8, 50, 57, 62, 176
"Active measures" of the KGB, xiii, xiv, 12, 76, 197, 203, 204, 206
African People's Socialist Party and the Uhuru Movement (APSP), 145
"Agents of influence," xxi, xxii, 78, 91, 155–185
Aldridge, Ira, 80
Alekperov, Vagit; *see also* LUKOIL, ix, 164, 181
Alfa Fellowship Program, 165, 166, 182
Alfa financial group (Alfa Bank), 164, 166
All-Union Society for Cultural Relations with Foreign Countries (VOKS); *see also* the Union of Soviet Societies of Friendship and Cultural Relations with Foreign Countries (SRTD), 167
Alterman, Jon, 170
Amar, Tarik Cyril, 114–115, 124, 135, 150
American Association for Advanced Slavic Studies (now the Association for Slavic, East European, and Eurasian Studies); *see also* the Joint Committee on Slavic Studies, xxiii, 2, 4, 147

American Council of Learned Societies (ACLS), xii, xvi, 3, 52, 205
American Revolution Bicentennial, 158, 179
American-Russian Cultural Cooperation Foundation, ix
American University, viii
Americanization/ Westernization, vii, 61, 187–199
Americans, The (American TV show), 83–86
Arbatov, Alexei, 160, 171, 179, 180
Arbatov, Georgi, KGB code name "Vasili," 21–24, 25, 57–58, 65, 100, 140, 193, 196
Arbatova, Nadezhda, 171
Army Specialized Training Program (ASTP), 1, 2
Andrew, Christopher, xiii, 46, 47, 87, 89, 191
Andrew W. Mellon Foundation, 57
Andropov, Yuri, 12
Anti-Globalization Movement of Russia (AGMR), 144, 145
Appatov, Semion, 93, 141
Aven, Petr; *see also* Alfa Bank, ix, 165–166, 181, 182
Averchev, Vladimir, 161

Bakalo, Ivan, 5
Barsky, Jack Philip (Albrecht Dittrich), 79, 88
Bauer, Raymond, 5
Bazhanov, L., 28, 43
Bekhterev, Gennadiy P., 10, 11, 12, 16
Bertelsen, Olga, xiv, xv, 182, 203
Billington, James, 156, 157, 159
Biden, Joe (Joseph), 169, 183
Black Panthers, 79, 80
Blavatnik, Len (Leonard), 164
Bogdanov, Radomir, 25, 32, 33, 43, 50, 138
Bolkhovitinov, Nikolai N., 39, 59, 64, 158, 159
Branson, Elena, ix
Brezhnev, Leonid I., x, 12, 56, 134, 142
Bridge of Spies, 84
Brooks, Jeffrey, 130, 139
Browder, Bill, 169
Bukovsky, Vladimir, 187
Budapest Treaty of 1994, 147
Burlinova, Natalia, 145, 146, 153
Butina, Maria, viii, x
"Butina-Fedyashin-Carmel" connections, viii-x
Bystritskiy, Andrey, 168

California Institute of Technology, 173
Carmel Institute of Russian Culture and History, viii, ix, 181
Carnegie Endowment for International Peace, 162, 169, 180
Carnegie Foundation, 4, 40, 47, 162, 188
Carter, Jimmy, 32, 64
Center for Urban History of East Central Europe in Lviv, 114
Central European University (Budapest, Hungary, Prague, Czechia, and Vienna, Austria), 113, 139, 161
Certeau, Michel de, 132, 149
Charap, Samuel, 170
Chatham House, xiv
Chemych, Stephan, 107

Chernobyl nuclear catastrophe, x, 126
CHMO (*chelovek Moskvy i Moskovskoi oblasti*), 176, 184–185
Chubarian, Aleksandr, 32
CIA; *see also* the Office of Strategic Services (OSS), 3, 5, 159
Clark University, 60
CNN television, 162, 170
Cold War, ix, xiii, xvi, 32, 39, 146, 162, 167
Cold War International History Project, 161
Colton, Timothy, 170
Columbia University, 1, 2, 3, 8, 9, 10, 11, 22, 26, 27, 81, 106, 111, 114–115
Cooper, James Fenimore, 31, 189, 195
Cooper, Julian M., 170
Corera, Gordon, 81, 87
Cornell University, 2, 3, 28, 52
Council of Foreign and Defense Policy (of Russia), 168

Darevich, Yu., 109
Dawisha, Karen, 164, 181
Diachenko, Aleksandr A. (Demidenko), 77
Diefenbaker, John, 111
Disinformation (*dezinformatsiya*), xiv, 25, 80, 115, 121, 144
Displaced Person(s) [DP], 5, 14, 103
Dmytryshyn, Basil, xvii, 113
Dobrynin, Anatoly, xviii
"Donetsk People's Republic," the, 145
Dougherty, Jill, 170, 183
Drexel University, 139
Duke University, 139, 152

Eisenhower, Dwight D., 8, 36
Eisenhower Exchange Fellowship, 36
Ellison, Herbert, 159
Emmons, Terrence, 34
Engerman, David C., xi, 7
Espionage; *see also* Industrial and technological espionage, xiv, 3, 19, 39, 64, 78, 191, 194

Etkind, Alexander, 139
Eurasian Research Institute, 4
European University (St. Petersburg, Russia), 171, 178

FBI, viii, ix, x, 62, 73–74, 79, 80, 81, 83, 84, 86, 144, 145–146
Fedenko, Panas, 5
Fedyashin, Anton, viii–x
Fischer, George, 5
Fitzpatrick, Sheila, 130, 136
Foley, Tracey Lee Ann (Elena Vavilova), 82–86
Foner, Eric, 115, 141
Ford Foundation, 4, 57, 58
Foucault, Michel, 132
Fields, Joel, 84
Fridman, Mikhail; see also Alfa Bank, ix, 164, 165, 166
"Front organizations" of Russian intelligence, xiv, xv, 155, 167–176
FSB (*federal'naia sluzhba bezopasnosti*), xi, 40, 71, 85–86, 111, 145, 162, 167, 176, 178, 182
Fuerst (Fürst), Juliane, 133–134
Fulbright scholarship program, 9, 15, 29, 30, 39, 58, 192
Fursenko, Alexander, 37, 55, 60–62, 141–142, 193

Gaddis, John Lewis, xiii, xvii, 32
Gaddy, Clifford, 170
Gaetskii, Yu., 109
Galkin, I., 28
Garthoff, Raymond, 58
Georgetown University, 11, 72, 81, 86, 170
George Mason University, 113
George Washington University; see also the National Security Archive, 28, 161, 170
Gleason, Abbott, 159
Goldfrank, David, xvii
Goldstein, Karma, 136
Goldstein, Moisei, 136

Golubev, Alexey, 139
Gorbachev, Mikhail; see also the perestroika, 9, 32, 63, 100, 101, 129, 142, 160, 173, 190
Gorchakov Fund, ix, 167, 175–176
Graves, Melissa, 165
Grigulevich (Lavretskii), Iosif R., 18, 19, 37
Gromyko, Alexei; see also Russkii Mir Foundation, 172
Gromyko, Andrei, 172
GRU (*glavnoye razvedyvatelnoye upravlenie*), xii, xvii, 2, 9, 10 18, 24, 25, 40, 49, 74, 79, 86, 112, 115, 135, 136, 162, 167, 168, 171, 172
Gurevich, Aron, 10, 16

Harman, Jane,169
Harriman Institute (W. Averell Harriman Institute for the Advanced Study of the Soviet Union); see also the Russian Institute, 2, 114
Harvard Refugee Interview Project (RIP), 5, 7
Harvard Ukrainian Research Institute (HURI), 107–109, 112
Harvard University, 2, 3, 4, 5–7, 8, 11, 12, 22, 49, 54, 72, 82, 107–109, 111, 114, 170
Haynes, John Earl, xiii
Heathfield, Donald (Andrei Bezrukov), 82–85
Hellie, Richard, 34
Higher Education Support Program; see also Soros Foundation, 39, 40, 161, 178
Himka, John-Paul, 105–106, 114
Hitler, Adolf, 197
Hofstadter, Richard, 26, 27
Holm, Julia, 53, 54
Holodomor, 100, 101, 135, 138
Holubnychy, Vsevolod, 5
Howard University, 79–80
Humphrey, Hubert, 163

Inkeles, Alex, 5
Inozemtsev, Nikolai, 21, 57, 98, 140, 141
Institute for Democracy and Cooperation; see also Andranik Migranian, 50, 143, 176
Institute for the Study of the History and Culture of the USSR in Munich, Germany, 4, 5, 6
Institute of African Studies of the USSR Academy of Science, 12, 18
Institute of Ethnography of the USSR Academy of Science, 26, 36, 37, 141, 161
Institute of History of the Ukrainian Academy of Sciences, 17, 24, 26, 101
Institute of Latin America of the USSR Academy of Science, 18, 19
Institute of Slavic Studies and Balkan Studies of the USSR Academy of Science, 17, 19
Institute of Oriental Studies of the USSR Academy of Science, 38
Institute of Social and Economic Problems of Foreign Countries (ISEPZK) of the Ukrainian SSR Academy of Sciences, 98–101
Institute of the USA and Canada (ISKAN) of the USSR Academy of Science, 21–23, 31, 32, 53, 55, 100, 137, 141, 159, 160, 161
Institute of the World Economy and International Relations (IMEMO) of the USSR Academy of Science, 17, 18, 21, 23, 51, 55, 56, 57, 98, 141, 160, 171
Institute of World History (IVI) of the USSR Academy of Science, 17, 20, 26, 36, 38, 64, 126, 141, 193
International Renaissance Foundation; see also Soros Foundation, 39–40, 161, 178

International Research and Exchanges Board (IREX), xii, xvi, 9, 28, 30, 39, 51–58, 62, b160, 192
Ionov, Aleksandr V., 144–145

Jones, Seth G., xiv
Johns Hopkins University, 138–139, 170
Johnson, Lyndon, 163
Joy-Lud Electronics, 163

Kalugin, Oleg D., xiii, xviii, 10–11, 12, 50, 63, 91, 163, 191
Katchanovski, Ivan, 113–114
Kasianov, Georgiy, 40
Kazakevich, Vladimir, 2, 18
Kasparov, Garry, 169
Kassof, Allen, 53, 62, 192
Keenan, Edward, 108
Kennan, George "the Elder," 157
Kennan, George F., 156, 157
Kennan Institute, ix, xiv, 156–158, 159, 160, 161, 162, 164, 165, 166, 169, 170, 177
KGB (*komitet gosudarstvennoi bezopasnosti*); see also Cheka, OGPU, NKVD, FSB, viii, 20, 49, 50, 77, 91–92, 105, 110, 163, 191–194
KGB curators ("*kuratory*"), 17, 26, 38, 39, 92, 109, 112
"KGB connections" of Soviet scholars, who travelled to the West, [the archivists' criteria], xvii–xviii
KGB mind-set, 71, 83
KGB spy station (*rezidentura*), 84
Khokhlov, Rem, 58
Khrushchev, Nikita S., x, 18, 21, 33, 75, 131, 142, 190
Khvostov, V. M., 27
Kiriliuk, Vadym, 72–73
Kislin, Semyon, 163
Kislyak, Sergey, ix
Kluckhohn, Clyde, 5
Kokoshin, Andrey, 161
Koleneko, Vadim, 38, 39, 59, 193

Kommunist (Communist), Soviet communist party's periodical, 22, 172
Kondufor, Yuri, 101
Korotich, Vitaly, 92, 102–105
Kostiuk, Hryhory, 5
Kotkin, Stephen, 114, 135
Kovacevich, Filip, xxii
Kozak, Dmitry, 171, 172
Krawchenko, Bohdan, 109
Krawchuk (Kravchuk), Peter (Petro), 92, 95, 96, 99, 101, 102, 103, 104, 105, 197
Krupnytsky, Borys, 5
Krylov, B. N., 19
Krylova, Anna, 138–139
Kulchytsky, Stanislav, 17, 40
Kupchan, Charles, 170
Kurilla, Ivan, xvii, 40, 79, 177–178
Kurinny, Petro, 5
Kuzio, Taras, xv, 188

Lacy, William S. B., 8
Laruelle, Marlene, 137, 170
Lavrentieva, Nadezhda, 168
Leffler, Melvyn, 32
Left (political); *see also* Marxists, 1, 3, 6, 11, 12, 39, 71, 85, 92, 103, 104, 105, 113, 117, 130, 163, 196
Lehrman, Susan Carmel, viii, ix
Leshchenko, Leonid A., xvi, xvii, xviii, 94, 97, 99, 102, 111, 112, 140–141
Levada, Yuri, 161
Library of Congress, ix, 4, 52
Lipman, Maria, 162
Litvin, Zalman (Ignatii Samuel Witchak), "the Mulatto," 18, 74, 87
London School of Economics and Political Science (LSE), 25, 114, 137, 162, 174
Los,' Fedir, 95
Lukin, Vladimir, 142
Lukyanov, Fyodor, 168
Lunt, Horace, 108
Lutsevich, Orysia, xiv

MacArthur Foundation, 162
Maidan Revolution, 113–115, 128, 130, 135, 173
Malia, Martin, 34
Marinich, A. M., 97
Martos, Borys, 97
Massachusetts Institute of Technology (MIT), 22, 53
Mayne Reid, Thomas, 31, 189
McGill University, 82
Mearsheimer, John J., 137, 170
Middlebury Institute of International Studies at Monterey, 162
Migranian, Andranik, 50, 143, 176
Mikhailov, Boris, 20
Military and Diplomatic Academy of the General Staff of the Soviet Armed Forces, 18
Miller, Alexei I.; *see also* Soros Foundation and Valdai Club, 40, 47, 160, 161, 171, 188
Miller, Christopher; *see also* Alfa Fellowship, 166
Miller, Ilia S., 17, 19, 26, 39, 160
Miller, Mykhailo, 5
Milshtein, Mikhail, 25
Minakov, Mikhail, 169
Mirchuk, Ivan, 5
Mitrokhin, Vasili, and "Mitrokhin Archive," xviii, 25
Modernity, 93, 139, 189, 190
Molotov, Vyacheslav, 172
Molotova, Svetlana, 172
Moore, Barrington Jr., 5
Morozov, Viacheslav, 177–178
Morris, Richard, 158
Moscow State Institute of International Relations (MGIMO), 21, 22, 172
Moscow State University (MGU), 26, 27, 29, 33, 34, 35, 58, 59, 138, 173
Murphy, Cynthia (Lydia Guryeva), 81
Muscovites, residents of Moscow, Russia; *see also* CHMO (*chelovek Moskvy i Moskovskoi oblasti*), 29,

99, 126, 129, 134, 139, 140, 141, 176–177

Narochnitskii, Aleksei L., 35
National Association of Manufacturers, 2
National Security Council, 169
Naval School of Military Government and Administration (NSMGA), 1, 3
Nevel, Jesse, 145
Nikonov, Alexei, 172
Nikonov, Vyacheslav; *see also* Russkii Mir Foundation, 50, 143, 160, 171, 172, 173, 174, 195
Nixon, Richard, xvi, 156

Oberlin College, 157
Operation Ghost Stories by the FBI, 82, 83
Osborn, Frederick, 4
Osobyi (Pervyi) otdel, xvii
Osokina, Elena, 138
Oushakine, Serguei, 139
Oxford Univeristy, 114

Parshin, Pavel, 161
Parsons, Talcott, 5
Paton, Borys E., 24
Patrushev, Nikolai, 167
PBS, American public television, 137–138
Pechatnov, Vladimir, 32
Petro, Nikolai N., 135
PICREADI, FSB "front organization," 145–146
Pinchuk, Victor, 146
Pipes, Richard, 2, 5, 108
Plekhanov, Sergei, 64
Plokhy (Plokhii), Serhii, 112, 113, 131, 146
Polonska-Vasylenko, Nataliia, 5
Pomerantz, William, 169
Poznyakov, Vladimir V., 39, 64, 65, 193
Popov, Yegor S., 145
Potekhin, Ivan, 18

Powers, Francis Gary, 72
Primakov, Yevgeniy M., KGB code name MAKSIM, 38, 39, 164
Primakov, Yevgeniy Y. Jr., 171
Princeton University, 49, 114, 135, 139
Pritsak (Prytsak), Omeljan, 106, 107, 108, 109
Prorector po rabote s inostrantsami (Dean of Foreign Students and Visitors), 50, 79, 178
Putin, Vladimir, x, xiii, xix, 83, 84, 113, 129, 133, 136, 143, 169

Raleigh, Donald, J., xvii, 63, 134
Rand Corporation, 22, 81, 170
Reddaway, Peter, 159
Redfin, 82
Remington, Thomas, 170
Renova financial group, 164
Rid, Thomas, xiii
Richmond, Yale, xvii, 27, 30
Rieber, Alfred, 64
Robinson, Geroid, 3
Rockefeller Foundation, 3, 4, 57
Rojansky, Matthew, 169
Roosevelt, Eleanor, 27, 40, 43
Rossutrudnichestvo, xiv, 167, 171, 175
Rudling, Per Anders, 114
"Russia Forum New York," ix
"Russia Today" (RT), Russian television channel, 115, 135
Russian academic imperialism, 125–153
Russian cultural diplomacy, 135, 155–185
Russian "*derzhavniki*" (state-builders), 142
Russian diaspora; *see also* Russian emigrants, 144, 174, 175, 176–178, 197
Russian International Affairs Council (RIAC), 168
Russian invasion in Ukraine, vii, 113, 125, 137, 145, 166

Russian oligarchs; *see also* Putin's Kleptocracy, ix, x, xv, xix, 86, 155–185
Russification, 7, 80, 111, 133, 188
Russkii Mir Foundation, xiii, xiv, xix, 40, 155, 167, 171–175
Russophiles, 3

Sakharov, Andrei N., 32
Sakwa, Richard, 135, 170
Saul, Norman, 52, 63, 64
SBU (*Sluzhba bezpeku Ukrainy*), the Service of Security of Ukraine, xii, xvi, 39
Schifrin, Nick, 137
Scott, Cynthia, 53
Schlesinger, Arthur Jr., 55
Sergeyev, Victor, 161
Sevostianov, Grigorii, xvii, 17, 19–20, 25, 26, 27, 33, 34, 35, 37, 38, 39, 51, 52, 57, 62, 64, 98, 193
Shcherbytskyi, Volodymyr, 24
Shestydesiatnyky, 103
Shevchenko, Fedir, 95
Shevchenko, Georgii N., 154
Shevchenko, Ihor, 108
Shevchenko, Taras G., 80, 187
Shevel, Heorhii (Georgii), 24
Shevel, Oxana, 112, 113
Shevtsova, Lilia, 162, 168
Shlepakov, Arnold M., xvi, 17, 24, 26, 38, 39, 40, 62, 64, 92–102, 105, 111, 140, 141, 196
Shulman, Marshall, 55
Simmons, Ernest, 3, 4
Sitnikov, Vasily, 50
Sivachev, Nikolai, xvii, 25, 26–30, 33, 37, 38, 39, 40, 58, 59, 62, 63, 64, 138, 140, 141, 142, 193
Skolnikoff, Eugene B., 53, 54
Slavophile "*pochvenniki*," 142
"Sleeping cells" ("Illegals") of Soviet and Russian intelligence; *see also* Soviet/Russian spies, 71–90
Slezkine, Lev, 136

Slezkine, Yuri, 131, 136–138, 139, 170, 175, 177
Sluzhba vneshnei razvedki (SVR) of the Russian Federation, a former the KGB First Chief Directorate, 79, 115, 162, 167, 168
Smagliy, Kateryna, 165, 169
SMERSH (*smert' shpionam*), 17, 171
Smith Richardson Foundation, 161
Snyder, Timothy, 146
Society for Cultural Relations with Ukrainians Abroad, 76, 95
Sogrin, Vladimir, 25, 30, 38, 39, 63, 64, 193
Solodovnikov, Vasily, 18
Solovei, Dmytro, 5
Soros, George, 40
Soros (Open Society) Foundation, 39, 40, 161, 178
Soviet Americanists (experts in the US-Canada studies), xvii, 9, 19–69, 161, 193
Soviet Peace Fund, 167
"Soviet (Russian) sympathizers," 2, 71, 102, 105
Soviet Vulnerability Project, 5
Spielberg, Steven, 84
Stalin, Joseph, xi, 61, 92, 101, 131, 135, 157, 189, 191
Starr, S. Frederick, 156, 157, 159
Stent, Angela, 170
Stites, Richard, xvii, xviii, 11, 127, 130
Stozhkov, Yuli N., 10, 11
Sukhodolov, Aleksey B., 145
SUSTA, "*Soyuz Ukrainskykh Studentskykh Tovarystv Ameryky*," 106–107
Sysyn, Frank, xvii, 106

Taubman, William, 32
Temple University, 137, 161, 174
Tishkov, Valery, xvii, 25, 33–37, 140, 141, 161
Trenin, Dmitri, 40, 162, 188
Truman, Harry S., 31

Trump, Donald, 188, 195
Tsygankov, Andrey, 171
Tufts University, 112, 166

Ukrainian Congress Committee of America (UCCA),169
Ukrainian diaspora in Northern America (Ukrainian Americans and Canadians), xii, 73, 76, 77, 91–124, 135, 144, 163, 196–197
Ukrainian Free Academy of Sciences, 6
Ukrainian History Global Initiative, 146
Ukrainian Review, 5
Ukrains'kyi zbirnyk, 5
Ukrains'kyi istorychnyi zhurnal, 95
UNESCO, 77, 97, 103, 104
United Nations Organization (UNO), x, 72, 73, 77, 78, 104
University of Alberta, 97, 106, 109, 114
University of California, Berkeley, 34, 52, 136, 137, 175, 177
University of Hamburg, 108
University of Houston, 139
University of Kansas, 52, 64
University of Memphis, 139
University of Michigan, 5, 53, 105
University of South Carolina, 138, 184
University of Southern California, 74
University of Tartu (Estonia), 177
US Air Force, 5
US Department of Justice, viii, ix, 80
US Russia Foundation, 169

Valdai Discussion Club, xiii, 40, 137, 155, 167–170, 188
Van Herpen, Marcel, 168
Vance, Cyrus, KGB code name "Visir," 25
Vavilova's memoirs, 85–86
Vekselberg, Victor, ix, 164–166
Vlasovites; *see also* ROA, 3
Voina, Oleksii (Olexa) D., 94, 95
Volgograd State University, 40, 79, 178
Von Laue, Theodore, 60, 61

Wagner group, 189
Wake Forest University, 136
Walkowitz, Daniel, 139
Walkowitz, Judith, 139
Wallace, Henry A., 30
Ward, John W., 57
Weintraub, Wiktor, 108
Weisberg, Joe, 84
Wesleyan University, 60
Wilson Center (Woodrow Wilson International Center for Scholars), ix, 155, 156, 157, 158, 159, 162, 165, 170
Wilson, Woodrow, 156, 165
Woodrow Wilson Award for Public Service, ix, 165

Yakovlev, Alexander N., 9, 10, 11
Yakovlev, Nikolai N., 30
Yale University, 52, 146
Yaz'kov, Evgenii, 34, 173
Yeshitela, Omali, 145
Yekelchyk, Serhy, 112, 113
Yeltsin, Boris, 100, 137, 142, 143, 173, 174
Yeltsin Center (Yekaterinburg, Russia), 137
Yevtukh, Volodymyr, 99
York University, 184
Yurchak, Alexei, 131–135

Zarubin, Georgiy Z., 8
Zaslavskiy, Ilya, xx, xxii
Zatirka, Iosif, 72–73, 163
Zayarnyuk, Andriy, xv
Zhmudskii, A. Z., 97
Zhukov, Evgenii M., 35
Znamenski, Andrei, xvii, 64, 131, 139
Zolotukhin, Vladimir, 55, 56
Zubkova, Elena, 133
Zubok, Lev, 31, 160
Zubok, Vladislav, xvii, 25, 32, 33, 40, 64, 131, 137, 160, 161, 162, 174

About the Author

Sergei I. Zhuk is professor of history at Ball State University, Indiana. A former Soviet expert in US history, he moved in 1997 to the United States and defended his American PhD dissertation about imperial Russian history at Johns Hopkins University in 2002. His research interests are imperialism and fascism in Russia past and present, Russian intelligence, international relations (especially US-Russia relations), knowledge production, cultural consumption, religion, popular culture, and identity in a history of the United States, imperial Russia, Ukraine, and the Soviet Union. His recent publications include *KGB Operations against the USA and Canada in Soviet Ukraine, 1953–1991* (2022) and *Soviet Americana: The Cultural History of Russian and Ukrainian Americanists* (2018).

Milton Keynes UK
Ingram Content Group UK Ltd.
UKHW031539300724
446331UK00003B/43